ABOUT THIS PUBLICATION

FOR SERVICE ASSISTANCE

Customer Service
1.704.898.0770

North Carolina General Statues is published by The Muliti-Media Group of Greater Charlotte in Charlotte, North Carolina. Copyright 2015 by the Multi-Media Group of Greater Charlotte. This book or parts thereof may not be reproduced in any form, stored in a retrieval system, or transmitted in any form by any means—electronic, mechanical, photocopy, recording or otherwise—without prior written permission of the publisher, except as provided by United States of America copyright law.

The records required by U.S. Code 2257(a) through (c) and the pertinent regulations 28 C.F.R. Cli. 1, Part 75 with respect to this publication and all materials associated with such records are maintained by The Multi-Media Group of Greater Charlotte, Publisher and available for review by Attorney General.

www.visionbooks.org

Copyright © 2015 by MMGGC
All rights reserved!

TID: 5061493
ISBN (10) digit: 1502913461
ISBN (13) digit: 978-1502913463

123-4-56789-01239-Paperback
123-4-56789-01239-Hardback

First Edition

090520140547

Printed in the United States of America

1

2015 EDITION

North Carolina Criminal Law And Procedure-Pamphlet # 37

Printed In conjunction with the Administration of the Courts

North Carolina Criminal Law and Procedure
Pamphlet Reference Guide

Chapters	Pamphlet
Chapter 1 Civil Procedure	1
Chapter 1 Civil Procedure (Continue)	2
Chapter 1A Rules of Civil Procedure	2
Chapter 1B Contribution.	2
Chapter 1C Enforcement of Judgments.	2
Chapter 1D Punitive Damages.	2
Chapter 1E Eastern Band of Cherokee Indians.	2
Chapter 1F North Carolina Uniform Interstate Depositions and Discovery Act.	2
Chapter 2 - Clerk of Superior Court [Repealed and Transferred.]	3
Chapter 3 - Commissioners of Affidavits and Deeds [Repealed.]	3
Chapter 4 - Common Law	3
Chapter 5 - Contempt [Repealed.]	3
Chapter 5A - Contempt	3
Chapter 6 - Liability for Court Costs	3
Chapter 7 - Courts [Repealed and Transferred.]	3
Chapter 7A – Judicial Department	3
Chapter 7A – Continuation (Judicial Department)	4
Chapter 7A – Continuation (Judicial Department)	5
Chapter 7B - Juvenile Code	5
Chapter 8 - Evidence	6
Chapter 8A - Interpreters for Deaf Persons [Recodified.]	6
Chapter 8B - Interpreters for Deaf Persons	6
Chapter 8C - Evidence Code	6
Chapter 9 - Jurors	6
Chapter 10 - Notaries [Repealed.]	6
Chapter 10A - Notaries [Recodified.]	6
Chapter 10B - Notaries	6
Chapter 11 - Oaths	6
Chapter 12 - Statutory Construction	6
Chapter 13 - Citizenship Restored	6
Chapter 14 - Criminal Law	7
Chapter 14 –Criminal Law (Continuation)	8
Chapter 15 - Criminal Procedure	9
Chapter 15A - Criminal Procedure Act (Continuation)	10
Chapter 15A - Criminal Procedure Act (Continuation)	11
Chapter 15B - Victims Compensation	11
Chapter 15C - Address Confidentiality Program	11
Chapter 16 - Gaming Contracts and Futures	11
Chapter 17 - Habeas Corpus	11

Chapter 17A - Law-Enforcement Officers [Recodified.]	11
Chapter 17B - North Carolina Criminal Justice Education and Training System [Recodified.] Chapter 17C - North Carolina Criminal Justice Education and Training Standards Commission	11 11
Chapter 17D - North Carolina Justice Academy	11
Chapter 17E - North Carolina Sheriffs' Education and Training Standards Commission	11
Chapter 18 - Regulation of Intoxicating Liquors [Repealed.]	12
Chapter 18A - Regulation of Intoxicating Liquors [Repealed.]	12
Chapter 18B - Regulation of Alcoholic Beverages	12
Chapter 18C - North Carolina State Lottery	12
Chapter 19 - Offenses against Public Morals	12
Chapter 19A - Protection of Animals	12
Chapter 20 - Motor Vehicles	13
Chapter 20 - Motor Vehicles (Continuation)	14
Chapter 20 - Motor Vehicles (Continuation)	15
Chapter 20 - Motor Vehicles (Continuation)	16
Chapter 21 - Bills of Lading	17
Chapter 22 - Contracts Requiring Writing	17
Chapter 22A - Signatures	17
Chapter 22B - Contracts Against Public Policy	17
Chapter 22C - Payments to Subcontractors	17
Chapter 23 - Debtor and Creditor.	17
Chapter 24 – Interest	17
Chapter 25 – Uniform Commercial Code	18
Chapter 25 – Uniform Commercial Code (Continuation)	19
Chapter 25A – Retail Installment Sales Act	20
Chapter 25B - Credit	20
Chapter 25C - Sales of Artwork	20
Chapter 26 - Suretyship	20
Chapter 27 - Warehouse Receipts [Repealed.]	20
Chapter 28 - Administration [Repealed.]	20
Chapter 28A - Administration of Decedents' Estates	20
Chapter 28B - Estates of Absentees in Military Service	20
Chapter 28C - Estates of Missing Persons	20
Chapter 29 - Intestate Succession	21
Chapter 30 - Surviving Spouses	21
Chapter 31 - Wills	21
Chapter 31A - Acts Barring Property Rights	21
Chapter 31B - Renunciation of Property and Renunciation of Fiduciary Powers Act	21
Chapter 31C - Uniform Disposition of Community Property Rights at Death Act	21
Chapter 32 - Fiduciaries	21
Chapter 32A - Powers of Attorney	21
Chapter 33 - Guardian and Ward [Repealed and Recodified.]	21

Chapter 33A - North Carolina Uniform Transfers to Minors Act	21
Chapter 33B - North Carolina Uniform Custodial Trust Act	21
Chapter 34 - Veterans' Guardianship Act	22
Chapter 35 - Sterilization Procedures	22
Chapter 35A - Incompetency and Guardianship	22
Chapter 36 - Trusts and Trustees [Repealed.]	22
Chapter 36A - Trusts and Trustees	22
Chapter 36B - Uniform Management of Institutional Funds Act [Repealed.]	22
Chapter 36C - North Carolina Uniform Trust Code	22
Chapter 36D - North Carolina Community Third Party Trusts, Pooled Trusts	23
Chapter 36E - Uniform Prudent Management of Institutional Funds Act	23
Chapter 37 - Allocation of Principal and Income [Repealed.]	23
Chapter 37A - Uniform Principal and Income Act	23
Chapter 38 - Boundaries	23
Chapter 38A - Landowner Liability	23
Chapter 39 - Conveyances	23
Chapter 39A - Transfer Fee Covenants Prohibited	23
Chapter 40 - Eminent Domain [Repealed.]	23
Chapter 40A - Eminent Domain	23
Chapter 41 - Estates	23
Chapter 41A - State Fair Housing Act	23
Chapter 42 - Landlord and Tenant	23
Chapter 42A - Vacation Rental Act	23
Chapter 43 - Land Registration	23
Chapter 44 - Liens	24
Chapter 44A - Statutory Liens and Charges	24
Chapter 45 - Mortgages and Deeds of Trust	24
Chapter 45A - Good Funds Settlement Act	24
Chapter 46 - Partition	24
Chapter 47 - Probate and Registration	25
Chapter 47A - Unit Ownership	25
Chapter 47B - Real Property Marketable Title Act	25
Chapter 47C - North Carolina Condominium Act	25
Chapter 47D - Notice of Settlement Act [Expired.]	25
Chapter 47E - Residential Property Disclosure Act	25
Chapter 47F - North Carolina Planned Community Act	25
Chapter 47G - Option to Purchase Contracts	25
Chapter 47H - Contracts for Deed	25
Chapter 48 - Adoptions +	26
Chapter 48A - Minors	26
Chapter 49 - Bastardy	26
Chapter 49A - Rights of Children	26
Chapter 50 - Divorce and Alimony	26
Chapter 50A - Uniform Child-Custody Jurisdiction and	

Enforcement Act	26
Chapter 50B - Domestic Violence	26
Chapter 50C - Civil No-Contact Orders	26
Chapter 51 - Marriage	26
Chapter 52 - Powers and Liabilities of Married Persons	27
Chapter 52A - Uniform Reciprocal Enforcement of Support Act [Repealed.]	27
Chapter 52B - Uniform Premarital Agreement Act	27
Chapter 52C - Uniform Interstate Family Support Act	27
Chapter 53 - Banks	27
Chapter 53A - Business Development Corporations and North Carolina Capital Resource Corporations	28
Chapter 53B - Financial Privacy Act	28
Chapter 54 - Cooperative Organizations	28
Chapter 54A - Capital Stock Savings and Loan Associations [Repealed.]	28
Chapter 54B - Savings and Loan Associations	29
Chapter 54C - Savings Banks	29
Chapter 55 - North Carolina Business Corporation Act	30
Chapter 55A - North Carolina Nonprofit Corporation Act	31
Chapter 55B - Professional Corporation Act	31
Chapter 55C - Foreign Trade Zones	31
Chapter 55D - Filings, Names, and Registered Agents for Corporations, Nonprofit Corporations, and Partnerships	31
Chapter 56 - Electric, Telegraph and Power Companies [Repealed.]	31
Chapter 57 - Hospital, Medical and Dental Service Corporations [Recodified.]	31
Chapter 57A - Health Maintenance Organization Act [Recodified.]	31
Chapter 57B - Health Maintenance Organization Act [Recodified.]	31
Chapter 57C - North Carolina Limited Liability Company Act.	31
Chapter 58 - Insurance.	32
Chapter 58 - Insurance (Continuation)	33
Chapter 58 - Insurance (Continuation)	34
Chapter 58 - Insurance (Continuation)	35
Chapter 58 - Insurance (Continuation)	36
Chapter 58 - Insurance (Continuation)	37
Chapter 58 - Insurance (Continuation)	38
Chapter 58A - North Carolina Health Insurance Trust Commission [Recodified.]	38
Chapter 59 - Partnership.	39
Chapter 59B - Uniform Unincorporated Nonprofit Association Act.	39
Chapter 60 - Railroads and Other Carriers [Repealed and Transferred.]	39
Chapter 61 - Religious Societies	39
Chapter 62 - Public Utilities	39

Chapter 62 - Public Utilities (Continuation)	40
Chapter 62A - Public Safety Telephone Service And Wireless Telephone Service	40
Chapter 63 - Aeronautics	40
Chapter 63A - North Carolina Global TransPark Authority	40
Chapter 64 - Aliens	40
Chapter 65 – Cemeteries	40
Chapter 66 - Commerce and Business	41
Chapter 67 - Dogs	41
Chapter 68 - Fences and Stock Law	41
Chapter 69 - Fire Protection	41
Chapter 70 - Indian Antiquities, Archaeological Resources and Unmarked Human Skeletal Remains Protection	42
Chapter 71 - Indians [Repealed.]	42
Chapter 71A - Indians	42
Chapter 72 - Inns, Hotels and Restaurants	42
Chapter 73 - Mills	42
Chapter 74 - Mines and Quarries	42
Chapter 74A - Company Police [Repealed.]	42
Chapter 74B - Private Protective Services Act [Repealed.]	42
Chapter 74C - Private Protective Services	42
Chapter 74D - Alarm Systems	42
Chapter 74E - Company Police Act	42
Chapter 74F - Locksmith Licensing Act	42
Chapter 74G - Campus Police Act	42
Chapter 75 - Monopolies, Trusts and Consumer Protection	42
Chapter 75A - Boating and Water Safety	43
Chapter 75B - Discrimination in Business	43
Chapter 75C - Motion Picture Fair Competition Act	43
Chapter 75D - Racketeer Influenced and Corrupt Organizations	43
Chapter 75E - Unlawful Activities in Connection With Certain Corporate Transactions	43
Chapter 76 - Navigation	43
Chapter 76A - Navigation and Pilotage Commissions	43
Chapter 77 - Rivers, Creeks, and Coastal Waters	43
Chapter 78 - Securities Law [Repealed.]	43
Chapter 78A - North Carolina Securities Act	43
Chapter 78B - Tender Offer Disclosure Act [Repealed.]	43
Chapter 78C - Investment Advisers	43
Chapter 78D - Commodities Act	43
Chapter 79 - Strays [Repealed.]	43
Chapter 80 - Trademarks, Brands, etc.	44
Chapter 81 - Weights and Measures [Recodified.]	44
Chapter 81A - Weights and Measures Act of 1975.	44
Chapter 82 - Wrecks [Repealed.]	44
Chapter 83 - Architects [Recodified.]	44

Chapter 83A - Architects	44
Chapter 84 - Attorneys-at-Law	44
Chapter 84A - Foreign Legal Consultants	44
Chapter 85 - Auctions and Auctioneers [Repealed.]	44
Chapter 85A - Bail Bondsmen and Runners [Recodified.]	44
Chapter 85B - Auctions and Auctioneers	44
Chapter 85C - Bail Bondsmen and Runners [Recodified.]	44
Chapter 86 - Barbers [Recodified.]	44
Chapter 86A - Barbers	44
Chapter 87 - Contractors	44
Chapter 88 - Cosmetic Art [Repealed.]	44
Chapter 88A - Electrolysis Practice Act	44
Chapter 88B - Cosmetic Art	45
Chapter 89 - Engineering and Land Surveying [Recodified.]	45
Chapter 89A - Landscape Architects	45
Chapter 89B - Foresters	45
Chapter 89C - Engineering and Land Surveying	45
Chapter 89D - Landscape Contractors	45
Chapter 89E - Geologists Licensing Act	45
Chapter 89F - North Carolina Soil Scientist Licensing Act	45
Chapter 89G - Irrigation Contractors	45
Chapter 90 - Medicine and Allied Occupations	45
Chapter 90 - Medicine and Allied Occupations (Continuation)	46
Chapter 90 - Medicine and Allied Occupations (Continuation)	47
Chapter 90 - Medicine and Allied Occupations (Continuation)	48
Chapter 90A - Sanitarians and Water and Wastewater Treatment Facility Operators	48
Chapter 90B - Social Worker Certification and Licensure Act	48
Chapter 90C - North Carolina Recreational Therapy Licensure Act	48
Chapter 90D - Interpreters and Transliterators	48
Chapter 91 - Pawnbrokers [Repealed.]	48
Chapter 91A - Pawnbrokers Modernization Act of 1989	48
Chapter 92 - Photographers [Deleted.]	48
Chapter 93 - Certified Public Accountants	48
Chapter 93A - Real Estate License Law	49
Chapter 93B - Occupational Licensing Boards	49
Chapter 93C - Watchmakers [Repealed.]	49
Chapter 93D - North Carolina State Hearing Aid Dealers and Fitters Board.	49
Chapter 93E - North Carolina Appraisers Act	49
Chapter 94 - Apprenticeship	49
Chapter 95 - Department of Labor and Labor Regulations	49
Chapter 95 - Department of Labor and Labor Regulations (Continuation)	50
Chapter 96 - Employment Security	50
Chapter 97 - Workers' Compensation Act	50
Chapter 97 - Workers' Compensation Act (Continuation)	51

Chapter 98 - Burnt and Lost Records	51
Chapter 99 - Libel and Slander	51
Chapter 99A - Civil Remedies for Criminal Actions	51
Chapter 99B - Products Liability	51
Chapter 99C - Actions Relating to Winter Sports Safety and Accidents	51
Chapter 99D - Civil Rights	51
Chapter 99E - Special Liability Provisions	51
Chapter 100 - Monuments, Memorials and Parks	51
Chapter 101 - Names of Persons	51
Chapter 102 - Official Survey Base	51
Chapter 103 - Sundays, Holidays and Special Days	51
Chapter 104 - United States Lands	51
Chapter 104A - Degrees of Kinship	51
Chapter 104B - Hurricanes or Other Acts of Nature	51
Chapter 104C - Atomic Energy, Radioactivity and Ionizing Radiation [Repealed and Recodified.]	51
Chapter 104D - Southern States Energy Compact	51
Chapter 104E - North Carolina Radiation Protection Act	51
Chapter 104F - Southeast Interstate Low-Level Radioactive Waste Management Compact [Repealed]	51
Chapter 104G - North Carolina Low-Level Radioactive Waste Management Authority Act of 1987 [Repealed]	51
Chapter 105 - Taxation	51
Chapter 105 - Taxation (Continuation)	52
Chapter 105 - Taxation (Continuation)	53
Chapter 105 - Taxation (Continuation)	54
Chapter 105A - Setoff Debt Collection Act	55
Chapter 105B - Defaulted Student Loan Recovery Act	55
Chapter 106 - Agriculture	55
Chapter 106 - Agriculture (Continue)	56
Chapter 106 - Agriculture (Continue)	57
Chapter 107 - Agricultural Development Districts [Repealed.]	57
Chapter 108 - Social Services [Repealed and Recodified.]	57
Chapter 108A - Social Services	57
Chapter 108B - Community Action Programs	58
Chapter 108C Medicaid and Health Choice Provider Requirements.	58
Chapter 108D Medicaid Managed Care for Behavioral Health Services.	58
Chapter 109 - Bonds [Recodified.]	58
Chapter 110 - Child Welfare	58
Chapter 111 - Aid to the Blind	58
Chapter 112 - Confederate Homes and Pensions [Repealed.]	58
Chapter 113 - Conservation and Development	58
Chapter 113 - Conservation and Development (Continuation)	59

Chapter 113A - Pollution Control and Environment	59
Chapter 113A - Pollution Control and Environment (Continuation)	60
Chapter 113B - North Carolina Energy Policy Act of 1975	60
Chapter 114 - Department of Justice	60
Chapter 115 - Elementary and Secondary Education [Repealed.]	60
Chapter 115A - Community Colleges, Technical Institutes, and Industrial Education Centers [Repealed.]	60
Chapter 115B - Tuition and Fee Waivers	60
Chapter 115C - Elementary and Secondary Education	60
Chapter 115C - Elementary and Secondary Education (Continuation)	61
Chapter 115C - Elementary and Secondary Education (Continuation)	62
Chapter 115C - Elementary and Secondary Education (Continuation)	63
Chapter 115D - Community Colleges	63
Chapter 115E - Private Educational Facilities Finance Act [Recodified]	63
Chapter 116 - Higher Education	63
Chapter 116 - Higher Education (Continuation)	63
Chapter 116A - Escheats and Abandoned Property [Repealed.]	64
Chapter 116B - Escheats and Abandoned Property	64
Chapter 116C - Continuum of Education Programs	64
Chapter 116D - Higher Education Bonds	64
Chapter 117 - Electrification	64
Chapter 118 - Firemen's and Rescue Squad Workers' Relief and Pension Funds [Recodified.]	64
Chapter 118A - Firemen's Death Benefit Act [Repealed.]	64
Chapter 118B - Members of a Rescue Squad Death Benefit Act [Repealed.]	64
Chapter 119 - Gasoline and Oil Inspection and Regulation	64
Chapter 120 - General Assembly	65
Chapter 120 - General Assembly (Continuation)	66
Chapter 120 - General Assembly (Continuation)	67
Chapter 120C - Lobbying	67
Chapter 121 - Archives and History	67
Chapter 122 - Hospitals for the Mentally Disordered [Repealed.]	67
Chapter 122A - North Carolina Housing Finance Agency	67
Chapter 122B - North Carolina Agricultural Facilities Finance Act [Repealed.]	67
Chapter 122C - Mental Health, Developmental Disabilities, and Substance Abuse Act of 1985	67
Chapter 122C - Mental Health, Developmental Disabilities, and Substance Abuse Act of 1985 (Continuation)	68
Chapter 122D - North Carolina Agricultural Finance Act	68

Chapter 122E - North Carolina Housing Trust and Oil Overcharge Act	68
Chapter 123 - Impeachment	69
Chapter 123A - Industrial Development [Repealed.]	69
Chapter 124 - Internal Improvements	69
Chapter 125 - Libraries	69
Chapter 126 - State Personnel System	69
Chapter 127 - Militia [Repealed.]	69
Chapter 127A - Militia	69
Chapter 127B - Military Affairs	69
Chapter 127C - Advisory Commission on Military Affairs	69
Chapter 128 - Offices and Public Officers	69
Chapter 128 - Offices and Public Officers (Continuation)	70
Chapter 129 - Public Buildings and Grounds	70
Chapter 130 - Public Health [Repealed.]	70
Chapter 130A - Public Health	70
Chapter 130A - Public Health (Continuation)	71
Chapter 130A - Public Health (Continuation)	72
Chapter 130B - Hazardous Waste Management Commission [Repealed.]	72
Chapter 131 - Public Hospitals [Repealed.]	72
Chapter 131A - Health Care Facilities Finance Act	72
Chapter 131B - Licensing of Ambulatory Surgical Facilities [Repealed.]	72
Chapter 131C - Charitable Solicitation Licensure Act [Repealed.]	72
Chapter 131D - Inspection and Licensing of Facilities	72
Chapter 131E - Health Care Facilities and Services	72
Chapter 131E - Health Care Facilities and Services (Continuation)	73
Chapter 131F - Solicitation of Contributions	73
Chapter 132 - Public Records	73
Chapter 133 - Public Works	74
Chapter 134 - Youth Development [Recodified.]	74
Chapter 134A - Youth Services [Repealed.]	74
Chapter 135 - Retirement System for Teachers and State Employees; Social Security; Health Insurance Program for Children	74
Chapter 135 - Retirement System for Teachers and State Employees; Social Security; Health Insurance Program for Children	75
Chapter 136 - Transportation	75
Chapter 136 - Transportation (Continuation)	76
Chapter 137 - Rural Rehabilitation [Repealed.]	76
Chapter 138 - Salaries, Fees and Allowances	76
Chapter 138A - State Government Ethics Act	76
Chapter 139 - Soil and Water Conservation Districts	76

Chapter 140 - State Art Museum; Symphony and Art Societies	76
Chapter 140A - State Awards System	76
Chapter 141 - State Boundaries	76
Chapter 142 - State Debt	76
Chapter 143 - State Departments, Institutions, and Commissions	77
Chapter 143 - State Departments, Institutions, and Commissions (Continuation)	78
Chapter 143 - State Departments, Institutions, and Commissions (Continuation)	79
Chapter 143 - State Departments, Institutions, and Commissions (Continuation)	80
Chapter 143A - State Government Reorganization	80
Chapter 143B - Executive Organization Act of 1973	80
Chapter 143B - Executive Organization Act of 1973 (Continuation)	81
Chapter 143B - Executive Organization Act of 1973 (Continuation)	82
Chapter 143C - State Budget Act	83
Chapter 143D - The State Governmental Accountability and Internal Control Act	83
Chapter 144 - State Flag, Official Governmental Flags, Motto, and Colors	83
Chapter 145 - State Symbols and Other Official Adoptions.	83
Chapter 146 - State Lands	83
Chapter 147 - State Officers	83
Chapter 148 - State Prison System	84
Chapter 149 - State Song and Toast	84
Chapter 150 - Uniform Revocation of Licenses [Repealed.]	84
Chapter 150A - Administrative Procedure Act [Recodified.]	84
Chapter 150B - Administrative Procedure Act	84
Chapter 151 - Constables [Repealed.]	84
Chapter 152 - Coroners	84
Chapter 152A - County Medical Examiner [Repealed.]	84
Chapter 152A - County Medical Examiner [Repealed.] (Continuation)	85
Chapter 153 - Counties and County Commissioners [Repealed.]	85
Chapter 153A - Counties	85
Chapter 153B - Mountain Resources Planning Act	85
Chapter 153C - Uwharrie Regional Resources Act	85
Chapter 154 - County Surveyor [Repealed.]	85
Chapter 155 - County Treasurer [Repealed.]	85
Chapter 156 - Drainage	85
Chapter 156 – Drainage (Continuation)	86

Chapter 157 - Housing Authorities and Projects	86
Chapter 157A - Historic Properties Commissions [Transferred.]	86
Chapter 158 - Local Development	86
Chapter 159 - Local Government Finance	86
Chapter 159 - Local Government Finance (Continuation)	87
Chapter 159A - Pollution Abatement and Industrial Facilities Financing Act [Unconstitutional.]	87
Chapter 159B - Joint Municipal Electric Power and Energy Act	87
Chapter 159C - Industrial and Pollution Control Facilities Financing Act	87
Chapter 159D - The North Carolina Capital Facilities Financing Act	87
Chapter 159E - Registered Public Obligations Act	87
Chapter 159F - North Carolina Energy Development Authority [Repealed.]	87
Chapter 159G - Water Infrastructure	87
Chapter 159H - [Reserved.]	87
Chapter 159I - Solid Waste Management Loan Program and Local Government Special Obligation Bonds	87
Chapter 160 - Municipal Corporations [Repealed And Transferred.]	87
Chapter 160A - Cities and Towns	88
Chapter 160A - Cities and Towns (Continuation)	89
Chapter 160B - Consolidated City-County Act	89
Chapter 160C - Baseball Park Districts [Repealed.]	90
Chapter 161 - Register of Deeds	90
Chapter 162 - Sheriff	90
Chapter 162A - Water and Sewer Systems	90
Chapter 162B Continuity of Local Government in Emergency.	90
Chapter 163 Elections and Election Laws.	90
Chapter 163 Elections and Election Laws. (Continuation)	91
Chapter 164 Concerning the General Statutes of North Carolina.	92
Chapter 165 Veterans.	92
Chapter 166 Civil Preparedness Agencies [Repealed.]	92
Chapter 166A North Carolina Emergency Management Act.	92
Chapter 167 State Civil Air Patrol [Repealed.]	92
Chapter 168 Persons with Disabilities.	92
Chapter 168A Persons With Disabilities Protection Act.	92

§ 58-58-61. Standard nonforfeiture law for individual deferred annuities.

(a) Title. - This section is and may be cited as the Standard Nonforfeiture Law for Individual Deferred Annuities.

(b) Applicability. - This section does not apply to any:

(1) Reinsurance.

(2) Group annuity purchased under a retirement plan or plan of deferred compensation established or maintained by an employer, including a partnership or sole proprietorship, or by an employee organization, or by both, other than a plan providing individual retirement accounts or individual retirement annuities under section 408 of the Internal Revenue Code, as amended.

(3) Premium deposit fund.

(4) Variable annuity.

(5) Investment annuity.

(6) Immediate annuity.

(7) Deferred annuity contract after annuity payments have commenced.

(8) Reversionary annuity.

(9) Contract delivered outside this State through an agent or other representative of the company issuing the contract.

(c) Nonforfeiture Requirements. - In the case of contracts issued on or after the operative date of this section as defined in subsection (o) of this section, no contract of annuity, except as stated in subsection (b) of this section, shall be delivered or issued for delivery in this State unless it contains in substance the following provisions, or corresponding provisions that in the opinion of the Commissioner are at least as favorable to the contract holder, upon cessation of payment of considerations under the contract:

(1) That upon cessation of payment of considerations under a contract, or upon the written request of the contract owner, the company shall grant a paid-

up annuity benefit on a plan stipulated in the contract of the value specified in subsections (g), (h), (i), (j), and (l) of this section.

(2) If a contract provides for a lump sum settlement at maturity or at any other time, that upon surrender of the contract at or before the commencement of any annuity payments, the company shall pay in lieu of a paid-up annuity benefit a cash surrender benefit of the amount specified in subsections (g), (h), (j), and (l) of this section. The company may reserve the right to defer the payment of the cash surrender benefit for a period not to exceed six months after demand for the payment with surrender of the contract after making written request and receiving written approval of the Commissioner. The request shall address the necessity and equitability to all policyholders of the deferral.

(3) A statement of the mortality table, if any, and interest rates used in calculating any minimum paid-up annuity, cash surrender, or death benefits that are guaranteed under the contract, together with sufficient information to determine the amounts of the benefits.

(4) A statement that any paid-up annuity, cash surrender, or death benefits that may be available under the contract are not less than the minimum benefits required by any statute of the state in which the contract is delivered and an explanation of the manner in which the benefits are altered by the existence of any additional amounts credited by the company to the contract, any indebtedness to the company on the contract, or any prior withdrawals from or partial surrenders of the contract.

Notwithstanding the requirements of this subsection, a deferred annuity contract may provide that if no considerations have been received under the contract for a period of two full years and the portion of the paid-up annuity benefit at maturity on the plan stipulated in the contract arising from prior considerations paid would be less than twenty dollars ($20.00) monthly, the company may at its option terminate the contract by payment in cash of the then-present value of the portion of the paid-up annuity benefit, calculated on the basis of the mortality table, if any, and interest rate specified in the contract for determining the paid-up annuity benefit, and by this payment shall be relieved of any further obligation under the contract.

(d) Minimum Values. - The minimum values specified in subsections (g), (h), (i), (j), and (l) of this section of any paid-up annuity, cash surrender, or death benefits available under an annuity contract shall be based upon minimum nonforfeiture amounts as defined in this section. The minimum nonforfeiture amount at any time at or before the commencement of any annuity payments shall be equal to an accumulation up to that time at rates of interest as indicated in subsection (e) of this section of the net considerations, as hereinafter defined, paid before that time, decreased by the sum of the following:

(1) Any prior withdrawals from or partial surrenders of the contract accumulated at rates of interest as indicated in subsection (e) of this section.

(2) An annual contract charge of fifty dollars ($50.00), accumulated at rates of interest as indicated in subsection (e) of this section.

(3) Any premium tax paid by the company for the contract, accumulated at rates of interest as indicated in subsection (e) of this section.

(4) The amount of any indebtedness to the company on the contract, including interest due and accrued.

The net considerations for a given contract year used to define the minimum nonforfeiture amount shall be an amount equal to eighty-seven and one-half percent (87 1/2%) of the gross considerations credited to the contract during that contract year.

(e) The interest rate used in determining minimum nonforfeiture amounts shall be an annual rate of interest determined as the lesser of three percent (3%) per annum and the following, which shall be specified in the contract if the interest rate will be reset:

(1) The five-year Constant Maturity Treasury Rate reported by the Federal Reserve as of a date, or average over a period, rounded to the nearest one-twentieth of one percent (0.05%), specified in the contract no longer than 15 months before the contract issue date or redetermination date under subdivision (4) of this subsection.

(2) Reduced by 125 basis points.

(3) Where the resulting interest guarantee is not less than one percent (1%).

(4) The interest rate shall apply for an initial period and may be redetermined for additional periods. The redetermination date, basis, and period, if any, shall be stated in the contract. The basis is the date or average

over a specified period that produces the value of the five-year Constant Maturity Treasury Rate to be used at each redetermination date.

(f)   During the period or term that a contract provides substantive participation in an equity indexed benefit, it may increase the reduction described in subdivision (e)(2) of this section by up to an additional 100 basis points to reflect the value of the equity index benefit. The present value at the contract issue date, and at each subsequent redetermination date, of the additional reduction shall not exceed the market value of the benefit. The Commissioner may require a demonstration that the present value of the additional reduction does not exceed the market value of the benefit. Absent a demonstration that is acceptable to the Commissioner, the Commissioner may disallow or limit the additional reduction. The Commissioner may adopt rules to implement the provisions of this subsection and to provide for further adjustments to the calculation of minimum nonforfeiture amounts for contracts that provide substantive participation in an equity index benefit and for other contracts for which the Commissioner determines adjustments are justified.

(g)   Computation of Present Value. - Any paid-up annuity benefit available under a contract shall be such that its present value on the date annuity payments are to commence is at least equal to the minimum nonforfeiture amount on that date. Present value shall be computed using the mortality table, if any, and the interest rates specified in the contract for determining the minimum paid-up annuity benefits guaranteed in the contract.

(h)   Calculation of Cash Surrender Value. - For contracts that provide cash surrender benefits, the cash surrender benefits available before maturity shall not be less than the present value as of the date of surrender of that portion of the maturity value of the paid-up annuity benefit that would be provided under the contract at maturity arising from considerations paid before the time of cash surrender reduced by the amount appropriate to reflect any prior withdrawals from or partial surrenders of the contract, such present value being calculated on the basis of an interest rate not more than one percent (1%) higher than the interest rate specified in the contract for accumulating the net considerations to determine maturity value, decreased by the amount of any indebtedness to the company on the contract, including interest due and accrued, and increased by any existing additional amounts credited by the company to the contract. In no event shall any cash surrender benefit be less than the minimum nonforfeiture amount at that time. The death benefit under such contracts shall be at least equal to the cash surrender benefit.

(i) Calculation of Paid-Up Annuity Benefits. - For contracts that do not provide cash surrender benefits, the present value of any paid-up annuity benefit available as a nonforfeiture option at any time before maturity shall not be less than the present value of that portion of the maturity value of the paid-up annuity benefit provided under the contract arising from considerations paid before the time the contract is surrendered in exchange for, or changed to, a deferred paid-up annuity, the present value being calculated for the period before the maturity date on the basis of the interest rate specified in the contract for accumulating the net considerations to determine maturity value, and increased by any additional amounts credited by the company to the contract. For contracts that do not provide any death benefits before the commencement of any annuity payments, present values shall be calculated on the basis of the interest rate and the mortality table specified in the contract for determining the maturity value of the paid-up annuity benefit. However, in no event shall the present value of a paid-up annuity benefit be less than the minimum nonforfeiture amount at that time.

(j) Maturity Date. - For the purpose of determining the benefits calculated under subsections (h) and (i) of this section, in the case of annuity contracts under which an election may be made to have annuity payments commence at optional maturity dates, the maturity date shall be the latest date for which election is permitted by the contract but not later than the anniversary of the contract next following the annuitant's seventieth birthday or the tenth anniversary of the contract, whichever is later.

(k) Disclosure of Limited Death Benefits. - A contract that does not provide cash surrender benefits or does not provide death benefits at least equal to the minimum nonforfeiture amount before the commencement of any annuity payments shall include a statement in a prominent place in the contract that those benefits are not provided.

(l) Inclusion of Lapse of Time Considerations. - Any paid-up annuity, cash surrender, or death benefits available at any time, other than on the contract anniversary under any contract with fixed scheduled considerations, shall be calculated with allowance for the lapse of time and the payment of any scheduled considerations beyond the beginning of the contract year in which cessation of payment of considerations under the contract occurs.

(m) Proration of Values; Additional Benefits. - For a contract that provides within the same contract, by rider or supplemental contract provision, both annuity benefits and life insurance benefits that are in excess of the greater of cash surrender benefits or a return of the gross considerations with interest, the minimum nonforfeiture benefits shall be equal to the sum of the minimum nonforfeiture benefits for the annuity portion and the minimum nonforfeiture benefits, if any, for the life insurance portion computed as if each portion were a separate contract. Notwithstanding the provisions of subsections (g), (h), (i), (j), and (l) of this section, additional benefits payable in the event of total and permanent disability, as reversionary annuity or deferred reversionary annuity benefits, or as other policy benefits additional to life insurance, endowment, and annuity benefits, and considerations for all such additional benefits, shall be disregarded in ascertaining the minimum nonforfeiture amounts, paid-up annuity, cash surrender, and death benefits that may be required by this section. The inclusion of those benefits shall not be required in any paid-up benefits, unless the additional benefits separately would require minimum nonforfeiture amounts, paid-up annuity, cash surrender, and death benefits.

(n)   Rules. - The Commissioner may adopt rules to implement the provisions of this section.

(o)   Effective Date. - On and after October 1, 2003, a company may elect to apply the provisions of this section to annuity contracts on a contract form-by-contract form basis before October 1, 2004. In all other instances, this section shall become operative with respect to annuity contracts issued by the company on and after October 1, 2004. (2003-144, s. 1.)

§ 58-58-65. Reinsurance of companies regulated.

The receiver of any life insurance company organized under the laws of this State, when the assets of the company are sufficient for that purpose, and the consent of two thirds of its policyholders has been secured in writing, may reinsure all the policy obligations of such company in some other solvent life insurance company, or, when the assets are insufficient to secure the reinsurance of all the policies in full, he may reinsure such a percentage of each and every policy outstanding as the assets will secure; but there must be no preference or discrimination as against any policyholder, and the contract for such reinsurance by the receiver must be approved by the Commissioner before it has effect. (1899, c. 54, s. 58; 1903, c. 536, s. 9; Rev., s. 4778; C.S., s. 6462; 1945, c. 379; 1991, c. 720, s. 61.)

Part 3. Insurable Interests and Other Rights.

§ 58-58-70. Insurable interest as between stockholders, partners, etc.

Where two or more persons have heretofore contracted or hereafter contract with one another for the purchase, at the death of one, by the survivor or survivors, of the stock, share or interest of the deceased in any corporation, partnership or business association of any kind, the person or persons making the contract of purchase shall be deemed to have, and are hereby declared to have, an insurable interest in the life or lives of the person or persons contracting to sell. (1941, c. 201; 1969, c. 751, s. 44.)

§ 58-58-75. Insurable interest in life and physical ability of employee or agent.

(a) An employer, whether a partnership, joint venture, business trust, mutual association, corporation, any other form of business organization, or one or more individuals, or any religious, educational, or charitable corporation, institution or body, has an insurable interest in and the right to insure the physical ability or the life, or both the physical ability and the life, of an employee for the benefit of such employer. Any principal shall have a life insurable interest in and the right to insure the physical ability or the life, or both the physical ability and the life, of an agent for the benefit of such principal.

(b) An employee described in subsection (a) of this section shall be insured for the benefit of an employer described in subsection (a) of this section only if the employee receives written notification from the insurer of the existence of the coverage or that coverage will be purchased. The notice shall be provided to the employee in connection with the application for coverage or within 30 days after the effective date of the coverage and shall include a statement that the employer may maintain the life insurance coverage on the employee even after employment is terminated.

(c) For nonkey or nonmanagerial employees, the aggregate amount of coverage shall be reasonably related to the benefits provided to the employees in the aggregate.

(d) With respect to employer-provided pension and welfare plans, the life insurance coverage purchased to finance the plans may only cover the lives of those employees and retirees who, at the time their lives were first insured under the plan, either are participants, or would be eligible to participate, upon the satisfaction of age, service, or similar eligibility criteria in the plan. (1951, c. 283, s. 1; 1957, c. 1086; 2005-234, s. 2.)

§ 58-58-80. Insurable interest in life and physical ability of partner.

Any partner has an insurable interest in and the right to insure the physical ability or the life, or both the physical ability and the life, of any other partner or partners who are members of the same partnership for his benefit, either alone or jointly with another partner or partners of the same partnership. A partnership has a like insurable interest in and the right to insure the physical ability or the life, or both the physical ability and the life, of one or more partners of the partnership. (1951, c. 283, s. 2.)

§ 58-58-85. Insurable interest in life of person covered by pension plan.

A trustee under a written document providing for a pension plan for payments of money or delivery of other benefits to be made to persons eligible to receive them under the terms and provisions of such written document shall be deemed to have and is hereby declared to have an insurable interest in the lives of any person or persons covered by the pension plan, to the extent that contracts or policies of insurance are in conformity with and in furtherance of the purposes of the pension plan. (1951, c. 283, s. 2 1/2.)

§ 58-58-86. Insurable interest of charitable organizations.

(a) If an organization described in section 501(c)(3) of the Internal Revenue Code purchases or receives by assignment, before, on, or after the effective date of this section, life insurance on an insured who consents to the purchase or assignment, the organization is deemed to have an insurable interest in the insured person's life.

(b) Expired effective October 1, 2007, pursuant to Session Laws 2004-124, s. 32F.2. (1991, c. 644, s. 2; 2004-124, ss. 32F.1, 32F.2.)

§ 58-58-90. Construction.

G.S. 58-58-75, 58-58-80, 58-58-85, and 58-58-86 do not limit or abridge any insurable interest or right to insure now existing at common law or by statute, and shall be construed liberally to sustain insurable interest, whether as a declaration of existing law or as an extension of or addition to existing law. (1951, c. 283, s. 3; 1991, c. 644, s. 3.)

§ 58-58-95. Rights of beneficiaries.

When a policy of insurance is effected by any person on his own life, or on another life in favor of some person other than himself having an insurable interest therein, the lawful beneficiary thereof, other than himself or his legal representatives, is entitled to its proceeds against the creditors and representatives of the person effecting the insurance. The person to whom a policy of life insurance is made payable may maintain an action thereon in his own name. A person may insure his or her own life for the sole use and benefit of his or her spouse, or children, or both, and upon his or her death the proceeds from the insurance shall be paid to or for the benefit of the spouse, or children, or both, or to a guardian, free from all claims of the representatives or creditors of the insured or his or her estate. Any insurance policy which insures the life of a person for the sole use and benefit of that person's spouse, or children, or both, shall not be subject to the claims of creditors of the insured during his or her lifetime, whether or not the policy reserves to the insured during his or her lifetime any or all rights provided for by the policy and whether or not the policy proceeds are payable to the estate of the insured in the event the beneficiary or beneficiaries predecease the insured. (Const., Art. X, s. 7; 1899, c. 54, s. 59; Rev., ss. 4771, 4772; C.S., s. 6464; 1977, c. 518, s. 1.)

§ 58-58-97. Provision of life insurance information upon notification of insured's death.

(a) Any person licensed to practice funeral directing or any employee of a funeral establishment licensed under the provisions of Article 13A of Chapter 90 of the General Statutes providing funeral service, as that term is defined in G.S. 90-210.20, for a deceased person insured or believed to be insured under a contract of life insurance or under a group life insurance policy may request information regarding the deceased person's life insurance contracts by providing an insurer with (i) a copy of a notification of death filed pursuant to G.S. 130A-112, (ii) written authorization from the person or persons with legal authority to direct disposition of the deceased's body as prescribed under G.S. 90-210.124 or G.S. 130A-420, and (iii) in the case of a person covered or believed to be covered under a group life insurance policy, the affiliation of the deceased entitling them to coverage under the group life insurance policy. As soon as possible after receipt of the request, the life insurance company shall inform the person authorized by this section to make an inquiry of the following:

(1)   The existence of any contract insuring the life of the deceased person.

(2)   Any beneficiaries on record under any life insurance contract insuring the life of the deceased person.

(3)   The amount of any liens or loans outstanding on the policy.

(4)   The amount of benefits payable to the beneficiaries.

(5)   Whether the policy has been reinstated within the last 24 months.

The insurer shall provide a claim form to any person or assignee making the request.

(b)   If any person making a written request under subsection (a) of this section who has provided all the information required by subsection (a) of this section does not receive a timely response from the insurer, then the person may refer the request to the Consumer Services Division of the Department, which shall treat the referral as a consumer complaint. The referral shall include all the information provided to the insurer under subsection (a) of this section as well as copies of all communications and information received from the insurer regarding the request for information.

(c)   If the beneficiary of record under the life insurance contract or group life insurance policy is not the estate of the deceased, then any person authorized to request information under subsection (a) of this section shall make reasonable efforts to locate the beneficiaries within 100 hours of receiving information from the insurance carrier regarding any life insurance contracts or group life insurance policies and shall provide to all beneficiaries all documents and information obtained from the insurance carrier. The person obtaining the information also shall inform all beneficiaries in writing in bold print that "THE BENEFICIARY OF A LIFE INSURANCE POLICY HAS NO LEGAL DUTY OR OBLIGATION TO SPEND ANY OF THAT MONEY ON THE FUNERAL, DEBTS, OR OBLIGATIONS OF THE DECEASED" and shall do so before discussing with the beneficiaries financial arrangements for burial of the deceased.

(d) Any licensee or employee of a funeral establishment licensed under Article 13A of Chapter 90 of the General Statutes who makes a false request for information under this section or fails to do that required by subsection (c) of this section shall be deemed guilty of fraud or misrepresentation in the practice of funeral service as defined in G.S. 90-210.25(e)(1)b. and unfit to practice funeral service.

(e) This section shall apply to life insurance companies as defined in G.S. 58-58-1 and to all contracts subject to the provisions of this Article. (2009-566, s. 23; 2011-229, s. 1.)

§ 58-58-100. Minors may enter into insurance or annuity contracts and have full rights, powers and privileges thereunder.

All minors in North Carolina of the age of 15 years and upwards shall have full power and authority to make contracts of insurance or annuity with any life insurance company authorized to do business in the State of North Carolina, either domestic or foreign, and to exercise all the powers, rights, and privileges of ownership conferred upon them under the terms of any and all such contracts applied for by and issued to them, and with full power to surrender, assign, modify, pledge, or change such contracts, and to receive any dividends thereon and generally to have the full power and authority in the premises that persons 18 years and upwards could and would have relative to any and all such contracts. (1945, c. 379; 1947, c. 721; 1971, c. 1231, s. 1.)

§ 58-58-105. Renunciation.

A beneficiary of a life insurance policy who did not possess the incidents of ownership under the policy at the time of death of the insured may renounce as provided in Chapter 31B of the General Statutes. (1975, c. 371, s. 5.)

§ 58-58-110. Interest payments on death benefits.

(a) Each insurer admitted to transact insurance in this State which, without the written consent of the beneficiary, fails or refuses to pay the death proceeds or death benefits in accordance with the terms of any policy providing a death benefit issued by it in this State within 30 days after receipt of satisfactory proof of loss because of the death, whether accidental or otherwise, of the insured shall pay interest, at a rate not less than the then current rate of interest on death proceeds left on deposit with the insurer computed from the date of the insured's death, on any moneys payable and unpaid after the expiration of the 30-day period. As used in this subsection, the phrase "satisfactory proof of loss because of the death" includes, but is not limited to, a certified copy of the death certificate; or a written statement by the attending physician at the time of death that contains the following information: (i) the name and address of the physician, who must be duly licensed to practice medicine in the United States; (ii) the name of the deceased; (iii) the date, time, and place of the death; and (iv) the immediate cause of the death.

(b) Within the meaning of this section, payment of proceeds or benefits shall be deemed to have been made on the date upon which a check, draft or other valid instrument equivalent to the payment of money was placed in the United States mails in a properly addressed, postpaid envelope, or, if not so posted, on the date of delivery of such instrument to the beneficiary.

(c) This section does not allow an insurer to withhold payment of money payable under any policy providing a death benefit to any beneficiary for a period longer than reasonably necessary to determine whether benefits are payable and to transmit the payment.

(d) This section shall not apply to policies of insurance issued prior to the effective date of this section to the extent that such policies contain specific provisions in conflict with this section. (1977, c. 395, s. 1; 1983, c. 749; 1985, c. 666, s. 45; 1991, c. 644, s. 8; 1995, c. 193, s. 46.)

§ 58-58-115. Creditors deprived of benefits of life insurance policies except in cases of fraud.

If a policy of insurance is effected by any person on his own life or on another life in favor of a person other than himself, or, except in cases of transfer with intent to defraud creditors, if a policy of life insurance is assigned or in any way made payable to any such person, the lawful beneficiary or assignee thereof, other than the insured or the person so effecting such insurance or the executor or administrator of such insured or of the person effecting such insurance, shall be entitled to its proceeds and avails against creditors and representatives of the insured and of the person effecting same, whether or not the right to change the beneficiary is reserved or permitted, and whether or not the policy is made payable to the person whose life is insured if the beneficiary or assignee shall predecease such person: Provided, that subject to the statute of limitations, the amount of any premiums for said insurance paid with the intent to defraud creditors, with interest thereon, shall inure to their benefit from the proceeds of the policy; but the company issuing the policy shall be discharged of all liability thereon by payment of its proceeds in accordance with its terms unless, before such payment, the company shall have written notice by or in behalf of the creditor, of a claim to recover for transfer made or premiums paid with intent to defraud creditors, with specifications of the amount claimed. (1931, c. 179, s. 1; 1947, c. 721.)

§ 58-58-120. Notice of nonpayment of premium required before forfeiture.

No life insurance corporation doing business in this State shall, within one year after the default in payment of any premium, installment, or interest, declare forfeited or lapsed any policy hereafter issued or renewed, except policies on which premiums are payable monthly or at shorter intervals and except group insurance contracts and term insurance contracts for one year or less, nor shall any such policy be forfeited or lapsed by reason of nonpayment, when due, of any premium, interest, or installment or any portion thereof required by the terms of the policy to be paid, within one year from the failure to pay such premium, interest, or installment, unless a written or printed notice stating the amount of such premium, interest, installment, or portion thereof due on such policy, the place where it shall be paid, and the person to whom the same is payable has been duly addressed and mailed, postage paid, to the person whose life is insured, or to the assignee or owner of the policy, or to the person designated in writing by such insured, assignee or owner, if notice of the assignment has been given to the corporation, at his or her last known post-office address in this State, by the corporation or by any officer thereof or person appointed by it to collect such premium, at least 15 and not more than 45 days prior to the day when the same is payable, as regards policies which do not contain a provision for grace or are not entitled to grace in the payment of premiums and at least five and not more than 45 days prior to the day when the same is payable as regards policies which do contain a provision for grace or are entitled to grace in the payment of premiums. The notice shall also state that unless such premium, interest, installment, or portion thereof then due shall be paid to the corporation or to the duly appointed agent or person authorized to collect such premium, by or before the day it falls due, the policy and all payments thereon will become forfeited and void, except as to the right to a surrender value or paid-up policy, as in the contract provided. If the payment demanded by such notice shall be made within its time limit therefor, it shall be taken to be in full compliance with the requirements of the policy in respect to the time of such payment; and no such policy shall in any case be forfeited or declared forfeited or lapsed until the expiration of 30 days after the mailing of such notice. The affidavit of any officer, clerk, or agent of the corporation, or of anyone authorized to mail such notice, that the notice required by this section has been duly addressed and mailed by the corporation issuing such policy, shall be presumptive evidence that such notice has been duly given. No action shall be maintained to recover under a forfeited policy unless the same is instituted within three years from the day upon which default was made in paying the premium, installment, interest, or portion thereof for which it is claimed that forfeiture ensued. (1909, c. 884; C.S., s. 6465; 1929, c. 308, s. 1; 1931, c. 317; 1945, c. 379.)

Part 4. Miscellaneous Provisions.

§ 58-58-125. Minimum premium rates for assessment life insurance companies.

No assessment life insurance corporation, organization or association of any kind issuing policies or contracts upon the life of any resident of this State shall hereafter be organized or licensed by the Commissioner unless such corporation, organization or association adopt premium rates based upon the attained age of the assured at the time of issuance of the contract and such rates shall not be less than those fixed by the American Experience Table of

Mortality or any other recognized table of mortality approved by the Commissioner. Nothing contained in this section shall be construed to affect burial associations regulated under G.S. 143B-472 through 143B-472.28 or railroad burial associations. (1939, c. 161; 1991, c. 720, ss. 4, 32.)

§ 58-58-130. Distribution of surplus in mutual companies.

Every life insurance company doing business in this State upon the principle of mutual insurance, or the members of which are entitled to share in the surplus funds thereof, may distribute the surplus annually, or once in two, three, four, or five years, as its directors determine. No payments shall be made to policyholders by way of dividends unless the company possesses admitted assets in the amount of such payments in excess of its capital and/or minimum required surplus and all other liabilities. (1903, c. 536, s. 10; Rev., s. 4776; C.S., s. 6466; 1945, c. 379.)

§ 58-58-135. "Group life insurance" defined.

No policy of group life insurance shall be delivered in this State unless it conforms to one of the following descriptions:

(1) A policy issued to an employer, or to the trustee of a fund established by an employer, which employer or trustee shall be deemed the policyholder, to insure employees of the employer for the benefit of persons other than the employer subject to the following requirements:

a. The employees eligible for insurance under the policy shall be all of the employees of the employer, or all of any class or classes thereof determined by conditions pertaining to their employment. The policy may provide that the term "employees" shall include the employees of one or more subsidiary corporations, and the employees, individual proprietors, and partners of one or more affiliated corporations, proprietors or partnerships if the business of the employer and of such affiliated corporations, proprietors or partnerships is under common control through stock ownership, contract, or otherwise. The policy may provide that the term "employees" shall include the individual proprietor or partners if the employer is an individual proprietor or a partnership. The policy may provide that the term "employees" shall include retired employees. The term "employer" as used herein may be deemed to include any county, municipality, or the proper officers, as such, of any unincorporated municipality or any department, division, agency, instrumentality or subdivision of a county, unincorporated municipality or municipality. In all cases where counties, municipalities or unincorporated municipalities or any officer, agent, division, subdivision or agency of the same have heretofore entered into contracts and purchased group life insurance for their employees, such transactions, contracts and insurance and the purchase of the same is hereby approved, authorized and validated.

b. The premium for the policy shall be paid either wholly or partly from the employer's funds or funds contributed by him, or wholly or partly from funds contributed by the insured employees, or by both. A policy on which all or part of the premium is to be derived from funds contributed by the insured employees may be placed in force provided the group is structured on an actuarially sound basis. A policy on which no part of the premium is to be derived from funds contributed by the insured employees must insure all eligible employees, or all except any as to whom evidence of individual insurability is not satisfactory to the insurer.

c. Repealed by Session Laws 2007-298, s. 7.6, effective October 1, 2007.

d. Repealed by Session Laws 1991 (Regular Session, 1992), c. 837, s. 6.

(2) A policy issued to a creditor, who shall be deemed the policyholder, to insure debtors of the creditor, subject to the following requirements:

a. The debtors eligible for insurance under the policy shall be all of the debtors of the creditor whose indebtedness is repayable in installments, or all of any class or classes thereof determined by conditions pertaining to the indebtedness or to the purchase giving rise to the indebtedness. The policy may provide that the term "debtors" shall include the debtors of one or more subsidiary corporations, and the debtors of one or more affiliated corporations, proprietors or partnerships if the business of the policyholder and of such affiliated corporations, proprietors or partnerships is under common control through stock ownership, contract or otherwise.

b. The premium for the policy shall be paid from the creditor's funds, from charges collected from the insured debtors, or from both. A policy on which part or all of the premium is to be derived from the collection from the insured debtors or identifiable charges not required of uninsured debtors shall not include, in the class or classes of debtors eligible for insurance, debtors under obligations outstanding at its date of issue without evidence of individual insurability unless the group is structured on an actuarially sound basis. A policy on which no part of the premium is to be derived from the collection of such identifiable charges must insure all eligible debtors, or all except any as to whom evidence of individual insurability is not satisfactory to the insurer.

c. The policy may be issued only if the group of eligible debtors is then receiving new entrants at the rate of at least 100 persons yearly, or may reasonably be expected to receive at least 100 new entrants during the first policy year, and only if the policy reserves to the insurer the right to require evidence of individual insurability if less than seventy-five percent (75%) of the new entrants become insured.

d, e. Repealed by Session Laws 1975, c. 660, s. 4.

(3) A policy issued to a labor union, which shall be deemed the policyholder, to insure members of such union for the benefit of persons other than the union or any of its officials, representatives or agents, subject to the following requirements:

a. The members eligible for insurance under the policy shall be all of the members of the union, or all of any class or classes thereof determined by conditions pertaining to their employment, or to membership in the union, or both.

b. The premium for the policy shall be paid either wholly or partly from the union's funds, or wholly or partly from funds contributed by the insured members specifically for their insurance, or by both. A policy on which all or part of the premium is to be derived from funds contributed by the insured members specifically for their insurance may be placed in force provided the group is structured on an actuarially sound basis. A policy on which no part of the premium is to be derived from funds contributed by the insured members specifically for their insurance must insure all eligible members, or all except any as to whom evidence of individual insurability is not satisfactory to the insurer.

c. The policy must cover at least 25 members at date of issue.

d. Repealed by Session Laws 1991 (Regular Session, 1992), c. 837, s. 6.

(4) A policy issued to the trustee of a fund established by two or more employers in the same industry or kind of business or by two or more labor unions, which trustee shall be deemed the policyholder, to insure employees of the employers or members of the unions for the benefit of persons other than the employers or the unions, subject to the following requirements:

a. The persons eligible for insurance shall be all of the employees of the employers or all of the members of the unions, or all of any class or classes thereof determined by conditions pertaining to their employment, or to memberships in the unions, or to both. The policy may provide that the term "employees" shall include the individual proprietor or partners if an employer is an individual proprietor or a partnership. The policy may provide that the term "employees" shall include the trustee or the employees of the trustee, or both, if their duties are principally connected with such trusteeship. The policy may provide that the term "employees" shall include retired employees.

b. The premium for the policy shall be paid wholly or partly from funds contributed by the participating employer, labor union, or the insured persons.

If none of the premium paid by the participating employer or labor union is to be derived from funds contributed by the insured persons specifically for the insurance, all eligible employees of that particular participating employer or labor union must be insured, or all except any as to whom evidence of insurability is not satisfactory to the insurer.

If part of the premium paid by the participating employer or labor union is to be derived from funds contributed by the insured persons specifically for their insurance, coverage may be placed in force on employees of a participating employer or on members of a participating labor union provided the group is structured on an actuarially sound basis.

c. The policy must cover at least 100 persons at date of issue.

d. Repealed by Session Laws 1991 (Regular Session, 1992), c. 837, s. 6.

(5) A policy issued to an association of persons having a common professional or business interest, which association shall be deemed the policyholder, to insure members of such association for the benefit of persons other than the association or any of its officials, representatives or agents, subject to the following requirements:

a. Such association shall have had an active existence for at least two years immediately preceding the purchase of such insurance, was formed for purposes other than procuring insurance and does not derive its funds principally from contributions of insured members toward the payment of premiums for the insurance.

b. The members eligible for insurance under the policy shall be all of the members of the association or all of any class or classes thereof determined by conditions pertaining to their employment, or the membership in the association, or both. The policy may provide that the term "members" shall include the employees of members, if their duties are principally connected with the member's business or profession.

c. The premium for the policy shall be paid either wholly or partly from the association's funds, or wholly or partly from funds contributed by the insured members specifically for their insurance, or by both. No policy may be issued if the Commissioner finds that the rate of insured members' contributions will exceed the maximum rate customarily charged employees insured under like group life insurance policies issued in accordance with the provisions of subdivision (1). A policy on which all or part of the premium is to be derived from funds contributed by the insured members specifically for their insurance may be placed in force provided the group is structured on an actuarially sound basis. A policy on which no part of the premium is to be derived from funds contributed by the insured members specifically for their insurance must insure all eligible members, or all except any as to whom evidence of individual insurability is not satisfactory to the insurer.

d. The policy must cover at least 25 members at date of issue.

e. Repealed by Session Laws 1991 (Regular Session, 1992), c. 837, s. 6.

(5a) A policy issued to a group other than those described in subdivisions (1) through (5) of this section, subject to the following requirements:

a. Either of the following is true:

1. The Commissioner has made the following findings:

I. The issuance of the group policy is not contrary to the best interest of the public.

II. The issuance of the group policy would result in economies of acquisition or administration.

III. The benefits are reasonable in relation to the premiums charged.

2. Another state having requirements substantially similar to those contained in sub-sub-subdivision 1. of this sub-subdivision has made a determination that the requirements have been met.

b. The premium for the policy shall be paid from either the policyholder's funds or funds contributed by the covered persons, or from both.

c. An insurer may exclude or limit the coverage on any person as to whom evidence of individual insurability is not satisfactory to the insurer.

(6) Notwithstanding the provisions of this section, or any other provisions of law to the contrary, a policy may be issued to the employees of the State or any other political subdivision where the entire amount of premium therefor is paid by such employees. (1925, c. 58, s. 1; 1931, c. 328; 1943, c. 597, s. 1; 1947, c. 834; 1951, c. 800; 1955, c. 1280; 1957, c. 998; 1959, c. 287; 1965, c. 869; 1971, c. 516; 1973, c. 249; 1975, c. 660, s. 4; 1977, c. 192, ss. 1-4; c. 835; 1987, c. 752, ss. 14-18; 1991 (Reg. Sess., 1992), c. 837, s. 6; 2007-298, s. 7.6; 2007-484, s. 43.5; 2011-215, s. 2.)

§ 58-58-140. Group life insurance standard provisions.

No policy of group life insurance shall be delivered in this State unless it contains in substance the following provisions, or provisions which in the Commissioner's opinion are more favorable to the persons insured, or at least as favorable to the persons insured and more favorable to the policyholder, provided, however, (i) that subdivisions (6) through (10) of this section do not apply to policies issued to a creditor to insure the creditor's debtors; (ii) that the standard provisions required for individual life insurance policies do not apply to group life insurance policies; and (iii) that if the group life insurance policy is on a plan of insurance other than the term plan, it shall contain a nonforfeiture provision or provisions that in the Commissioner's opinion is or are equitable to the insured persons and to the policyholder, but nothing in this section requires group life insurance policies to contain the same nonforfeiture provisions that are required for individual life insurance policies:

(1) A provision that the policyholder is entitled to a grace period of 31 days for the payment of any premium due except the first, during which grace period the death benefit coverage shall continue in force, unless the policyholder has given the insurer written notice of discontinuance before the date of discontinuance and in accordance with the terms of the policy. The policy may provide that the policyholder shall be liable to the insurer for the payment of a pro rata premium for the time the policy was in force during the grace period.

(2) A provision that the validity of the policy shall not be contested, except for nonpayment of premiums, after it has been in force for two years from its date of issue; and that no statement made by any person insured under the policy relating to that person's insurability shall be used in contesting the validity of the insurance with respect to which the statement was made after the insurance has been in force before the contest for a period of two years during the person's lifetime nor unless it is contained in a written instrument signed by the person.

(3) A provision that a copy of the application, if any, of the policyholder shall be attached to the policy when issued, that all statements made by the policyholder or by the persons insured shall be considered representations and not warranties; and that no statement made by any person insured shall be used in any contest unless a copy of the instrument containing the statement is or has been furnished to the person or to the person's beneficiary.

(4) A provision setting forth the conditions, if any, under which the insurer reserves the right to require a person eligible for insurance to furnish evidence of individual insurability satisfactory to the insurer as a condition to part or all of the person's coverage.

(5) A provision specifying an equitable adjustment of premiums or benefits, or both, to be made if the age of a person insured has been misstated; the provision to contain a clear statement of the method of adjustment to be used.

(6) A provision that any sum becoming due because of the death of the person insured shall be payable to the beneficiary designated by the person insured, subject to the provisions of the policy if there is no designated beneficiary as to all or any part of the sum living at the death of the person insured, and subject to any right reserved by the insurer in the policy and set forth in the certificate to pay at its option a part of the sum not exceeding two hundred fifty dollars ($250.00) to any person appearing to the insurer to be

equitably entitled thereto by having incurred funeral or other expenses incident to the last illness or death of the person insured.

(7)   A provision that the insurer will issue to the policyholder, for delivery to each person insured, an individual certificate setting forth a statement as to the insurance protection to which the person is entitled, to whom the insurance benefits are payable, and the rights and conditions set forth in subdivisions (8), (9) and (10) of this section.

(8)   A provision that if the insurance, or any portion of it, on a person covered under the policy ceases because of termination of employment or of membership in the classes eligible for coverage under the policy, the person shall be entitled to be issued by the insurer, without evidence of insurability, an individual policy of life insurance without disability or other supplementary benefits, provided application for the individual policy shall be made, and the first premium paid to the insurer, within 31 days after such termination, and provided further that,

a.   The individual policy shall, at the option of the person, be on any one of the forms, except term insurance, then customarily issued by the insurer at the age and for the amount applied for;

b.   The individual policy shall be in an amount not in excess of the amount of life insurance which ceases because of the termination, provided that any amount of insurance which shall have matured on or before the date of the termination as an endowment payable to the person insured, whether in one sum or in installments or in the form of an annuity, shall not, for the purposes of this provision, be included in the amount which is considered to cease because of the termination; and

c.   The premium on the individual policy shall be at the insurer's then customary rate applicable to the form and amount of the individual policy, to the class of risk to which the person then belongs, and to the person's age on the effective date of the individual policy.

(9)   A provision that if the group policy terminates or is amended so as to terminate the insurance of any class of insured persons, every person insured under the policy at the date of the termination whose insurance terminates and who has been so insured for at least five years before the termination date shall be entitled to be issued by the insurer an individual policy of life insurance, subject to the conditions and limitations in (8) above, except that the group

policy may provide that the amount of the individual policy shall not exceed the smaller of (i) the amount of the person's life insurance protection ceasing because of the termination or amendment of the group policy, less the amount of any life insurance for which the person is or becomes eligible under any group policy issued or reinstated by the same or another insurer within 31 days after termination, and (ii) ten thousand dollars ($10,000).

(10) A provision that if a person insured under the group policy dies during the period within which the person would have been entitled to have been issued an individual policy in accordance with (8) or (9) above and before such an individual policy shall have become effective, the amount of life insurance which the person would have been entitled to have been issued under the individual policy shall be payable as a claim under the group policy, whether or not application for the individual policy or the payment of the first premium therefor has been made. (1925, c. 58, s. 2; 1943, c. 597, s. 2; 1947, c. 834; 1991, c. 644, s. 9.)

§ 58-58-141. Portability of group life insurance.

(a) Definition. - For purposes of this section, "portability" means the prerogative to continue existing group life insurance coverage, or access alternate group life insurance coverage, that may be provided by a group life insurance policy to an individual insured after the individual's affiliation with the initial group terminates.

(b) Applicability. - This section applies to all certificates issued under group policies that are used in this State. This section also applies to a certificate issued under a policy issued and delivered to a trust or to an association outside of this State and covering persons residing in this State.

(c) Prohibitions. - The use of health questions, underwriting, or eligibility requirements that pertain to health status is prohibited when an individual insured elects to access a portability option provided by a group life insurance policy. (2007-298, s. 2.6.)

§ 58-58-145. Group annuity contracts defined; requirements; issuance of individual certificates.

(a)   Any policy or contract, except a joint, reversionary or survivorship annuity contract, whereby annuities are payable to more than one person, is a group annuity contract. The person, firm or corporation to whom or to which the contract is issued, is the holder of the contract. The term "annuitant" means any person to whom or which payments are made under the group annuity contract. No authorized insurer shall deliver or issue for delivery in this State any group annuity contract except upon a group of annuitants that conforms to the following: under a contract issued to an employer, or to the trustee of a fund established by an employer or two or more employers in the same industry or kind of business, the stipulated payments on which shall be paid by the holder of the contract either wholly from the employer's funds or funds contributed by the employer, or partly from the funds and partly from funds contributed by the employees covered by such contract, and providing a plan of retirement annuities under a plan which permits all of the employees of such employer or of any specified class or classes thereof to become annuitants. Any such group of employees may include retired employees, and may include officers and managers as employees, and may include the employees of subsidiary or affiliated corporations of a corporation employer, and may include the individual proprietors, partners and employees of affiliated individuals and firms controlled by the holders through stock ownership, contract or otherwise.

(b)   The insurer of a group annuity contract shall issue to the policyholder or to the annuitant directly, within 30 days of the annuitant's enrollment in the group annuity contract, an individual certificate for each annuitant which:

(1)   Identifies the annuity to which the annuitant is entitled.

(2)   States the name of the person to whom the annuity is payable.

(3)   Discloses all of the rights and obligations of the insurer, the policyholder, the annuitant, and the persons to whom the annuity is payable with respect to the group annuity contract.

G.S. 58-3-150 applies to the form of the individual certificate required by this subsection.

(c)   Each group annuity contract shall include a provision that the insurer will issue to the policyholder within 30 days of the effective date of the contract, for delivery to each annuitant, an individual certificate setting forth the information described in subsection (b) of this section.

(d) This section does not apply to annuities used to fund:

(1) An employee pension plan that is covered by the Employee Retirement Income Security Act of 1974 (ERISA);

(2) A plan described in sections 401(a), 401(k), 403(b), or 457 of the Internal Revenue Code, where the plan, as defined in ERISA, is established or maintained by an employer;

(3) A governmental or church plan defined in section 414 of the Internal Revenue Code or a deferred compensation plan of a state or local government or a tax-exempt organization under section 457 of the Internal Revenue Code; or

(4) A nonqualified deferred compensation arrangement established or maintained by an employer or plan sponsor. (1947, c. 721; 1993, c. 506, s. 3; 2005-234, s. 3; 2006-105, s. 2.9.)

§ 58-58-146. Application for annuities required.

(a) Each individual (nongroup) annuity contract shall be issued only upon application of the annuitant or proposed owner. Any application form, whether paper or electronic, is subject to G.S. 58-3-150, and if taken by an agent, broker, or other producer shall include the certificate of the agent, broker, or other producer that the agent, broker, or other producer has truly and accurately recorded on the application form the information provided by the annuitant or proposed owner. Every annuity contract subject to this section shall contain as part of the contract the original or reproduction of the application required by this section.

(b) The application copy required by this section may be either a photo copy of the original completed application, or a paper print of the completed application form, or a document that represents a compilation of information from the application process. Nothing in this subsection prohibits use of electronic application forms provided the format complies with these requirements. (2007-298, s. 1.2; 2009-382, s. 14.)

§ 58-58-147. Surrender fees on death benefits.

No authorized insurer shall deliver or issue for delivery in this State any deferred annuity contract that contains a provision that reduces the death benefit of the contract by a surrender fee when death occurs during the surrender period. (2007-298, s. 1.2.)

§ 58-58-150. Employee life insurance defined.

Employee life insurance is hereby declared to be that plan of life insurance other than salary savings life insurance under which individual policies are issued to the employees of any employer where such policies are issued on the life of more than one employee at date of issue. Premiums for such policies shall be paid by the employer or the trustee of a fund established by the employer either wholly from the employer's funds, or funds contributed by him, or partly from such funds and partly from funds contributed by the insured employees. (1947, c. 721; 1957, c. 1008.)

§ 58-58-155. Assignment of interest in group policies and annuity contracts.

Any individual insured under a group insurance policy or group annuity contract shall have the right, unless expressly prohibited under the terms of the policy or contract of insurance, to assign to any other person his rights and benefits under the policy or contract, including, but not limited to the right to designate the beneficiary or beneficiaries and the right of conversion guaranteed by G.S. 58-58-140, and, subject to the provisions of the policy relating to assignments thereunder, any such assignment, made either before or after April 28, 1969, shall be valid for the purpose of vesting in the assignee all such rights and benefits so assigned. (1969, c. 319.)

§ 58-58-160. Voting power under policies of group life insurance.

In every group policy issued by a domestic life insurance company, the employer shall be deemed to be the policyholder for all purposes within the meaning of Articles 1 through 64 of this Chapter, and, if entitled to vote at meetings of the company, shall be entitled to one vote thereat. (1925, c. 58, s. 3.)

§ 58-58-165. Exemption from execution.

No policy of group insurance, nor the proceeds thereof, when paid to any employee or employees thereunder, shall be liable to attachment, garnishment, or other process, or to be seized, taken, appropriated or applied by any legal or equitable process or operation of law, to pay any debt or liability of such employee, or his beneficiary, or any other person who may have a right thereunder, either before or after payment; but the proceeds thereof, when made payable to the estate of the employee insured, shall constitute a part of the estate of such employee available for the payment of debts. (1925, c. 58, s. 4; 1957, c. 1361.)

§ 58-58-170. Contestability after reinstatement.

A reinstated policy of life insurance or annuity contract may be contested on account of fraud or misrepresentation of facts material to the reinstatement only for the same period following reinstatement and with the same conditions and exceptions as the policy provides with respect to contestability after original issuance. The reinstatement application shall be deemed to be a part of the policy whether or not attached thereto. (1987, c. 752, s. 13.)

§§ 58-58-175 through 58-58-195: Reserved for future codification purposes.

Part 5. Viatical Settlements.

§ 58-58-200. Short title.

This Part may be cited as the Viatical Settlements Act. (2001-436, s. 3.)

§ 58-58-205. Definitions.

As used in this Article:

(1) "Advertising" means any written, electronic, or printed communication or any communication by means of recorded telephone messages or transmitted on radio, television, the Internet, or similar communications media, including filmstrips, motion pictures, and videos, published, disseminated, circulated, or placed before the public, directly or indirectly, for the purpose of creating an interest in or inducing a person to sell a life insurance policy under a viatical settlement contract.

(2) "Business of viatical settlements" means an activity involved in, but not limited to, the offering, solicitation, negotiation, procurement, effectuation, purchasing, investing, financing, monitoring, tracking, underwriting, selling, transferring, assigning, pledging, hypothecating, or in any other manner, of viatical settlement contracts. "Business of viatical settlements" does not include an activity involving viatical settlement contracts as investments as regulated by Chapter 78A of the General Statutes.

(3) "Chronically ill" means:

a. Being unable to perform at least two activities of daily living (i.e., eating, toileting, transferring, bathing, dressing, or continence);

b. Requiring substantial supervision to protect the individual from threats to health and safety due to severe cognitive impairment; or

c. Having a level of disability similar to that described in sub-subdivision a. of this subdivision as determined by the Secretary of Health and Human Services.

(4) "Financing entity" means an underwriter, placement agent, lender, purchaser of securities, purchaser of a policy from a viatical settlement provider, credit enhancer, or any entity that has a direct ownership in a policy that is the subject of a viatical settlement contract, but:

a. Whose principal activity related to the transaction is providing funds to effect the viatical settlement or purchase of one or more viaticated policies; and

b. Who has an agreement in writing with one or more licensed viatical settlement providers to finance the acquisition of viatical settlement contracts.

"Financing entity" does not include a nonaccredited investor or viatical settlement purchaser.

(5) "Fraudulent viatical settlement act" includes:

a. Acts or omissions committed by any person who, knowingly and with intent to defraud, for the purpose of depriving another of property or for pecuniary gain, commits, or permits its employees or its agents to engage in acts including:

1. Presenting, causing to be presented, or preparing with knowledge or belief that it will be presented to or by a viatical settlement provider, viatical settlement broker, viatical settlement purchaser, financing entity, insurer, insurance producer, viator, insured or any other person false material information, or concealing material information, as part of, in support of, or concerning a fact material to one or more of the following:

I. An application for the issuance of a viatical settlement contract or insurance policy.

II. The underwriting of a viatical settlement contract or insurance policy.

III. A claim for payment or benefit under a viatical settlement contract or insurance policy.

IV. Premiums paid on an insurance policy.

V. Payments and changes in ownership or beneficiary made in accordance with the terms of a viatical settlement contract or insurance policy.

VI. The reinstatement or conversion of an insurance policy.

VII. The solicitation, offer, effectuation, or sale of a viatical settlement contract or insurance policy.

VIII. The issuance of written evidence of viatical settlement contract or insurance.

IX. A financing transaction.

2. Employing any device, scheme, or artifice to defraud related to viaticated policies.

b. In the furtherance of a fraud or to prevent the detection of a fraud, any person commits or permits the person's employees or agents to:

1. Remove, conceal, alter, destroy, or sequester from the Commissioner the assets or records of a licensee or other person engaged in the business of viatical settlements;

2. Misrepresent or conceal the financial condition of a licensee, financing entity, insurer, or other person;

3. Transact the business of viatical settlements in violation of laws requiring a license, certificate of authority, or other legal authority for the transaction of the business of viatical settlements; or

4. File with the Commissioner or the insurance regulator of another jurisdiction a document containing false information or otherwise conceal information about a material fact from the Commissioner.

c. Embezzlement, theft, misappropriation, or conversion of monies, funds, premiums, credits, or other property of a viatical settlement provider, insurer, insured, viator, insurance policy owner, or any other person engaged in the business of viatical settlements or insurance; or

d. Attempting to commit, assisting, aiding, or abetting in the commission of, or conspiracy to commit, the acts or omissions specified in this subdivision.

(6) "Policy" means an individual or group life insurance policy, group life insurance certificate, group life insurance contract, or any other arrangement of life insurance affecting the rights of a resident of this State or bearing a reasonable relation to this State, regardless of whether delivered or issued for delivery in this State.

(7) "Related provider trust" means a titling trust or other trust established by a licensed viatical settlement provider or a financing entity for the sole purpose

of holding the ownership or beneficial interest in purchased policies in connection with a financing transaction.

(8) "Special purpose entity" means a corporation, partnership, trust, limited liability company, or other similar entity formed solely to provide either directly or indirectly access to institutional capital markets for a financing entity or licensed viatical settlement provider.

(9) "Terminally ill" means having an illness or sickness that can reasonably be expected to result in death in 24 months or fewer.

(10) "Viatical settlement broker" or "broker" means a person that on behalf of a viator and for a fee, commission, or other valuable consideration offers or attempts to negotiate viatical settlement contracts between a viator and one or more viatical settlement providers. The term does not include an attorney, certified public accountant, or a financial planner accredited by a nationally recognized accreditation agency who is retained to represent the viator and whose compensation is not paid directly or indirectly by the viatical settlement provider or purchaser.

(11) "Viatical settlement contract" means a written agreement establishing the terms under which compensation or anything of value will be paid, which compensation or value is less than the expected death benefit of the policy, in return for the viator's assignment, transfer, sale, or devise of the death benefit or ownership of any portion of the policy. A viatical settlement contract also includes a contract for a loan or other financing transaction with a viator secured primarily by a policy, other than a loan by a life insurance company under the terms of the life insurance contract, or a loan secured by the cash value of a policy. A viatical settlement contract includes an agreement with a viator to transfer ownership or change the beneficiary designation at a later date regardless of the date that compensation is paid to the viator.

(12) "Viatical settlement provider" or "provider" means a person, other than a viator, that enters into or effectuates a viatical settlement contract on residents of this State or residents of another state from offices within this State. "Viatical settlement provider" or "provider" does not include:

a. A bank, savings bank, savings and loan association, credit union, or other licensed lending institution that takes an assignment of a life insurance policy as collateral for a loan;

b. The issuer of a life insurance policy providing accelerated benefits under rules adopted by the Commissioner and under the contract;

c. An authorized or eligible insurer that provides stop-loss coverage to a viatical settlement provider, purchaser, financing entity, special purpose entity, or related provider trust;

d. A natural person who enters into or effectuates no more than one agreement in a calendar year for the transfer of life insurance policies for any value less than the expected death benefit;

e. A financing entity;

f. A special purpose entity;

g. A related provider trust;

h. A viatical settlement purchaser; or

i. An accredited investor or qualified institutional buyer as defined respectively in Regulation D, Rule 501 or Rule 144A of the Federal Securities Act of 1933, as amended, and who purchases a viaticated policy from a viatical settlement provider.

(13) "Viatical settlement purchase agreement" or "purchase agreement" means an agreement, entered into by a viatical settlement purchaser, to which the viator is not a party, to purchase a life insurance policy or an interest in a life insurance policy, that is entered into for the purpose of deriving an economic benefit.

(14) "Viatical settlement purchaser" or "purchaser" means a person who gives a sum of money as consideration for a life insurance policy or an interest in the death benefits of a life insurance policy or a person who owns or acquires or is entitled to a beneficial interest in a trust that owns a viatical settlement contract or is the beneficiary of a life insurance policy that has been or will be the subject of a viatical settlement contract for the purpose of deriving an economic benefit. "Viatical settlement purchaser" does not include:

a. A licensee under this Part;

b.   An accredited investor or qualified institutional buyer as defined respectively in Regulation D, Rule 501 or Rule 144A of the Federal Securities Act of 1933, as amended;

c.   A financing entity;

d.   A special purpose entity; or

e.   A related provider trust.

(15)   "Viaticated policy" means a policy that has been acquired by a viatical settlement provider under a viatical settlement contract.

(16)   "Viator" means the owner of a policy or a certificate holder under a group policy who enters or seeks to enter into a viatical settlement contract. For the purposes of this Part, a viator shall not be limited to an owner of a life insurance policy or a certificate holder under a group policy insuring the life of an individual with a terminal or chronic illness or condition except where specifically addressed. "Viator" does not include:

a.   A licensee under this Part;

b.   An accredited investor or qualified institutional buyer as defined respectively in Regulation D, Rule 501 or Rule 144A of the Federal Securities Act of 1933, as amended;

c.   A financing entity;

d.   A special purpose entity; or

e.   A related provider trust. (2001-436, s. 3; 2007-298, s. 7.7; 2007-484, s. 43.5; 2011-284, s. 56.)

§ 58-58-210. License requirements.

(a)   No person shall operate as a provider or broker without first obtaining a license from the insurance regulator of the state of residence of the viator. If there is more than one viator on a single policy and the viators are residents of different states, the viatical settlement shall be governed by the law of the state in which the viator having the largest percentage ownership resides or, if the viators hold equal ownership, the state of residence of one viator agreed upon in writing by all viators.

(b)	Application for a provider or broker license shall be made to the Commissioner by the applicant on a form prescribed by the Commissioner, and these applications shall be accompanied by a fee of five hundred dollars ($500.00).

(c)	Licenses may be renewed from year to year on the anniversary date upon payment of the annual renewal fee of five hundred dollars ($500.00). Failure to pay the fees by the renewal date results in expiration of the license.

(d)	The applicant shall provide information on forms required by the Commissioner. The Commissioner may require the applicant to fully disclose the identity of all stockholders, partners, officers, members, and employees; and the Commissioner may refuse to issue a license in the name of a legal entity if not satisfied that any officer, employee, stockholder, partner, or member of the legal entity who may materially influence the applicant's conduct meets the standards of this Part.

(e)	A license issued to a legal entity authorizes all partners, officers, members, and designated employees to act as providers or brokers, as applicable, under the license; and all those persons shall be named in the application and any supplements to the application.

(f)	Upon the filing of an application and the payment of the license fee, the Commissioner shall investigate each applicant and issue a license if the Commissioner finds that the applicant:

(1)	If a provider, has provided a detailed plan of operation.

(2)	Is competent and trustworthy and intends to act in good faith in the capacity involved by the license applied for.

(3)	Has a good business reputation and has had experience, training, or education so as to be qualified in the business for which the license is applied.

(4)	If a legal entity, provides a certificate of good standing from the state of its domicile.

(g) The Commissioner shall not issue a license to a nonresident applicant unless a written designation of an agent for service of process is filed and maintained with the Commissioner or the applicant has filed with the Commissioner the applicant's written irrevocable consent that any action against the applicant may be commenced against the applicant by service of process on the Commissioner.

(h) A provider or broker shall provide to the Commissioner new or revised information about officers, ten percent (10%) or more stockholders, partners, directors, members, or designated employees within 20 days after any change in the constituent membership of that respective category of persons. (2001-436, s. 3; 2009-451, s. 21.17(a).)

§ 58-58-215. License revocation and denial.

The Commissioner may suspend, revoke, or refuse to issue or renew the license of a provider or broker if the Commissioner finds that:

(1) There was any material misrepresentation in the application for the license;

(2) The licensee or any officer, partner, member, or key management personnel has been convicted of fraudulent or dishonest practices, is subject to a final administrative action, or is otherwise shown to be untrustworthy or incompetent;

(3) The provider demonstrates a pattern of unreasonable payments to viators;

(4) The licensee or any officer, partner, member, or key management personnel has been found guilty of, or has pleaded guilty or nolo contendere to, any felony, or to a misdemeanor involving fraud or moral turpitude, regardless of whether a judgment of conviction has been entered by the court;

(5) The provider has entered into any viatical settlement contract that has not been approved pursuant to this Part;

(6) The provider has failed to honor contractual obligations set out in a viatical settlement contract;

(7) The licensee no longer meets the requirements for initial licensure;

(8) The provider has assigned, transferred, or pledged a viaticated policy to a person other than a provider licensed in this State, viatical settlement purchaser, an accredited investor, or qualified institutional buyer as defined respectively in Regulation D, Rule 501 or Rule 144A of the Federal Securities Act of 1933, as amended, financing entity, special purpose entity, or related provider trust; or

(9) The licensee or any officer, partner, member, or key management personnel has violated any provision of this Part. (2001-436, s. 3.)

§ 58-58-220. Approval of viatical settlement contracts and disclosure statements.

A person shall not use a contract or provide to a viator a disclosure statement form in this State unless filed with and approved by the Commissioner. The Commissioner shall disapprove a contract form or disclosure statement form if, in the Commissioner's opinion, the contract or provisions contained therein are unreasonable, contrary to the interests of the public, or otherwise misleading or unfair to the viator. The Commissioner may also require the submission of advertising material. (2001-436, s. 3.)

§ 58-58-225. Reporting requirements and privacy.

(a) Each licensee shall file with the Commissioner on or before June 1 of each year an annual statement containing such information as the Commissioner prescribes by administrative rule.

(b) Except as otherwise allowed or required by law, a provider, broker, insurance company, insurance producer, information bureau, rating agency or company, or any other person with actual knowledge of an insured's identity shall not disclose that identity as an insured, or the insured's financial or medical information, to any other person unless the disclosure:

(1) Is necessary to effect a viatical settlement between the viator and a provider and the viator and insured have provided prior written consent to the disclosure;

(2) Is provided in response to an investigation or examination by the Commissioner or any other governmental officer or agency or pursuant to the requirements of G.S. 58-58-270;

(3) Is a term of or condition to the transfer of a policy by one provider to another provider;

(4) Is necessary to permit a financing entity, related provider trust, or special purpose entity to finance the purchase of policies by a provider and the viator and insured have provided prior written consent to the disclosure;

(5) Is necessary to allow the provider or broker or its authorized representatives to make contacts for the purpose of determining health status; or

(6) Is required to purchase stop-loss coverage. (2001-436, s. 3.)

§ 58-58-230. Examinations.

(a) The Commissioner may conduct an examination of a licensee as often as the Commissioner considers appropriate.

(b) An examination under this Part shall be conducted in accordance with the Examination Law.

(c) In lieu of an examination of any foreign or alien person licensed under this Part, the Commissioner may accept an examination report on the licensee prepared by the appropriate viatical settlement regulator for the licensee's state of domicile or port-of-entry state.

(d) When making an examination under this Part, the Commissioner may retain attorneys, appraisers, independent actuaries, independent certified public accountants, or other professionals and specialists as examiners, the reasonable cost of which shall be borne by the licensee that is the subject of the examination. (2001-436, s. 3.)

§ 58-58-235. Record retention requirements.

(a) A person licensed under this Part shall retain copies for five years of all:

(1) Proposed, offered, or executed contracts, purchase agreements, underwriting documents, policy forms, and applications from the date of the proposal, offer, or execution of the contract or purchase agreement, whichever is later.

(2) Checks, drafts, or other evidence and documentation related to the payment, transfer, deposit, or release of funds from the date of the transaction.

(3) Other records and documents related to the requirements of this Part.

(b) This section does not relieve a person of the obligation to produce these documents to the Commissioner after the retention period has expired if the person has retained the documents.

(c) Records required to be retained by this section must be legible and complete and may be retained in paper, photograph, microprocessor, magnetic, mechanical, or electronic media, or by any process that accurately reproduces or forms a durable medium for the reproduction of a record. (2001-436, s. 3.)

§ 58-58-240. Investigative authority of the Commissioner.

The Commissioner may investigate suspected fraudulent viatical settlement acts and persons engaged in the business of viatical settlements. (2001-436, s. 3.)

§ 58-58-245. Disclosure.

(a) With each application for a viatical settlement, the provider or broker shall provide the viator with at least the following disclosures no later than the time the application for the contract is signed by all parties. The disclosures shall be provided in a separate document that is signed by the viator and the provider or broker and shall provide the following information:

(1) There are possible alternatives to contracts including any accelerated death benefits or policy loans offered under the viator's policy.

(2) Some or all of the proceeds of the viatical settlement may be taxable under federal income tax and state franchise and income taxes, and assistance should be sought from a professional tax advisor.

(3) Proceeds of the viatical settlement could be subject to the claims of creditors.

(4) Receipt of the proceeds of a viatical settlement may adversely affect the viator's eligibility for Medicaid or other government benefits or entitlements, and advice should be obtained from the appropriate government agencies.

(5) The viator has the right to rescind a contract for 10 business days after the receipt of the viatical settlement proceeds by the viator, as provided in G.S. 58-58-250(h). If the insured dies during the rescission period, the settlement contract shall be deemed to have been rescinded, subject to repayment of all viatical settlement proceeds and any premiums, loans, and loan interest to the provider or purchaser.

(6) Funds will be sent to the viator within three business days after the provider has received the insurer or group administrator's acknowledgment that ownership of the policy or interest in the certificate has been transferred and the beneficiary has been designated.

(7) Entering into a contract may cause other rights or benefits, including conversion rights and waiver of premium benefits that may exist under the policy, to be forfeited by the viator. Assistance should be sought from a financial adviser.

(8) Disclosure to a viator shall include distribution of a brochure describing the process of viatical settlements. The NAIC's form for the brochure shall be used unless the Commissioner develops one.

(9) The disclosure document shall contain the following language: "All medical, financial, or personal information solicited or obtained by a provider or broker about an insured, including the insured's identity or the identity of family

members, a spouse or a significant other may be disclosed as necessary to effect the viatical settlement between the viator and the provider. If you are asked to provide this information, you will be asked to consent to the disclosure. The information may be provided to someone who buys the policy or provides funds for the purchase. You may be asked to renew your permission to share information every two years.

(10) The insured may be contacted by either the provider or broker or its authorized representative for the purpose of determining the insured's health status. This contact is limited to once every three months if the insured has a life expectancy of more than one year, and no more than once per month if the insured has a life expectancy of one year or less.

(b) A provider shall provide the viator with at least the following disclosures no later than the date the contract is signed by all parties. The disclosures shall be conspicuously displayed in the contract or in a separate document signed by the viator and the provider or broker, and provide the following information:

(1) State the affiliation, if any, between the provider and the issuer of the insurance policy to be viaticated.

(2) The document shall include the name, address, and telephone number of the provider.

(3) A broker shall disclose to a prospective viator the amount and method of calculating the broker's compensation. The term "compensation" includes anything of value paid or given to a broker for the placement of a policy.

(4) If an insurance policy to be viaticated has been issued as a joint policy or involves family riders or any coverage of a life other than the insured under the policy to be viaticated, the viator shall be informed of the possible loss of coverage on the other lives under the policy and shall be advised to consult with his or her insurance producer or the insurer issuing the policy for advice on the proposed viatical settlement.

(5) State the dollar amount of the current death benefit payable to the provider under the policy. If known, the provider shall also disclose the availability of any additional guaranteed insurance benefits, the dollar amount of any accidental death and dismemberment benefits under the policy, and the provider's interest in those benefits.

(6) State the name, business address, and telephone number of the independent third-party escrow agent and the fact that the viator or owner may inspect or receive copies of the relevant escrow or trust agreements or documents.

(c) If the provider transfers ownership or changes the beneficiary of the insurance policy, the provider shall communicate the change in ownership or beneficiary to the insured within 20 days after the change. (2001-436, s. 3.)

§ 58-58-250. General rules.

(a) A provider entering into a contract shall first obtain:

(1) If the viator is the insured, a written statement from a licensed attending physician that the viator is of sound mind and under no constraint or undue influence to enter into a contract.

(2) A document in which the insured consents to the release of his or her medical records to a provider or broker and, if the policy being viaticated has been in effect for less than five years, to the insurance company that issued the policy covering the life of the insured.

(b) Within 20 days after a viator executes documents necessary to transfer any rights under a policy or within 20 days after entering any agreement, option, promise, or any other form of understanding, expressed or implied, to viaticate the policy, the provider shall give written notice to the insurer that issued that policy that the policy has or will become a viaticated policy. The notice shall be accompanied by the documents required by subsection (c) of this section.

(c) If the policy being viaticated has been in effect for less than five years, the viatical provider shall deliver a copy of the medical release required under subdivision (a)(2) of this section, a copy of the viator's application for the contract, the notice required under subsection (b) of this section, and a request for verification of coverage to the insurer that issued the policy that is the subject of the viatical settlement. The NAIC's form for verification shall be used unless the Commissioner develops standards for verification.

(d) The insurer shall respond to a request for verification of coverage submitted on an approved form by a provider within 30 days after the date the request is received and shall indicate whether, based on the medical evidence and documents provided, the insurer intends to pursue an investigation at this time regarding the validity of the policy.

(e) Before or at the time of execution of the contract, the provider shall obtain a witnessed document in which the viator consents to the contract, represents that the viator has a full and complete understanding of the contract, that he or she has a full and complete understanding of the benefits of the policy, acknowledges that he or she is entering into the contract freely and voluntarily and, for persons with a terminal or chronic illness or condition, acknowledges that the insured has a terminal or chronic illness or condition and that the terminal or chronic illness or condition was first diagnosed after the policy was issued.

(f) If a broker performs any of these activities required of the provider, the provider is deemed to have fulfilled the requirements of this section.

(g) All medical information solicited or obtained by any licensee is subject to the applicable provisions of federal and North Carolina law relating to confidentiality of medical information.

(h) All contracts entered into in this State shall provide the viator with an unconditional right to rescind the contract for at least 10 business days after the receipt of the viatical settlement proceeds. If the insured dies during the rescission period, the contract shall be deemed to have been rescinded, subject to repayment to the provider or purchaser of all viatical settlement proceeds, and any premiums, loans, and loan interest that have been paid by the provider or purchaser.

(i) The provider shall instruct the viator to send the executed documents required to effect the change in ownership, assignment, or change in beneficiary directly to the independent escrow agent. Within three business days after the date the escrow agent receives the documents, or from the date the provider receives the documents, if the viator erroneously provides the documents directly to the provider, the provider shall pay or transfer the proceeds of the viatical settlement into an escrow or trust account maintained in a state or federally chartered financial institution, the deposits of which are insured by the Federal Deposit Insurance Corporation (FDIC) or any successor entity. Upon payment of the settlement proceeds into the escrow account, the escrow agent shall deliver the original change in ownership, assignment, or change in beneficiary forms to the provider or related provider trust. Upon the escrow agent's receipt of the acknowledgment of the properly completed transfer of ownership, assignment, or designation of beneficiary from the insurance company, the escrow agent shall pay the settlement proceeds to the viator.

(j)   Failure to tender consideration to the viator for the contract within the time required under G.S. 58-58-245(a)(6) renders the contract voidable by the viator for lack of consideration until the time consideration is tendered to and accepted by the viator.

(k)   Contacts with the insured for the purpose of determining the health status of the insured by the provider or broker after the viatical settlement has occurred shall only be made by the provider or broker licensed in this State or its authorized representatives and shall be limited to once every three months for insureds with a life expectancy of more than one year, and to no more than once per month for insureds with a life expectancy of one year or less. The provider or broker shall explain the procedure for these contacts at the time the contract is entered into. The limitations set forth in this subsection shall not apply to any contacts with an insured for reasons other than determining the insured's health status. Providers and brokers shall be responsible for the actions of their authorized representatives.

(l)   Every related provider trust shall have a written agreement with the licensed viatical settlement provider under which the licensed viatical settlement provider is responsible for ensuring compliance with all statutory and regulatory requirements and under which the trust agrees to make all records and files related to viatical settlement transactions available to the Commissioner as if those records and files were maintained directly by the licensed viatical settlement provider.

(m)   Notwithstanding the manner in which a viatical settlement broker is compensated, a broker is deemed to represent only the viator and owes a fiduciary duty to the viator to act according to the viator's instructions and in the best interest of the viator. (2001-436, s. 3.)

§ 58-58-255. Prohibited practices.

(a)   It is a violation of this Part for any person to enter into a contract within a two-year period commencing with the date of issuance of the policy unless the viator certifies to the provider that one or more of the following conditions have been met within the two-year period:

(1)   The policy was issued upon the viator's exercise of conversion rights arising out of a policy, provided the total time covered under the conversion policy plus the time covered under the prior policy is at least 24 months, or the contestability and suicide time periods have been waived by the insurer. The time covered under a group policy shall be calculated without regard to any change in insurance carriers, provided the coverage has been continuous and under the same group sponsorship.

(2)   The viator is a charitable organization exempt from taxation under 26 U.S.C. § 501(c)(3).

(3)   The viator is not a natural person (e.g., the owner is a corporation, limited liability company, partnership, etc.).

(4)   The viator submits independent evidence to the provider that one or more of the following conditions have been met within the two-year period:

a.   The viator or insured is terminally or chronically ill.

b.   The viator's spouse dies.

c.   The viator divorces his or her spouse.

d.   The viator retires from full-time employment.

e.   The viator becomes physically or mentally disabled and a physician determines that the disability prevents the viator from maintaining full-time employment.

f.   The viator was the insured's employer at the time the policy was issued and the employment relationship terminated.

g.   A final order, judgment, or decree is entered by a court of competent jurisdiction, on the application of a creditor of the viator, adjudicating the viator bankrupt or insolvent, or approving a petition seeking reorganization of the viator or appointing a receiver, trustee, or liquidator to all or a substantial part of the viator's assets.

h. The viator experiences a significant decrease in income that is unexpected and that impairs the viator's reasonable ability to pay the policy premium.

i. The viator or insured disposes of his or her ownership interests in a closely held corporation.

(b) Copies of the independent evidence described in subdivision (a)(4) of this section and documents required by G.S. 58-58-250(a) shall be submitted to the insurer when the provider submits a request to the insurer for verification of coverage. The copies shall be accompanied by a letter of attestation from the provider that the copies are true and correct copies of the documents received by the provider.

(c) If the provider submits to the insurer a copy of the owner or insured's certification described in subdivision (a)(4) and subsection (b) of this section when the provider submits a request to the insurer to effect the transfer of the policy to the provider, the copy shall be deemed to conclusively establish that the contract satisfies the requirements of this section, and the insurer shall timely respond to the request. (2001-436, s. 3.)

§ 58-58-260. Advertising for viatical settlements.

(a) The purpose of this section is to provide prospective viators with clear and unambiguous statements in the advertisement of viatical settlements and to assure the clear, truthful, and adequate disclosure of the benefits, risks, limitations, and exclusions of any contract. This purpose is intended to be accomplished by the establishment of guidelines and standards of permissible and impermissible conduct in the advertising of viatical settlements to assure that product descriptions are presented in a manner that prevents unfair, deceptive, or misleading advertising and is conducive to accurate presentation and description of viatical settlements through the advertising media and material used by viatical settlement licensees.

(b) This section shall apply to any advertising of contracts or related products or services intended for dissemination in this State, including Internet advertising viewed by persons located in this State. Where disclosure requirements are established pursuant to federal regulation, this section shall be interpreted so as to minimize or eliminate conflict with federal regulation wherever possible.

(c) Every viatical settlement licensee shall establish and at all times maintain a system of control over the content, form, and method of dissemination of all advertisements of its contracts, products, and services. All advertisements, regardless of by whom written, created, designed, or presented, shall be the responsibility of the viatical settlement licensee, as well as the individual who created or presented the advertisement. A system of control shall include regular routine notification, at least once a year, to agents and others, authorized by the viatical settlement licensee, who disseminate advertisements of the requirements and procedures for approval before the use of any advertisements not furnished by the viatical settlement licensee.

(d) Advertisements shall be truthful and not misleading in fact or by implication. The form and content of an advertisement of a contract shall be sufficiently complete and clear so as to avoid deception. It shall not have the capacity or tendency to mislead or deceive. Whether an advertisement has the capacity or tendency to mislead or deceive shall be determined by the Commissioner from the overall impression that the advertisement may be reasonably expected to create upon a person of average education or intelligence within the segment of the public to which it is directed.

(e) All information required to be disclosed under this Part shall be set out conspicuously and in close conjunction with the statements to which such information relates or under appropriate captions of such prominence that it shall not be minimized, rendered obscure, or presented in an ambiguous fashion or intermingled with the context of the advertisement so as to be confusing or misleading.

(f) An advertisement shall not:

(1) Omit material information or use words, phrases, statements, references, or illustrations if the omission or use has the capacity, tendency, or effect of misleading or deceiving viators as to the nature or extent of any benefit, loss covered, premium payable, or state or federal tax consequence. The fact that the contract offered is made available for inspection before consummation of the sale, or an offer is made to refund the payment if the viator is not satisfied or that the contract includes a "free look" period that satisfies or exceeds legal requirements, does not remedy misleading statements.

(2) Use the name or title of a life insurance company or a policy unless the insurer has approved the advertisement.

(3) State or imply that interest charged on an accelerated death benefit or a policy loan is unfair, inequitable, or in any manner an incorrect or improper practice.

(4) State or imply that a contract, benefit, or service has been approved or endorsed by a group of individuals, society, association, or other organization unless that is the fact and unless any relationship between an organization and the viatical settlement licensee is disclosed. If the entity making the endorsement or testimonial is owned, controlled, or managed by the viatical settlement licensee, or receives any payment or other consideration from the viatical settlement licensee for making an endorsement or testimonial, that fact shall be disclosed in the advertisement.

(5) Contain statistical information unless it accurately reflects recent and relevant facts. The source of all statistics used in an advertisement shall be identified.

(6) Disparage insurers, providers, brokers, insurance producers, policies, services, or methods of marketing.

(7) Use a trade name, group designation, name of the parent company of a viatical settlement licensee, name of a particular division of the viatical settlement licensee, service mark, slogan, symbol, or other device or reference without disclosing the name of the viatical settlement licensee, if the advertisement would have the capacity or tendency to mislead or deceive as to the true identity of the viatical settlement licensee, or to create the impression that a company other than the viatical settlement licensee would have any responsibility for the financial obligation under a contract.

(8) Use any combination of words, symbols, or physical materials that by their content, phraseology, shape, color, or other characteristics are so similar to a combination of words, symbols, or physical materials used by a government program or agency or otherwise appear to be of such a nature that they tend to mislead prospective viators into believing that the solicitation is in some manner connected with a government program or agency.

(9) Create the impression that the provider, its financial condition or status, the payment of its claims, or the merits, desirability, or advisability of its contracts are recommended or endorsed by any government entity.

(g) The words "free", "no cost", "without cost", "no additional cost", "at no extra cost", or words of similar import shall not be used with respect to any benefit or service unless true. An advertisement may specify the charge for a benefit or a service, may state that a charge is included in the payment, or use other appropriate language.

(h) Testimonials, appraisals, or analyses used in advertisements must be genuine; represent the current opinion of the author; be applicable to the contract, product, or service advertised, if any; and be accurately reproduced with sufficient completeness to avoid misleading or deceiving prospective viators as to the nature or scope of the testimonials, appraisals, analyses, or endorsements. In using testimonials, appraisals, or analyses, the viatical settlement licensee makes as its own all the statements contained therein, and the statements are subject to all the provisions of this section.

(i) If the individual making a testimonial, appraisal, analysis, or an endorsement has a financial interest in the provider or related entity as a stockholder, director, officer, employee, or otherwise, or receives any benefit directly or indirectly other than required union scale wages, that fact shall be prominently disclosed in the advertisement.

(j) When an endorsement refers to benefits received under a contract, all pertinent information shall be retained for a period of five years after its use.

(k) The name of the viatical settlement licensee shall be clearly identified in all advertisements about the licensee or its contracts, products, or services, and if any specific contract is advertised, the contract shall be identified either by form number or some other appropriate description. If an application is part of the advertisement, the name of the provider or broker shall be shown on the application.

(l) An advertisement may state that a viatical settlement licensee is licensed in the state where the advertisement appears, provided it does not exaggerate that fact or suggest or imply that a competing viatical settlement licensee may not be so licensed. The advertisement may ask the audience to consult the licensee's web site or contact the Department to find out if the state requires licensing and, if so, whether the provider or broker is licensed.

(m)   The name of the actual licensee shall be stated in all of its advertisements. An advertisement shall not use a trade name, any group designation, name of any affiliate or controlling entity of the licensee, service mark, slogan, symbol, or other device in a manner that would have the capacity or tendency to mislead or deceive as to the true identity of the actual licensee or create the false impression that an affiliate or controlling entity would have any responsibility for the financial obligation of the licensee.

(n)   An advertisement shall not directly or indirectly create the impression that any state or federal governmental agency endorses, approves, or favors:

(1)   Any viatical settlement licensee or its business practices or methods of operation;

(2)   The merits, desirability, or advisability of any contract;

(3)   Any contract; or

(4)   Any policy or life insurance company.

(o)   If the advertiser emphasizes the speed with which the viatication will occur, the advertising must disclose the average time frame from completed application to the date of offer and from acceptance of the offer to receipt of the funds by the viator.

(p)   If the advertising emphasizes the dollar amounts available to viators, the advertising shall disclose the average purchase price as a percent of face value obtained by viators contracting with the licensee during the past six months. (2001-436, s. 3.)

§ 58-58-265. Fraudulent viatical settlement acts, interference, and participation of convicted felons prohibited.

(a)   A person who commits a fraudulent viatical settlement act is guilty of a Class H felony.

(b) A person shall not knowingly or intentionally interfere with the enforcement of the provisions of this Part or investigations of suspected or actual violations of this Part.

(c) A person in the business of viatical settlements shall not knowingly or intentionally permit any person convicted of a felony involving dishonesty or breach of trust to participate in the business of viatical settlements. (2001-436, s. 3.)

§ 58-58-267. Fraud warning required.

(a) Viatical settlement contracts and purchase agreement forms and applications for viatical settlements, regardless of the form of transmission, shall contain the following statement or a substantially similar statement:

"Any person who knowingly presents false information in an application for insurance or viatical settlement contract or a viatical settlement purchase agreement is guilty of a felony and may be subject to fines and confinement in prison."

(b) The lack of a statement as required in subsection (a) of this section does not constitute a defense in any prosecution for a fraudulent viatical settlement act. (2001-436, s. 3.)

§ 58-58-268. Viatical settlement antifraud initiatives.

(a) Viatical settlement providers and viatical settlement brokers shall have in place antifraud initiatives reasonably calculated to detect, prosecute, and prevent fraudulent viatical settlement acts. At the discretion of the Commissioner, the Commissioner may order, or a licensee may request and the Commissioner may grant, such modifications of the following required initiatives as necessary to ensure an effective antifraud program. The modifications may be more or less restrictive than the required initiatives so long as the modifications may reasonably be expected to accomplish the purpose of this section.

(b) Antifraud initiatives shall include:

(1) Fraud investigators, who may be viatical settlement provider employees or viatical settlement broker employees or independent contractors; and

(2) An antifraud plan, which shall be submitted to the Commissioner. The antifraud plan shall include, but not be limited to:

a. A description of the procedures for detecting and investigating possible fraudulent viatical settlement acts and procedures for resolving material inconsistencies between medical records and insurance applications;

b. A description of the procedures for reporting possible fraudulent viatical settlement acts to the Commissioner;

c. A description of the plan for antifraud education and training of underwriters and other personnel; and

d. A description or chart outlining the organizational arrangement of the antifraud personnel who are responsible for the investigation and reporting of possible fraudulent viatical settlement acts and investigating unresolved material inconsistencies between medical records and insurance applications.

(c) Antifraud plans submitted to the Commissioner are privileged and confidential, are not public records, and are not subject to discovery or subpoena in a civil or criminal action. (2001-436, s. 3.)

§ 58-58-270. Report to Commissioner.

Whenever any person licensed under this Part knows or has reasonable cause to believe that any other person has violated any provision of this Part, it is the duty of that person, upon acquiring the knowledge, to notify the Commissioner and provide the Commissioner with a complete statement of all of the relevant facts and circumstances. The report is a privileged communication and when made without actual malice does not subject the person making the report to any liability whatsoever. The Commissioner may suspend, revoke, or refuse to renew the license of any person who willfully fails to comply with this section. (2001-436, s. 3.)

§ 58-58-275. Reporting and investigation of suspected viatical settlement fraudulent acts; immunity from liability.

(a) As used in this section, "Commissioner" includes an employee, agent, or designee of the Commissioner. A person, or an employee or agent of that person, acting without actual malice, is not subject to civil liability for libel, slander, or any other cause of action by virtue of furnishing to the Commissioner, under the requirements of law or at the direction of the Commissioner, reports or other information relating to any known or suspected viatical settlement fraudulent act.

(b) The Commissioner, acting without actual malice, is not subject to civil liability for libel or slander by virtue of an investigation of any known or suspected viatical settlement fraudulent act; or by virtue of the publication or dissemination of any official report related to any such investigation, which report is published or disseminated in the absence of fraud, bad faith, or actual malice on the part of the Commissioner.

(c) During the course of an investigation of a known or suspected viatical settlement fraudulent act, the Commissioner may request any person to furnish copies of any information relative to the known or suspected viatical settlement fraudulent act. The person shall release the information requested and cooperate with the Commissioner under this section. (2001-436, s. 3.)

§ 58-58-280. Confidentiality.

(a) Information and evidence provided under G.S. 58-58-270 or G.S. 58-58-275 or obtained by the Commissioner in an investigation of suspected or actual fraudulent viatical settlement acts shall be privileged and confidential, is not a public record, and is not subject to discovery or subpoena in a civil or criminal action.

(b) Subsection (a) of this section does not prohibit release by the Commissioner of documents and evidence obtained in an investigation of suspected or actual fraudulent viatical settlement acts:

(1) In administrative or judicial proceedings to enforce laws administered by the Commissioner;

(2) To federal, state, or local law enforcement or regulatory agencies, to an organization established for the purpose of detecting and preventing fraudulent viatical settlement acts, or to the NAIC; or

(3) At the discretion of the Commissioner, to a person in the business of viatical settlements that is aggrieved by a fraudulent viatical settlement act.

(c) Release of documents and evidence under subsection (b) of this section does not abrogate or modify the privilege granted in subsection (a) of this section. (2001-436, s. 3.)

§ 58-58-285. Other law enforcement or regulatory authority.

This Part does not:

(1) Preempt the authority or relieve the duty of other law enforcement or regulatory agencies to investigate, examine, and prosecute suspected violations of law.

(2) Prevent or prohibit a person from disclosing voluntarily information concerning viatical settlement fraud to a law enforcement or regulatory agency other than the Commissioner.

(3) Limit the powers granted elsewhere by the laws of this State to the Commissioner to investigate and examine possible violations of law and to take appropriate action against wrongdoers. (2001-436, s. 3.)

§ 58-58-290. Injunctions; civil remedies; cease and desist orders.

(a) In addition to the penalties and other enforcement provisions of this Part, if any person violates this Part or any rule implementing this Part, the Commissioner may seek an injunction in a court of competent jurisdiction and may apply for temporary and permanent orders that the Commissioner determines are necessary to restrain the person from committing the violation.

(b) Any person damaged by the acts of a person in violation of this Part may bring a civil action against the person committing the violation in a court of competent jurisdiction.

(c) The Commissioner may issue, in accordance with G.S. 58-63-32, a cease and desist order upon a person that violates any provision of this Part, any rule or order adopted by the Commissioner, or any written agreement entered into with the Commissioner. The cease and desist order may be subject to judicial review under G.S. 58-63-35.

(d) When the Commissioner finds that an activity in violation of this Part presents an immediate danger to the public that requires an immediate final order, the Commissioner may issue an emergency cease and desist order reciting with particularity the facts underlying the findings. The emergency cease and desist order is effective immediately upon service of a copy of the order on the respondent and remains effective for 90 days. If the Commissioner begins nonemergency cease and desist proceedings, the emergency cease and desist order remains effective, absent an order by a court of competent jurisdiction in accordance with G.S. 58-63-35.

(e) In addition to the penalties and other enforcement provisions of this Part, any person who violates this Part is subject to G.S. 58-2-70. (2001-436, s. 3.)

§ 58-58-295. Unfair trade practices.

A violation of this Part is an unfair trade practice under Article 63 of this Chapter. (2001-436, s. 3.)

§ 58-58-300. Authority to adopt rules.

The Commissioner may:

(1) Adopt rules implementing this Part.

(2) Establish standards for evaluating reasonableness of payments under contracts for persons who are terminally or chronically ill, including standards for the amount paid in exchange for assignment, transfer, sale, or devise of a benefit under a policy.

(3) Establish appropriate licensing requirements, fees, and standards for continued licensure for providers.

(4) Require a bond or other mechanism for financial accountability for providers and brokers.

(5) Adopt rules governing the relationship and responsibilities of insurers, providers, and brokers during the viatication of a policy. (2001-436, s. 3; 2011-284, s. 57.)

§ 58-58-305. Jurisdictional limitations.

Nothing in this Part affects the North Carolina Securities Act or the jurisdiction of the North Carolina Secretary of State. (2001-436, s. 3.)

§ 58-58-310. Effective date.

A provider or broker transacting business in this State, pursuant to G.S. 58-58-42, on the effective date of this Part may continue to do so pending approval of the provider's or broker's application for a license as long as the application is filed with the Commissioner no later than July 1, 2002. If the application is disapproved, then the provider or broker shall cease transacting viatical business in this State. (2001-436, s. 3.)

Part 6. Dishonest and Predatory Sales to Military Personnel.

§ 58-58-320. Purpose.

(a) The purpose of this Part is to set forth standards to protect service members of the Armed Forces from dishonest and predatory insurance sales practices by declaring certain identified practices to be false, misleading, deceptive, or unfair.

(b) Nothing in this Part shall be construed to create or imply a private cause of action for a violation of this Part. (2007-535, s. 1.)

§ 58-58-325. Scope.

This Part applies only to the solicitation or sale of any life insurance or annuity product by an insurer or insurance producer to an active duty service member of the Armed Forces. (2007-535, s. 1; 2011-183, s. 44.)

§ 58-58-330. Exemptions.

(a) This Part does not apply to solicitations or sales involving:

(1) Credit insurance.

(2) Group life insurance or group annuities where there is no in-person, face-to-face solicitation of individuals by an insurance producer or where the contract or certificate does not include a side fund.

(3) An application to the existing insurer that issued the existing policy or contract when (i) a contractual change or a conversion privilege is being exercised, (ii) the existing policy or contract is being replaced by the same insurer pursuant to a program filed with and approved by the Commissioner, or (iii) a term conversion privilege is exercised among corporate affiliates.

(4) Contracts offered by Servicemembers' Group Life Insurance or Veterans' Group Life Insurance, as authorized by 38 U.S.C. § 1965, et seq.

(5) Individual stand-alone health policies, including disability income policies.

(6) Life insurance contracts offered through or by a nonprofit military association, qualifying under section 501(c)(23) of the Internal Revenue Code (IRC), and that are not underwritten by an insurer.

(7) Contracts used to fund:

a. An employee pension or welfare benefit plan that is covered by the Employee Retirement and Income Security Act (ERISA).

b. A plan described by sections 401(a), 401(k), 403(b), 408(k) or 408(p) of the Internal Revenue Code, if established or maintained by an employer.

c. A government or church plan defined in section 414 of the Internal Revenue Code, a government or church welfare benefit plan, or a deferred compensation plan of a state or local government or tax exempt organization under section 457 of the Internal Revenue Code.

d. A nonqualified deferred compensation arrangement established or maintained by an employer or plan sponsor.

e. Settlements of or assumptions of liabilities associated with personal injury litigation or any dispute or claim resolution process.

f. Prearranged funeral contracts.

(b) Nothing in this Part shall be construed to abrogate the ability of nonprofit organizations (and/or other organizations) to educate members of the Armed Forces in accordance with Department of Defense "DoD Instruction 1344.07 - Personal Commercial Solicitation on DoD Installations" or successor directive.

(c) For purposes of this Part, general advertisements, direct mail, and Internet marketing do not constitute "solicitation." Telephone marketing does not constitute "solicitation," provided the caller explicitly and conspicuously discloses that the product concerned is life insurance and makes no statements that avoid a clear and unequivocal statement that life insurance is the subject matter of the solicitation. Provided, however, nothing in this subsection shall be construed to exempt an insurer or insurance producer from this Part in any in-person, face-to-face meeting established as a result of the "solicitation" exemptions identified in this subsection. (2007-535, s. 1; 2011-183, s. 45.)

§ 58-58-335. Definitions.

As used in this Part:

(1) "Active duty" means full-time duty in the active military service of the United States and includes service by members of the reserve component (National Guard and Reserve) while serving under published orders for active duty or full-time training. "Active duty" does not include service by members of the reserve component who are performing active duty or active duty for training under military calls or orders specifying periods of less than 31 calendar days.

(1a) "Armed Forces" means all components of the United States Army, Navy, Air Force, Marine Corps, and Coast Guard.

(2) "Department of Defense personnel" means all active duty service members and all civilian employees, including nonappropriated fund employees and special government employees, of the Department of Defense.

(3) "Door to door" means a solicitation or sales method whereby an insurance producer proceeds randomly or selectively from household to household without prior specific appointment.

(4) "General advertisement" means an advertisement having as its sole purpose the promotion of the reader's or viewer's interest in the concept of insurance or the promotion of the insurer or the insurance producer.

(5) "Insurance producer" means a person required to be licensed under Article 33 of this Chapter to sell, solicit, or negotiate life insurance, including annuities.

(6) "Insurer" means an insurance company required to be licensed under this Chapter to provide life insurance products, including annuities.

(7) "Known" or "knowingly" means, depending on its use in this Part, the insurance producer or insurer had actual awareness, or in the exercise of ordinary care should have known, at the time of the act or practice complained of, that the person solicited is or was:

a. A service member; or

b.   A service member with a pay grade of E-4 or below.

(8)   "Life insurance" means insurance coverage on human lives, including benefits of endowment and annuities, and may include benefits in the event of death or dismemberment by accident and benefits for disability income; and unless otherwise specifically excluded, includes individually issued annuities.

(9)   "Military installation" means any federally owned, leased, or operated base, reservation, post, camp, building, or other facility to which service members are assigned for duty, including barracks, transient housing, and family quarters.

(10)   "MyPay" means the Defense Finance and Accounting Service (DFAS) Web-based system that enables service members to process certain discretionary pay transactions or provide updates to personal information data elements without using paper forms.

(11)   "Service member" means any active duty commissioned officer, any active duty warrant officer, or any active duty enlisted member of the Armed Forces.

(12)   "SGLI" means Servicemembers' Group Life Insurance, as authorized by 38 U.S.C. § 1965, et seq.

(13)   "Side fund" means a fund or reserve that is part of or otherwise attached to a life insurance policy (excluding individually issued annuities) by rider, endorsement, or other mechanism that accumulates premium or deposits with interest or by other means. "Side fund" does not include:

a.   Accumulated value or cash value or secondary guarantees provided by a universal life policy;

b.   Cash values provided by a whole life policy which are subject to standard nonforfeiture law for life insurance; or

c.   A premium deposit fund that:

1.   Contains only premiums paid in advance that accumulate at interest.

2.   Imposes no penalty for withdrawal.

3. Does not permit funding beyond future required premiums.

4. Is not marketed or intended as an investment.

5. Does not carry a commission, either paid or calculated.

(14) "Specific appointment" means a prearranged appointment agreed upon by both parties and definite as to place and time.

(15) Repealed by Session Laws 2011-183, s. 46, effective June 20, 2011.

(16) "VGLI" means Veterans' Group Life Insurance, as authorized by 38 U.S.C. § 1965, et seq. (2007-535, s. 1; 2011-183, s. 46.)

§ 58-58-340. Practices declared false, misleading, deceptive, or unfair on a military installation.

(a) The following acts or practices when committed on a military installation by an insurer or insurance producer with respect to the in-person, face-to-face solicitation of life insurance are declared to be false, misleading, deceptive, or unfair:

(1) Knowingly soliciting the purchase of any life insurance product "door to door" or without first establishing a specific appointment for each meeting with the prospective purchaser.

(2) Soliciting service members in a group or "mass" audience or in a "captive" audience where attendance is not voluntary.

(3) Knowingly making appointments with or soliciting service members during their normally scheduled duty hours.

(4) Making appointments with or soliciting service members in barracks, day rooms, unit areas, or transient personnel housing or other areas where the installation commander has prohibited solicitation.

(5) Soliciting the sale of life insurance without first obtaining permission from the installation commander or the commander's designee.

(6)   Posting unauthorized bulletins, notices, or advertisements.

(7)   Failing to present DD Form 2885, Personal Commercial Solicitation Evaluation, to service members solicited or encouraging service members solicited not to complete or submit a DD Form 2885.

(8)   Knowingly accepting an application for life insurance or issuing a policy of life insurance on the life of an enlisted member of the Armed Forces without first obtaining for the insurer's files a completed copy of any required form that confirms that the applicant has received counseling or fulfilled any other similar requirement for the sale of life insurance established by regulations, directives, or rules of the Department of Defense or any branch of the Armed Forces.

(b)   The following acts or practices when committed on a military installation by an insurer or insurance producer constitute corrupt practices, improper influences or inducements and are declared to be false, misleading, deceptive, or unfair:

(1)   Using Department of Defense personnel, directly or indirectly, as a representative or agent in any official or business capacity with or without compensation with respect to the solicitation or sale of life insurance to service members.

(2)   Using an insurance producer to participate in any Armed Forces sponsored education or orientation program. (2007-535, s. 1; 2011-183, s. 47.)

§ 58-58-345. Practices declared false, misleading, deceptive, or unfair regardless of location.

(a)   The following acts or practices by an insurer or insurance producer constitute corrupt practices, improper influences or inducements and are declared to be false, misleading, deceptive, or unfair:

(1)   Submitting, processing, or assisting in the submission or processing of any allotment form or similar device used by the Armed Forces to direct a service member's pay to a third party for the purchase of life insurance. The foregoing includes, but is not limited to, using or assisting in using a service member's MyPay account or other similar Internet or electronic medium for such

purposes. This subdivision does not prohibit assisting a service member by providing insurer or premium information necessary to complete any allotment form.

(2) Knowingly receiving funds from a service member for the payment of premium from a depository institution with which the service member has no formal banking relationship. For purposes of this section, a formal banking relationship is established when the depository institution:

a. Provides the service member a deposit agreement and periodic statements and makes the disclosures required by the Truth in Savings Act, 12 U.S.C. § 4301, et seq. and the regulations promulgated thereunder; and

b. Permits the service member to make deposits and withdrawals unrelated to the payment or processing of insurance premiums.

(3) Employing any device or method or entering into any agreement whereby funds received from a service member by allotment for the payment of insurance premiums are identified on the service member's Leave and Earnings Statement or equivalent or successor form as "Savings" or "Checking" and where the service member has no formal banking relationship as defined in subdivision (a)(2) of this section.

(4) Entering into any agreement with a depository institution for the purpose of receiving funds from a service member whereby the depository institution, with or without compensation, agrees to accept direct deposits from a service member with whom it has no formal banking relationship.

(5) Using Department of Defense personnel, directly or indirectly, as a representative or agent in any official or unofficial capacity with or without compensation with respect to the solicitation or sale of life insurance to service members who are junior in rank or grade or to the family members of such personnel.

(6) Offering or giving anything of value, directly or indirectly, to Department of Defense personnel to procure their assistance in encouraging, assisting, or facilitating the solicitation or sale of life insurance to another service member.

(7) Knowingly offering or giving anything of value to a service member with a pay grade of E-4 or below for his or her attendance to any event where an application for life insurance is solicited.

(8) Advising a service member with a pay grade of E-4 or below to change his or her income tax withholding or state of legal residence for the sole purpose of increasing disposable income to purchase life insurance.

(b) The following acts or practices by an insurer or insurance producer lead to confusion regarding source, sponsorship, approval, or affiliation and are declared to be false, misleading, deceptive, or unfair:

(1) Making any representation, or using any device, title, descriptive name, or identifier that has the tendency or capacity to confuse or mislead a service member into believing that the insurer, insurance producer, or product offered is affiliated, connected or associated with, endorsed, sponsored, sanctioned, or recommended by the U.S. Government, the Armed Forces, or any state or federal agency or government entity. Examples of prohibited insurance producer titles include, but are not limited to, "Battalion Insurance Counselor," "Unit Insurance Advisor," "Servicemen's Group Life Insurance Conversion Consultant," or "Veteran's Benefits Counselor." Nothing in this subdivision prohibits a person from using a professional designation awarded after the successful completion of a course of instruction in the business of insurance by an accredited institution of higher learning. Those designations include, but are not limited to, Chartered Life Underwriter (CLU), Chartered Financial Consultant, (ChFC), Certified Financial Planner (CFP), Master of Science in Financial Services (MSFS), or Masters of Science Financial Planning (MS).

(2) Soliciting the purchase of any life insurance product through the use of or in conjunction with any third party organization that promotes the welfare of or assists members of the Armed Forces in a manner that has the tendency or capacity to confuse or mislead a service member into believing that either the insurer, insurance producer, or insurance product is affiliated, connected or associated with, endorsed, sponsored, sanctioned, or recommended by the U.S. Government or the Armed Forces.

(c) The following acts or practices by an insurer or insurance producer lead to confusion regarding premiums, costs, or investment returns and are declared to be false, misleading, deceptive, or unfair:

(1) Using or describing the credited interest rate on a life insurance policy in a manner that implies that the credited interest rate is a net return on premium paid.

(2) Excluding individually issued annuities, misrepresenting the mortality costs of a life insurance product, including stating or implying that the product "costs nothing" or is "free."

(d) The following acts or practices by an insurer or insurance producer regarding SGLI or VGLI are declared to be false, misleading, deceptive, or unfair:

(1) Making any representation regarding the availability, suitability, amount, cost, exclusions, or limitations to coverage provided to a service member or dependents by SGLI or VGLI that is false, misleading, or deceptive.

(2) Making any representation regarding conversion requirements, including the costs of coverage, or exclusions or limitations to coverage of SGLI or VGLI to private insurers that is false, misleading, or deceptive.

(3) Suggesting, recommending, or encouraging a service member to cancel or terminate his or her SGLI policy or issuing a life insurance policy that replaces an existing SGLI policy unless the replacement shall take effect upon or after the service member's separation from the Armed Forces.

(e) The following acts or practices by an insurer and/or insurance producer regarding disclosure are declared to be false, misleading, deceptive, or unfair:

(1) Deploying, using, or contracting for any lead generating materials designed exclusively for use with service members that do not clearly and conspicuously disclose that the recipient will be contacted by an insurance producer, if that is the case, for the purpose of soliciting the purchase of life insurance.

(2) Failing to disclose that a solicitation for the sale of life insurance will be made when establishing a specific appointment for an in-person, face-to-face meeting with a prospective purchaser.

(3) Excluding individually issued annuities, failing to clearly and conspicuously disclose the fact that the product being sold is life insurance.

(4) Failing to make, at the time of sale or offer to an individual known to be a service member, the written disclosures required by section 10 of the Military Personnel Financial Services Protection Act, Pub. L. No. 109-290, p.16.

(5) Excluding individually issued annuities, when the sale is conducted in-person, face-to-face with an individual known to be a service member, failing to provide the applicant at the time the application is taken:

a. An explanation of any free look period with instructions on how to cancel if a policy is issued; and

b. Either a copy of the application or a written disclosure. The copy of the application or the written disclosure shall clearly and concisely set out the type of life insurance, the death benefit applied for, and its expected first year cost. A basic illustration that meets the requirements of rules adopted by the Commissioner concerning life insurance illustrations are sufficient to meet this requirement for a written disclosure.

(f) The following acts or practices by an insurer or insurance producer with respect to the sale of certain life insurance products are declared to be false, misleading, deceptive, or unfair:

(1) Excluding individually issued annuities, recommending the purchase of any life insurance product which includes a side fund to a service member in pay grades E-4 and below unless the insurer has reasonable grounds for believing that the life insurance death benefit, standing alone, is suitable.

(2) Offering for sale or selling a life insurance product which includes a side fund to a service member in pay grades E-4 and below who is currently enrolled in SGLI is presumed unsuitable unless, after the completion of a needs assessment, the insurer demonstrates that the applicant's SGLI death benefit, together with any other military survivor benefits, savings and investments, survivor income, and other life insurance are insufficient to meet the applicant's insurable needs for life insurance. As used in this subdivision, "insurable needs" are the risks associated with premature death taking into consideration the financial obligations and immediate and future cash needs of the applicant's estate and/or survivors or dependents; and "other military survivor benefits" include, but are not limited to: the Death Gratuity, Funeral Reimbursement, Transition Assistance, Survivor and Dependents' Educational Assistance, Dependency and Indemnity Compensation, TRICARE Healthcare Benefits, Survivor Housing Benefits and Allowances, Federal Income Tax Forgiveness, and Social Security Survivor Benefits.

(3) Excluding individually issued annuities, offering for sale or selling any life insurance contract which includes a side fund:

a. Unless interest credited accrues from the date of deposit to the date of withdrawal and permits withdrawals without limit or penalty;

b. Unless the applicant has been provided with a schedule of effective rates of return based upon cash flows of the combined product. For this disclosure, the effective rate of return will consider all premiums and cash contributions made by the policyholder and all cash accumulations and cash surrender values available to the policyholder in addition to life insurance coverage. This schedule will be provided for at least each policy year from one to 10 and for every fifth policy year thereafter ending at age 100, policy maturity, or final expiration; and

c. Which by default diverts or transfers funds accumulated in the side fund to pay, reduce, or offset any premiums due.

(4) Excluding individually issued annuities, offering for sale or selling any life insurance contract which after considering all policy benefits, including, but not limited to, endowment, return of premium, or persistency, does not comply with standard nonforfeiture law for life insurance.

(5) Selling any life insurance product to an individual known to be a service member that excludes coverage if the insured's death is related to war, declared or undeclared, or any act related to military service except for an accidental death coverage, e.g., double indemnity, which may be excluded. (2007-535, s. 1; 2011-183, s. 48(a), (b), (c).)

§ 58-58-350. Procedures and sanctions.

(a) The provisions of G.S. 58-63-20, 58-63-25, 58-63-32, 58-63-35, 58-63-50, and 58-63-60 apply to this Part and are incorporated into this Part by reference.

(b) A violation of this Part is a ground for license suspension, probation, revocation, nonrenewal, or denial under G.S. 58-33-46 and subjects the violator to G.S. 58-2-70. (2007-535, s. 1.)

Article 59.

Registered Policies.

§ 58-59-1. Deposits to secure registered policies.

Any life insurance company, incorporated under the laws of this State, may deposit with the Commissioner securities of the kind authorized for the investment of the funds of life insurance companies, which shall be legally transferred by it to him as Commissioner and his successors for the common benefit of all the holders of its "registered" policies and annuity bonds issued under the provisions of this Article; and these securities shall be held by him and his successors in office in trust for the purposes and objects specified herein.

All securities offered to the Commissioner for deposit under this section shall be received and held pursuant to regulations promulgated by the Commissioner. (1905, c. 504, s. 12; Rev., s. 4780; 1909, c. 920, ss. 1, 2; 1911, c. 140, s. 1; 1917, c. 191, s. 2; C.S., s. 6467; 1945, c. 379.)

§ 58-59-5. Additional deposits may be required.

Each company which has made deposits herein provided for shall make additional deposits from time to time, as the Commissioner prescribes, in amounts of not less than five thousand dollars ($5,000) and of such securities as are described in the preceding section [G.S. 58-59-1], so that the admitted value of the securities deposited shall equal the net value of the registered policies and annuity bonds issued by the company, less such liens not exceeding such value as the company has against it. The Commissioner shall annually value or cause to be valued such policies and shall prepare an estimate based upon probable changes in the minimum amounts to be kept on deposit for each month of the ensuing year. (1905, c. 504, s. 15; Rev., s. 4781; 1909, c. 920, s. 3; 1911, c. 140, s. 2; 1917, c. 191, s. 3; C.S., s. 6468; 1945, c. 379; 1991, c. 720, s. 4.)

§ 58-59-10. Withdrawal of deposits.

Any such company whose deposits exceed the net value of all registered policies and annuity bonds it has in force, less such liens not exceeding such value as the company holds against them, may withdraw such excess or it may withdraw any of such securities at any time by depositing in their place others of equal value and of the character authorized by law; and as long as such company remains solvent and keeps up its deposits, as herein required, it may collect the interest and coupons on the securities deposited as they accrue; and any life insurance company may withdraw such securities by and with the consent of the policyholder only; and in case of such withdrawal, the certificate of registration in each case must be surrendered for cancellation, or a receipt from the policyholder, satisfactory to the Commissioner, must be produced before such withdrawal of deposits shall be allowed. (1905, c. 504, s. 18; Rev., s. 4782; 1911, c. 134; C.S., s. 6469; 1991, c. 720, s. 4.)

§ 58-59-15. Record of securities kept by Commissioner; deficit made good.

The Commissioner shall keep a careful record of the securities deposited by each company, and when furnishing the annual certificates of value required in this Article, he may enter thereon the face and market value of the securities deposited by such company. If at any time it appears from such certificate or otherwise that the value of securities held on deposit is less than the net value of the registered policies and annuity bonds issued by such companies, it is not lawful for the Commissioner to execute the certificate on any additional policies or annuity bonds of such company until it has made good the deficit. If any company fails or neglects to make such deposits for 60 days the Commissioner may suspend its license to do business until such deposit be made. (1905, c. 504 s. 16; Rev., s. 4784; C.S., s. 6471; 1945, c. 379; 1991, c. 720, s. 4.)

§ 58-59-20. Registered policies certified.

After making the deposits provided for in this Article no company may issue a policy of insurance or endowment or an annuity bond known or designated as "registered" unless it has upon its face a certificate in the following words: "This policy or annuity bond is registered and secured by pledge of bonds, stocks, or securities deposited with this Department as provided by law," which certificate shall be signed by the Commissioner and sealed with the seal of his office.

Such policies and bonds shall be known as "registered" policies and annuity bonds, and a sample copy of such kind, class, and issue shall be kept in the office of the Commissioner. All policies and bonds of each kind and class issued, and the copies thereof, filed in the office of the Commissioner must have imprinted thereon some appropriate designating letter, combination of letters or terms identifying the special forms of contract, together with the year of adoption of such form, and whenever any change or modification is made in the form of contracts, policy, or bond, the designating letters or terms and year of adoption thereon shall be changed accordingly. (1905, c. 504, s. 13; Rev., s. 4785; C.S., s. 6472; 1991, c. 720, s. 4.)

§ 58-59-25. Power of Commissioner in case of insolvency.

If at any time the affairs of a life insurance company which has deposited securities under the provisions of this Article, in the opinion of the Commissioner, appear in such condition as to render the issuing of additional policies and annuity bonds by such company injurious to the public interest, the Commissioner may take such proceedings against the company as are authorized by law to be taken against other insolvent companies, and said companies are in all respects subject to the provisions of law affecting other companies. (1905, c. 504, s. 20; Rev., s. 4788; C.S., s. 6475; 1991, c. 720, s. 4.)

§ 58-59-30. Fees for registering policies.

Every company making deposits under the provisions of this Article must pay to the Commissioner for each certificate on registered policies or annuity bonds, including seal, a fee of fifty cents (50¢) for those exceeding ten thousand dollars ($10,000) in amount and twenty-five cents (25¢) for all under ten thousand dollars ($10,000) in amount, except policies for one hundred dollars ($100.00) and not exceeding five hundred dollars ($500.00) the fee shall be fifteen cents (15¢); for policies of one hundred dollars ($100.00) or less the fee shall be ten cents (10¢). (1905, c. 504, s. 21; Rev., s. 4789; C.S., s. 6476; 1945, c. 379; 1991, c. 720, s. 4.)

§ 58-59-35. Registration of policies.

After January 1, 1947, the Commissioner shall not register any new policies that are issued by any company, nor accept any deposits covering reserves on business thereafter written. (1945, c. 379.)

Article 60.

Standards of Disclosure for Annuities and Life Insurance.

Part 1. Regulation of Life Insurance Solicitation.

§ 58-60-1. Short title; purpose.

(a)   This Part may be cited as the "Life Insurance Disclosure Act".

(b)   The purpose of this Part is to require insurers to deliver to purchasers of life insurance, information which will improve the buyer's ability to select the most appropriate plan of life insurance for the buyer's needs, improve the buyer's understanding of the basic features of the policy which has been purchased or which is under consideration and to improve the ability of the buyer to evaluate the relative costs of similar plans of life insurance.

This Part does not prohibit an insurer from using additional material that is not in violation of Articles 1 through 64 of this Chapter nor any other statute or regulation. (1979, c. 447; 2005-234, s. 1.3.)

§ 58-60-5. Scope; exemptions.

(a)   Except as otherwise provided in this Part, this Part applies to any solicitation, negotiation or procurement of life insurance occurring within this State. This Part applies to any issuer of a life insurance contract, including fraternal benefit societies.

(b)   Unless otherwise specifically included, this Part does not apply to:

(1) Individual and group annuity contracts.

(2) Credit life insurance.

(3) Group life insurance (except for disclosures relating to preneed funeral contracts or prearrangements; these disclosure requirements shall extend to the issuance or delivery of certificates as well as to the master policy).

(4) Life insurance policies issued in connection with pension and welfare plans as defined by and that are subject to the federal Employee Retirement Income Security Act of 1974 (ERISA).

(5) Variable life insurance under which the death benefits and cash values vary in accordance with unit values of investments held in a separate account.

(c) The policy summary in this Part is not required for policies that are sold subject to rules adopted by the Commissioner for life insurance illustrations. (1979, c. 447; 1998-211, s. 14; 2005-234, s. 1.4.)

§ 58-60-10. Definitions.

Unless the context of use indicates a different meaning, for the purposes of this Part, the following definitions shall apply:

(1) Buyer's Guide. - A Buyer's Guide is a document furnished pursuant to G.S. 58-60-15, which shall contain all the requirements of and be in substantial compliance with G.S. 58-60-25.

(2) Cash Dividend. - A Cash Dividend is the current illustrated dividend which can be applied toward payment of gross premium.

(3) Equivalent Level Annual Dividend. - The Equivalent Level Annual Dividend is calculated by applying the following steps:

a. Accumulate the annual cash dividends at five percent (5%) interest compounded annually to the end of the 10th and 20th policy years;

b.   Divide each accumulation of paragraph a of this subdivision by an interest factor that converts it into one equivalent level annual amount that, if paid at the beginning of each year, would accrue to the values in paragraph a of this subdivision over the respective periods stipulated in paragraph a of this subdivision. If the period is 10 years, the factor is 13.207 and if the period is 20 years, the factor is 34.719.

c.   Divide the results of paragraph b of this subdivision by the number of thousands of the Equivalent Level Death Benefit to arrive at the Equivalent Level Annual Dividend.

(4)   Equivalent Level Death Benefit. - The Equivalent Level Death Benefit of a policy or term life insurance rider is an amount calculated as follows:

a.   Accumulate the guaranteed amount payable upon death, regardless of the cause of death, at the beginning of each policy year for 10 and 20 years at five percent (5%) interest compounded annually to the end of the 10th and 20th policy years respectively;

b.   Divide each accumulation of paragraph a of this subdivision by an interest factor that converts it into one equivalent level annual amount that, if paid at the beginning of each year, would accrue to the value in paragraph a of th s subdivision over the respective periods stipulated in paragraph a of this subdivision. If the period is 10 years, the factor is 13.207 and if the period is 20 years, the factor is 34.719.

(5)   Generic Name. - Generic Name means a short title which is descriptive of the premium and benefit patterns of a policy or a rider.

(6)   Life Insurance Cost Indexes. -

a.   Life Insurance Surrender Cost Index. The Life Insurance Surrender Cost Index is calculated by applying the following steps:

1.   Determine the guaranteed cash surrender value, if any, available at the end of the 10th and 20th policy years;

2.   For participating policies, add the terminal dividend payable upon surrender, if any, to the accumulation of the annual Cash Dividends at five percent (5%) interest compounded annually to the end of the period selected and add this sum to the amount determined in subdivision a;

3. Divide the result of subparagraph 2 (subparagraph 1 for guaranteed-cost policies) by an interest factor that converts it into an equivalent level annual that, if paid at the beginning of each year, would accrue to the value in subparagraph 2 (subparagraph 1 for guaranteed-cost policies) over the respective periods stipulated in subparagraph 1. If the period is 10 years, the factor is 13.207 and if the period is 20 years, the factor is 34.719;

4. Determine the equivalent level premium by accumulating each annual premium payable for the basic policy or rider at five percent (5%) interest compounded annually to the end of the period stipulated in subparagraph 1 and dividing the result by the respective factors stated in subparagraph 3 (this amount is the annual premium payable for a level premium plan);

5. Subtract the result of subparagraph 3 from subparagraph 4;

6. Divide the result of subparagraph 5 by the number of thousands of the Equivalent Level Death Benefit to arrive at the Life Insurance Surrender Cost Index.

b. Life Insurance Net Payment Cost Index. The Life Insurance Net Payment Cost Index is calculated in the same manner as the comparable Life Insurance Cost Index except that the cash surrender value and any terminal dividend are set at zero.

(7) Policy Summary. - Policy Summary means a written statement describing the elements of the policy including but not limited to:

a. A prominently placed title in at least 10-point boldface capital letters as follows: STATEMENT OF POLICY COST AND BENEFIT INFORMATION;

b. The name and address of the insurance agent, or, if no agent is involved, a statement of the procedure to be followed in order to receive responses to inquiries regarding the Policy Summary;

c. The full name and home office or administrative office address of the company in which the life insurance policy is to be or has been written;

d. The Generic Name of the basic policy and each rider;

e. The following amounts, where applicable, for the first five policy years and representative policy years thereafter sufficient to clearly illustrate the premium and benefit patterns, including, but not necessarily limited to, the years for which Life Insurance Cost Indexes are displayed and at least one age from 60 through 65 or maturity, whichever is earlier:

1. The annual premium for the basic policy;

2. The annual premium for each optional rider;

3. Guaranteed amount payable upon death, at the beginning of the policy year regardless of the cause of death other than suicide, or other specifically enumerated exclusions, which is provided by the basic policy and each optional rider, with benefits provided under the basic policy and each rider shown separately;

4. Total guaranteed cash surrender values at the end of the year with values shown separately for the basic policy and each rider;

5. Cash Dividends payable at the end of the year with values shown separately for the basic policy and each rider. (Dividends need not be displayed beyond the 20th policy year);

6. Guaranteed endowment amounts payable under the policy which are not included under guaranteed cash surrender values above.

f. The effective policy loan annual percentage interest rate, if the policy contains this provision, specifying whether this rate is applied in advance or in arrears. If the policy loan interest rate is variable, the Policy Summary includes the maximum annual percentage rate;

g. Life Insurance Cost Indexes for 10 and 20 years but in no case beyond the premium paying period. Separate indexes must be displayed for the basic policy and for each optional term life insurance rider. Such indexes need not be included for optional riders which are limited to benefits such as accidental death benefits, disability waiver of premium, preliminary term life insurance coverage of less than 12 months and guaranteed insurability benefits nor for basic policies or optional riders covering more than one life;

h. The Equivalent Level Annual Dividend, in the case of participating policies and participating optional term life insurance riders, under the same circumstances and for the same durations at which Life Insurance Cost Indexes are displayed;

i. A Policy Summary which includes dividends shall also include a statement that dividends are based on the company's current dividend scale and are not guaranteed in addition to a statement in close proximity to the Equivalent Level Annual Dividend as follows: An explanation of the intended use of the Equivalent Level Annual Dividend is included in the Life Insurance Buyer's Guide;

j. A statement in close proximity to the Life Insurance Cost Indexes as follows: An explanation of the intended use of these indexes is provided in the Life Insurance Buyer's Guide.

k. The date on which the Policy Summary is prepared.

The Policy Summary must consist of a separate document. All information required to be disclosed must be set out in such a manner as to not minimize or render any portion thereof obscure. Any amounts which remain level for two or more years of the policy may be represented by a single number if it is clearly indicated what amounts are applicable for each policy year. Amounts in subparagraph e of this paragraph shall be listed in total, not on a per thousand nor per unit basis. If more than one insured is covered under one policy or rider, guaranteed death benefits shall be displayed separately for each insured or for each class of insureds if death benefits do not differ within the class. Zero amounts shall be displayed as zero and shall not be displayed as a blank space. If the insurer makes a material revision in the terms and conditions under which it will limit its right to change any nonguaranteed factor, it shall, no later than the first policy anniversary following the revision, advise each affected policy owner residing in this State. (1979, c. 447; 2005-234, ss. 1.5, 1.6.)

§ 58-60-15. Disclosure requirements.

(a) The insurer shall provide to all prospective purchasers a Buyer's Guide and a Policy Summary prior to accepting any applicant's initial premium deposit, unless the policy for which application is made contains an unconditional refund provision of at least 10 days or unless the Policy Summary contains such an unconditional refund offer, in which event the Buyer's Guide and Policy Summary must be delivered with the policy or prior to delivery of the policy.

(b) The insurer shall provide a Buyer's Guide and a Policy Summary to any prospective purchaser upon request.

(c) In the case of policies whose Equivalent Level Death Benefit does not exceed five thousand dollars ($5,000), the requirement for providing a Policy Summary will be satisfied by delivery of a written statement containing the information described in G.S. 58-60-10(7), subdivisions b, c, d, e1, e2, e3, f, g, j, and k. (1979, c. 447; 1993, c. 553, s. 21.)

§ 58-60-20. General rules relating to solicitation.

(a) Each insurer subject to this Part shall maintain at its home office or principal office a complete file containing one copy of each document authorized by the insurer for use pursuant to this Part. Such file shall contain one copy of each authorized form for a period of three years following the date of its last authorized use.

(b) An agent shall inform the prospective purchaser, prior to commencing a life insurance sales presentation, that he is acting as a life insurance agent and inform the prospective purchaser of the full name of the insurance company which he is representing to the buyer. In sales situations in which an agent is not involved, the insurer shall identify its full name.

(c) Terms such as financial planner, investment advisor, financial consultant, or financial counseling shall not be used in such a way as to imply that the insurance agent is generally engaged in an advisory business in which compensation is unrelated to sales unless such is actually the case.

(d) Any reference to policy dividends must include a statement that dividends are not guaranteed.

(e) A system or presentation which does not recognize the time value of money through the use of appropriate interest adjustments shall not be used for comparing the cost of two or more life insurance policies. Such a system may be used for the purpose of demonstrating the cash-flow pattern of a policy if such presentation is accompanied by a statement disclosing that the presentation does not recognize that, because of interest, a dollar in the future has less value than a dollar today.

(f)   A presentation of benefits shall not display guaranteed and nonguaranteed benefits as a single sum unless they are shown separately in close proximity thereto.

(g)   A statement regarding the use of the Life Insurance Cost Indexes shall include an explanation to the effect that the indexes are useful only for the comparison of the relative costs of two or more similar policies.

(h)   A Life Insurance Cost Index which reflects dividends or an Equivalent Level Annual Dividend shall be accompanied by a statement that it is based on the insurer's current dividend scale and is not guaranteed.

(i)   For the purposes of this Part, the annual premium for a basic policy or rider, for which the insurer reserves the right to change the premium, shall be the maximum annual premium. (1979, c. 447; 2005-234, ss. 1.7, 1.8.)

§ 58-60-25. Adoption of Buyer's Guide; requirements.

Any insurer soliciting life insurance in this State on or after December 1, 1979, shall adopt and use a Buyer's Guide, and the adoption and use by an insurer of the Buyer's Guide promulgated by the National Association of Insurance Commissioners in the NAIC Model Life Insurance Solicitation Regulations shall be in compliance with the requirements of this Part. (1979, c. 447; 2005-234, s. 1.9.)

§ 58-60-30. Failure to comply.

The failure of an insurer to provide or deliver a Buyer's Guide, or a Policy Summary as provided in G.S. 58-60-15(a) and (b) shall constitute an omission which misrepresents the benefits, advantages, conditions or terms of an insurance policy within the meaning of G.S. 58-58-40 and Article 63 (Unfair Trade Practice Act) of this Chapter. (1979, c. 447.)

§ 58-60-35. Disclosure of prearrangement insurance policy provisions.

(a) As used in this section:

(1) "Prearrangement" means any contract, agreement, or mutual understanding, or any series or combination of contracts, agreements or mutual understandings, whether funded by trust deposits or prearrangement insurance policies, or any combination thereof, which has for a purpose the furnishing or performance of specific funeral services, or the furnishing or delivery of specific personal property, merchandise, or services of any nature in connection with the final disposition of a dead human body, to be furnished or delivered at a time determinable by the death of the person whose body is to be disposed of, but does not mean the furnishing of a cemetery lot, crypt, niche, mausoleum, grave marker or monument.

(2) "Prearrangement insurance policy" means a life insurance policy, annuity contract, or other insurance contract, or any series of contracts or agreements in any form or manner, issued on a group or individual basis by an insurance company authorized by law to do business in this State, which, whether by assignment or otherwise, has for its sole purpose the funding of a specific preneed funeral contract or a specific insurance-funded funeral or burial prearrangement, the insured being the person for whose service the funds were paid.

(b) The following information shall be adequately disclosed by the insurance agent or limited representative at the time an application is made, prior to accepting the applicant's initial premium, for a prearrangement insurance policy:

(1) The fact that a prearrangement insurance policy is involved or being used to fund a prearrangement;

(2) The nature of the relationship among the insurance agent or limited representative, the provider of the funeral or cemetery merchandise or services, the administrator, and any other person;

(3) The relationship of the prearrangement insurance policy to the funding of the prearrangement and the nature and existence of any guarantees relating to the prearrangement;

(4) The effect on the prearrangement of (i) any changes in the prearrangement insurance policy, including but not limited to, changes in the assignment, beneficiary designation, or use of the policy proceeds; (ii) any

penalties to be incurred by the insured as a result of failure to make premium payments; and (iii) any penalties to be incurred or monies to be received as a result of cancellation or surrender of the prearrangement insurance policy;

(5) All relevant information concerning what occurs and whether any entitlements or obligations arise if there is a difference between the policy proceeds and the amount actually needed to fund the prearrangement; and

(6) Any penalties or restrictions, including geographic restrictions or the inability of the provider to perform, on the delivery of merchandise, services, or the prearrangement guarantee. (1989, c. 738, s. 1; 1991, c. 644, s. 10; 1995, c. 517, s. 32.)

Part 2. Regulation of Small Face Amount Life Insurance Solicitation.

§ 58-60-90. Title and reference.

This Part may be cited as the "Small Face Amount Life Insurance Disclosure Act". (2005-234, s. 1.10.)

§ 58-60-95. Purpose; intent; and scope.

(a) The purpose of this Part is to establish standards that ensure meaningful information is provided to the purchasers of small face amount policies.

(b) This Part applies to any life insurance policy or certificate with an initial face amount of fifteen thousand dollars ($15,000) or less.

(c) This Part does not apply to:

(1) Variable life insurance.

(2) Individual and group annuity contracts.

(3) Credit life insurance.

(4) Group or individual policies of life insurance issued to members of an employer group or other permitted group where:

a. Every plan of coverage was selected by the employer or other group representative;

b. Some portion of the premium is paid by the group or through payroll deduction; and

c. Group underwriting or simplified underwriting is used.

(5) Policies and certificates where an illustration has been provided pursuant to the requirements of Title 11, Chapter 4, Section .0500 of the North Carolina Administrative Code. (2005-234, s. 1.10.)

§ 58-60-100. Disclosure requirements.

(a) An insurer issuing a small face amount policy where, over the term of the policy, the cumulative policy premiums paid may exceed the face amount of the policy, shall clearly and prominently disclose, on or before policy delivery, the length of time until the cumulative policy premiums paid may exceed the face amount of the policy.

(b) If an insurer is required to provide a disclosure under subsection (a) of this section, the insurer shall clearly and prominently disclose, on or before policy delivery, available premium payment plan and product alternatives. If no alternatives exist, the insurer shall clearly and prominently disclose that there are no such alternatives.

(c) Cumulative premiums shall include premiums paid for riders. However, the face amount shall not include the benefits attributable to the riders. (2005-234, s. 1.10.)

§ 58-60-105. Insurer duties.

The insurer and its producers shall have a duty to provide information to policyholders or certificate holders that ask questions about the disclosure statement. (2005-234, s. 1.10.)

Part 3. Regulation of Annuity Solicitation.

§ 58-60-120. Title and reference.

This Part may be cited as the "Annuity Disclosure Act". (2005-234, s. 1.11.)

§ 58-60-125. Purpose; intent; scope.

(a) The purpose of this Part is to provide standards for the disclosure of certain minimum information about annuity contracts to protect consumers and foster consumer education. This Part specifies the minimum information that must be disclosed and the method for disclosing it in connection with the sale of annuity contracts. The goal of this Part is to ensure that purchasers of annuity contracts understand certain basic features of annuity contracts.

(b) This Part applies to all group and individual annuity contracts and certificates except:

(1) Registered or nonregistered variable annuities or other registered products.

(2) Immediate and deferred annuities that contain no nonguaranteed elements.

(3) Annuities used to fund any of the following:

a. An employee pension plan, which is covered by the Employee Retirement Income Security Act (ERISA).

b. A plan described by section 401(a), 401(k), or 403(b) of the Internal Revenue Code, where the plan, for purposes of ERISA, is established or maintained by an employer.

c. A governmental or church plan defined in section 414 of the Internal Revenue Code or a deferred compensation plan of a state or local government or a tax-exempt organization under section 457 of the Internal Revenue Code.

d. A nonqualified deferred compensation arrangement established or maintained by an employer or plan sponsor.

e. Structured settlement annuities.

f. Charitable gift annuities.

g. Funding agreements.

(c) This Part shall apply to annuities used to fund a plan or arrangement that is funded solely by contributions an employee elects to make, whether on a pretax or after-tax basis, and where the insurance company has been notified that plan participants may choose from among two or more fixed annuity providers, and there is a direct solicitation of an individual employee by a producer for the purchase of an annuity contract. As used in this subsection, direct solicitation shall not include any meeting held by a producer solely for the purpose of educating or enrolling employees in the plan or arrangement. (2005-234, s. 1.11.)

§ 58-60-130. Definitions.

As used in this Part:

(1) "Annuity buyer's guide" or "buyer's guide" means the current NAIC Model Buyer's Guide to Fixed Deferred Annuities, including any appendix thereto.

(2) "Charitable gift annuity" means a transfer of cash or other property by a donor to a charitable organization in return for an annuity payable over one or two lives, under which the actuarial value of the annuity is less than the value of the cash or other property transferred and the difference in value constitutes a charitable deduction for federal tax purposes but does not include a charitable remainder trust or a charitable lead trust or other similar arrangement where the charitable organization does not issue an annuity and incur a financial obligation to guarantee annuity payments.

(3) "Contract owner" means the owner named in the annuity contract or certificate holder in the case of a group annuity contract.

(4) "Determinable elements" means elements that are derived from processes or methods that are guaranteed at issue and not subject to company discretion but where the values or amounts cannot be determined until some point after issue. These elements include the premiums, credited interest rates (including any bonus), benefits, values, noninterest-based credits, charges, or elements of formulas used to determine any of these. These elements may be described as guaranteed but not determined at issue. An element is considered determinable if it was calculated from underlying determinable elements only or from both determinable and guaranteed elements.

(5) "Disclosure document" means the document the contents of which are described in G.S. 58-60-140.

(6) "Funding agreement" means an agreement for an insurer to accept and accumulate funds and to make one or more payments at future dates in amounts that are not based on mortality or morbidity contingencies.

(7) "Generic name" means a short title descriptive of the annuity contract being applied for or illustrated such as "single premium deferred annuity".

(8) "Guaranteed elements" means the premiums, credited interest rates, including any bonus, benefits, values, noninterest-based credits, charges, or elements of formulas used to determine any of these, that are guaranteed and determined at issue. An element is considered guaranteed if all of the underlying elements that go into its calculation are guaranteed.

(9) "Nonguaranteed elements" means the premiums, credited interest rates (including any bonus), benefits, values, noninterest-based credits, charges, or elements of formulas used to determine any of these that are subject to company discretion and are not guaranteed at issue. An element is considered nonguaranteed if any of the underlying nonguaranteed elements are used in its calculation.

(10) "Structured settlement annuity" means a "qualified funding asset" as defined in section 130(d) of the Internal Revenue Code or an annuity that would be a qualified funding asset under section 130(d) of the Internal Revenue Code

but for the fact that it is not owned by an assignee under a qualified assignment. (2005-234, s. 1.11.)

§ 58-60-135. Standards for the disclosure document and buyer's guide.

(a) Where the application for an annuity contract is taken in a face-to-face meeting, the applicant, at or before the time of application, shall be given both the disclosure document described in G.S. 58-60-140 and a copy of the buyer's guide.

(b) Where the application for an annuity contract is taken by means other than in a face-to-face meeting, the applicant shall be sent both the disclosure document and the buyer's guide no later than five business days after the completed application is received by the insurer.

(1) With respect to an application received as a result of a direct solicitation through the mail:

a. Providing a buyer's guide in a mailing inviting prospective applicants to apply for an annuity contract shall be deemed to satisfy the requirement that the buyer's guide be provided no later than five business days after receipt of the application.

b. Providing a disclosure document in a mailing inviting a prospective applicant to apply for an annuity contract shall be deemed to satisfy the requirement that the disclosure document be provided no later than five business days after receipt of the application.

(2) With respect to an application received via the Internet:

a. Taking reasonable steps to make the buyer's guide available for viewing and printing on the insurer's Web site shall be deemed to satisfy the requirement that the buyer's guide be provided no later than five business days after receipt of the application.

b. Taking reasonable steps to make the disclosure document available for viewing and printing on the insurer's Web site shall be deemed to satisfy the requirement that the disclosure document be provided no later than five business days after receipt of the application.

(3) A solicitation for an annuity contract provided in other than a face-to-face meeting shall include a statement that the proposed applicant may contact the Department for a free annuity buyer's guide. In lieu of the foregoing statement, an insurer may include a statement that the prospective applicant may contact the insurer for a free annuity buyer's guide.

(c) Where the buyer's guide and disclosure document are not provided at or before the time of application, a free-look period of no less than 15 days shall be provided for the applicant to return the annuity contract without penalty. This free-look period shall run concurrently with any other free-look period provided under State law or regulation. (2005-234, s. 1.11.)

§ 58-60-140. Contents of disclosure document.

At a minimum, all of the following information shall be included in the disclosure document required under this Part:

(1) The generic name of the contract, the company product name, if different, and form number, and the fact that it is an annuity.

(2) The insurer's name and address.

(3) A description of the contract and its benefits, emphasizing its long-term nature, including the following, if appropriate:

a. The guaranteed, nonguaranteed, and determinable elements of the contract, and their limitations, if any, and an explanation of how they operate.

b. An explanation of the initial crediting rate, specifying any bonus or introductory portion, the duration of the rate, and the fact that rates may change from time to time and are not guaranteed.

c. Periodic income options both on a guaranteed and nonguaranteed basis.

d. Any value reductions caused by withdrawals from or surrender of the contract.

e. How values in the contract can be accessed.

f. The death benefit, if available, and how it will be calculated.

g. A summary of the federal tax status of the contract and any penalties applicable on withdrawal of values from the contract.

h. The impact of any rider, such as a long-term care rider.

(4) The specific dollar amount or percentage charges and fees with an explanation of how they apply.

(5) Information about the current guaranteed rate for new contracts that contains a clear notice that the rate is subject to change.

Insurers shall define terms used in the disclosure statement in language that facilitates the understanding by a typical person within the segment of the public to which the disclosure statement is directed. (2005-234, s. 1.11.)

§ 58-60-145. Report to contract owners.

For annuities in the payout period with changes in nonguaranteed elements and for the accumulation period of a deferred annuity, the insurer shall provide each contract owner with a report, at least annually, on the status of the contract that contains at least all of the following information:

(1) The beginning and end dates of the current report period.

(2) The accumulation and cash-surrender value, if any, at the end of the previous report period and at the end of the current report period.

(3) The total amounts, if any, that have been credited, charged to the contract value, or paid during the current report period.

(4) The amount of outstanding loans, if any, as of the end of the current report period. (2005-234, s. 1.11.)

Part 4. Suitability in Annuity Transactions.

§ 58-60-150. Title and reference.

This Part may be cited as the "Suitability in Annuity Transactions Act". (2007-298, s. 1.1.)

§ 58-60-155. Purpose; scope.

(a) The purpose of this Part is to set forth standards and procedures for recommendations to consumers that result in a transaction involving annuity products so that the insurance needs and financial objectives of consumers at the time of the transaction are appropriately addressed.

(b) This Part shall apply to any recommendation to purchase or exchange an annuity made to a consumer by an insurance producer, or an insurer where no producer is involved, that results in the purchase or exchange recommended. (2007-298, s. 1.1.)

§ 58-60-160. Exemptions.

Unless otherwise specifically included, this Part does not apply to recommendations involving any of the following:

(1) Direct response solicitations where there is no recommendation based on information collected from the consumer pursuant to this Part.

(2) Contracts used to fund any of the following:

a. An employee pension or welfare benefit plan that is covered by the Employee Retirement and Income Security Act (ERISA).

b. A plan described by section 401(a), 401(k), 403(b), 408(k), or 408(p) of the Internal Revenue Code if established or maintained by an employer.

c. A government or church plan defined in section 414 of the Internal Revenue Code, a government or church welfare benefit plan, or a deferred compensation plan of a state or local government or tax-exempt organization under section 457 of the Internal Revenue Code.

d. A nonqualified deferred compensation arrangement established or maintained by an employer or plan sponsor.

e. Settlements of or assumptions of liabilities associated with personal injury litigation or any dispute or claim resolution process.

f. Formal prepaid funeral contracts. (2007-298, s. 1.1.)

§ 58-60-165. Definitions.

As used in this Part:

(1) "Annuity" means a fixed annuity or variable annuity that is individually solicited, whether the product is classified as an individual or group annuity.

(2) "Insurance producer" has the same meaning as in G.S. 58-33-10(7).

(3) "Recommendation" means advice provided by an insurance producer, or an insurer where no producer is involved, to an individual consumer that results in a purchase or exchange of an annuity in accordance with that advice. (2007-298, s. 1.1.)

§ 58-60-170. Duties of insurers and insurance producers.

(a) In recommending to a consumer the purchase of an annuity or the exchange of an annuity that results in another insurance transaction or series of insurance transactions, the insurance producer, or the insurer where no producer is involved, shall have reasonable grounds for believing that the reccmmendation is suitable for the consumer on the basis of the facts disclosed by the consumer as to the consumer's investments and other insurance procucts and as to the consumer's financial situation and needs.

(b) Before recommending the purchase or exchange of an annuity resulting from a recommendation, the insurance producer, or the insurer where no producer is involved, shall make reasonable efforts to obtain information about the particular consumer's circumstances, including, but not limited to, all of the following:

(1)   The consumer's financial status.

(2)   The consumer's tax status.

(3)   The consumer's investment objectives.

(4)   Any other information used or considered to be reasonable by the insurance producer, or the insurer where no producer is involved, in making recommendations to the consumer.

(c)   Except as provided under subdivision (1) of this subsection, neither an insurance producer, nor an insurer where no producer is involved, shall have any obligation to a consumer under subsection (a) of this section related to any recommendation if a consumer does any of the following:

(1)   Refuses to provide relevant information requested by the insurer or insurance producer. An insurer or insurance producer's recommendation subject to this subdivision shall be reasonable under all the circumstances actually known to the insurer or insurance producer at the time of the recommendation.

(2)   Decides to enter into an insurance transaction that is not based on a recommendation of the insurer or insurance producer.

(3)   Fails to provide complete or accurate information requested by the insurer or insurance producer.

(d)   An insurer either shall assure that a system to supervise recommendations that is reasonably designed to achieve compliance with this Part is established and maintained by complying with subsections (e), (f), and (g) of this section, or shall establish and maintain such a system, including:

(1)   Maintaining written procedures.

(2)   Conducting periodic reviews of its records that are reasonably designed to assist in detecting and preventing violations of this Part.

(e) A general agent and independent agency either shall adopt a system established by an insurer to supervise recommendations of its insurance producers that is reasonably designed to achieve compliance with this Part, or shall establish and maintain such a system, including:

(1) Maintaining written procedures.

(2) Conducting periodic reviews of records that are reasonably designed to assist in detecting and preventing violations of this Part.

(f) An insurer may contract with a third party, including a general agent or independent agency, to establish and maintain a system of supervision as required by subsection (d) of this section with respect to insurance producers under contract with, or employed by, the third party. An insurer shall make reasonable inquiry to assure that the third-party contracting under this subsection is performing the functions required under subsection (d) of this section and shall take any action that is reasonable under the circumstances to enforce the contractual obligation to perform the functions. An insurer may comply with its obligation to make reasonable inquiry by doing all of the following:

(1) The insurer annually obtains a certification from a third-party senior manager who has responsibility for the delegated functions that the manager has a reasonable basis to represent, and does represent, that the third party is performing the required functions. No person may provide a certification under this subdivision unless (i) the person is a senior manager with responsibility for the delegated functions; and (ii) the person has a reasonable basis for making the certification.

(2) The insurer, based on reasonable selection criteria, periodically selects third parties contracting under this subsection for a review to determine whether the third parties are performing the required functions. The insurer shall perform those procedures to conduct the review that are reasonable under the circumstances.

An insurer that contracts with a third party, and that complies with the requirements to supervise the third party pursuant to this subsection, shall have fulfilled its responsibilities under subsection (d) of this section.

A general agent or independent agency contracting with an insurer shall promptly, when requested by the insurer pursuant to this subsection, give a certification as described in this subsection or give a clear statement that it is unable to meet the certification criteria.

(g) An insurer, general agent, or independent agency is not required by subsections (d) or (e) of this section to:

(1) Review, or provide for review of, all insurance producer solicited transactions; or

(2) Include in its system of supervision an insurance producer's recommendations to consumers of products other than the annuities offered by the insurer, general agent, or independent agency.

(h) Compliance with the Financial Industry Regulatory Authority Conduct Rules pertaining to suitability shall satisfy the requirements under this section for the recommendation of annuities subject to the Conduct Rules. Nothing in this subsection limits the Commissioner's ability to enforce the provisions of this Article. (2007-298, s. 1.1; 2009-382, s. 36.)

§ 58-60-175. Mitigation of responsibility.

(a) The Commissioner may order:

(1) An insurer to take reasonably appropriate corrective action for any consumer harmed by the insurer's, or by its insurance producer's, violation of this Part.

(2) An insurance producer to take reasonably appropriate corrective action for any consumer harmed by the insurance producer's violation of this Part.

(3) A general agency or independent agency that employs or contracts with an insurance producer to sell, or solicit the sale, of annuities to consumers, to take reasonably appropriate corrective action for any consumer harmed by the insurance producer's violation of this Part.

(b) Any applicable penalty under G.S. 58-2-70 for a violation of subsection (a) or (b) of G.S. 58-60-170 may be reduced or eliminated if corrective action for the consumer was taken promptly after a violation was discovered.

(c) A violation of this Part is an unfair method of competition and unfair and deceptive act or practice in the business of insurance in violation of G.S. 58-63-10 (2007-298, s. 1.1.)

§ 58-60-180. Record keeping.

(a) Insurers, general agents, independent agencies, and insurance producers shall maintain or be able to make available to the Commissioner records of the information collected from the consumer and other information used in making the recommendations that were the basis for insurance transactions for five years after the insurance transaction is completed by the insurer. An insurer is permitted, but shall not be required, to maintain documentation on behalf of an insurance producer.

(b) Records required to be maintained by this Part may be maintained in paper, photographic, microprocess, magnetic, mechanical, or electronic media or by any process that accurately reproduces the actual document. (2007-298, s. 1.1.)

Article 61.

Regulation of Interest Rates on Life Insurance Policy Loans.

§ 58-61-1. Purpose.

The purpose of this Article is to permit and set guidelines for life insurers to include in life insurance policies issued after the effective date of this Article a provision for periodic adjustment of policy loan interest rates. Nothing in this Article shall be construed to prohibit a life insurer from issuing a policy that contains only the provision specified in G.S. 58-61-10(a)(1) with respect to policy loan interest rates. (1981, c. 841, s. 1.)

§ 58-61-5. Definitions.

For purposes of this Article the "Published Monthly Average" means:

(1) The Monthly Average of the Composite Yield on Seasoned Corporate Bonds as published by Moody's Investors Service, Inc., or any successor thereto; or

(2) In the event that the Monthly Average of the Composite Yield on Seasoned Corporate Bonds is no longer published, a substantially similar average, established by regulation issued by the Commissioner. (1981, c. 841, s. 1.)

§ 58-61-10. Maximum rate of interest on policy loans.

(a) Policies issued on or after September 1, 1981 shall provide for policy loan interest rates as follows:

(1) A provision permitting a maximum interest rate of not more than eight percent (8%) per annum; or

(2) A provision permitting an adjustable maximum interest rate established from time to time by the life insurer as permitted by law.

(b) The rate of interest on a policy loan made under subsection (a)(2) shall not exceed the higher of the following:

(1) The published monthly average for the calendar month ending two months before the date on which the rate is determined; or

(2) The rate used to compute the cash surrender values under the policy during the applicable period plus one percent (1%) per annum.

(c) If the maximum rate of interest is determined pursuant to subsection (a)(2), the policy shall contain a provision setting forth the frequency at which the rate is to be determined for that policy.

(d) The maximum rate for each policy must be determined at regular intervals at least once every 12 months, but not more frequently than once in any three-month period. At the intervals specified in the policy:

(1) The rate being charged may be increased whenever such increase as determined under subsection (b) would increase that rate by one-half percent (1/2%) or more per annum;

(2) The rate being charged must be reduced whenever such reduction as determined under subsection (b) would decrease that rate by one-half percent (1/2%) or more per annum.

(e) The life insurer shall:

(1) Notify the policyholder at the time a cash loan is made of the initial rate of interest on the loan;

(2) Notify the policyholder with respect to premium loans of the initial rate of interest on the loan as soon as it is reasonably practical to do so after making the initial loan. Notice need not be given to the policyholder when a further premium loan is added, except as provided in (3) below;

(3) Send to policyholders with loans reasonable advance notice of any increase in the rate; and

(4) Include in the notices required above the substance of the pertinent provisions of subsections (a) and (c).

(f) No policy shall terminate in a policy year as the sole result of change in the interest rate during that policy year, and the life insurer shall maintain coverage during that policy year until the time at which it would otherwise have terminated if there had been no change during that policy year.

(g) The substance of the pertinent provisions of subsections (a) and (c) shall be set forth in the policies to which they apply.

(h) For purposes of this section:

(1) The rate of interest on policy loans permitted under this section includes the interest rate charged on reinstatement of policy loans for the period during and after any lapse of a policy.

(2) The term "policy loan" includes any premium loan made under a policy to pay one or more premiums that were not paid to the life insurer as they fell due.

(3) The term "policyholder" includes the owner of the policy or the person designated to pay premiums as shown on the records of the life insurer.

(4) The term "policy" includes certificates issued by a fraternal benefit society and annuity contracts which provide for policy loans.

(i) No other provision of law shall apply to policy loan interest rates unless made specifically applicable to such rates. (1981, c. 841, s. 1.)

§ 58-61-15. Applicability to existing policies.

The provisions of this Article shall not apply to any insurance contract issued before September 1, 1981. (1981, c. 841, s. 1.)

Article 62.

Life and Health Insurance Guaranty Association.

§ 58-62-1: Repealed by Session Laws 1991, c. 681, s. 57.

§ 58-62-2. Title.

This Article shall be known and may be cited as the North Carolina Life and Health Insurance Guaranty Association Act. (1991, c. 681, s. 56.)

§ 58-62-5: Repealed by Session Laws 1991, c. 681, s. 57.

§ 58-62-6. Purpose.

(a)   The purpose of this Article is to protect, subject to certain limitations, the persons specified in G.S. 58-62-21(a) against failure in the performance of contractual obligations, under life and health insurance policies and annuity contracts specified in G.S. 58-62-21(b), because of the delinquency of the member insurer that issued the policies.

(b)   To provide this protection, an association of insurers is created to pay benefits and to continue coverages as limited herein, and members of the Association are subject to assessment to provide funds to carry out the purpose of this Article. (1991, c. 681, s. 56.)

§ 58-62-10: Repealed by Session Laws 1991, c. 681, s. 57.

§ 58-62-11. Construction.

This Article shall be liberally construed to effect the purpose under G.S. 58-62-6, which shall constitute an aid and guide to interpretation. (1991, c. 681, s. 56.)

§ 58-62-15: Repealed by Session Laws 1991, c. 681, s. 57.

§ 58-62-16. Definitions.

As used in this Article:

(1)   "Account" means any of the two accounts created under G.S. 58-62-26.

(2)   "Association" means the North Carolina Life and Health Insurance Guaranty Association created under G.S. 58-62-26.

(3) "Board" means the board of directors of the Association established under G.S. 58-62-31.

(4) "Contractual obligation" means any obligation under a policy or certificate under a group policy, or part thereof, for which coverage is provided under G.S. 58-62-21.

(5) "Covered policy" means any policy within the scope of this Article under G.S. 58-62-21.

(6) "Delinquent insurer" means an impaired insurer or an insolvent insurer; and "delinquency" means an insurer impairment or insolvency.

(7) "Health insurance" includes hospital or medical service corporation contracts, accident and health insurance, accident insurance, and disability insurance.

(8) "Impaired insurer" means a member insurer that, after the effective date of this Article, is not an insolvent insurer, and (i) is deemed by the Commissioner to be potentially unable to fulfill its contractual obligations or (ii) is placed under an order of rehabilitation or conservation by a court of competent jurisdiction.

(9) "Insolvent insurer" means a member insurer that, after the effective date of this Article, is placed under an order of liquidation with a finding of insolvency by a court of competent jurisdiction.

(10) "Insurance regulator" means the official or agency of another state that is responsible for the regulation of a foreign insurer.

(11) "Member insurer" means any insurer and any hospital or medical service corporation that is governed by Article 65 of this Chapter and that is licensed or that holds a license to transact in this State any kind of insurance for which coverage is provided under G.S. 58-62-21; and includes any insurer whose license in this State may have been suspended, revoked, not renewed or voluntarily withdrawn, but does not include an entity governed by Article 67 of this Chapter; fraternal order or fraternal benefit society; mandatory State pooling plan; mutual assessment company or any entity that operates on an assessment basis; insurance exchange; or any entity similar to any of the foregoing.

(12) "Moody's Corporate Bond Yield Average" means the Monthly Average Corporates as published by Moody's Investors Service, Inc., or any successor thereto.

(13) "Person" includes an individual, corporation, company, partnership, association, or aggregation of individuals.

(14) "Plan" means the plan of operation established under G.S. 58-62-46.

(15) "Policy" includes a master group contract and subscriber contract under Article 65 of this Chapter, a contract of insurance and an annuity contract.

(16) "Premiums" means amounts received in any calendar year on covered policies less premiums, considerations, and deposits returned thereon, and less dividends and experience credits thereon. "Premiums" does not include any amounts received for any policies or for the parts of any policies for which coverage is not provided under G.S. 58-62-21(b); except that assessable premium shall not be reduced on account of G.S. 58-62-21(c)(3) relating to interest limitations and G.S. 58-62-21(d)(2) relating to limitations with respect to any one individual, any one participant, and any one contract holder.

(17) "Resident" means any person who resides in this State when a member insurer is determined to be a delinquent insurer and to whom a contractual obligation is owed. A person may be a resident of only one state, which in the case of a person other than a natural person shall be its principal place of business. "Resident" also means a U.S. citizen residing outside of the United States who owns a covered policy that was purchased from a member insurer while that person resided in this State.

(17a) "Structured settlement annuities" means any contracts or certificates for annuities issued to fund, in whole or in part, a settlement agreement for a matter involving personal injury or illness, including any settlement agreement permitted under Chapter 97 of the General Statutes.

(18) "Unallocated annuity contract" means any annuity contract or group annuity certificate that is not issued to and owned by an individual, except to the extent of any annuity benefits guaranteed to an individual by an insurer under the contract or certificate. (1991, c. 681, s. 56; 1993, c. 452, s. 60; 1995, c. 177, s. 1; 2009-448, s. 1.)

§ 58-62-20: Repealed by Session Laws 1991, c. 681, s. 57.

§ 58-62-21. Coverage and limitations.

(a) This Article provides coverage for the policies and contracts specified in subsection (b) of this section:

(1) To persons other than persons specified in subdivisions (3) and (4) of this subsection who, regardless of where they reside (except for nonresident certificate holders under group policies), are the beneficiaries, assignees, or payees of the persons covered under subdivision (2) of this subsection;

(2) To persons other than persons specified in subdivisions (3) and (4) of this subsection who are owners or certificate holders under the policies, or in the case of unallocated annuity contracts to the persons who are the contract holders, and who are residents of this State, or who are not residents of this State, but only under all of the following conditions: (i) the insurers that issued the policies are domiciled in this State; (ii) the insurers never held a license in the states in which the persons reside; (iii) the states have associations similar to the association created by this Article; and (iv) the persons are not eligible for coverage by the associations;

(3) To persons who are payees (or beneficiaries of payees if the payees are deceased) under structured settlement annuities if the payees are residents of this State, regardless of where the contract owners of the structured settlement annuities reside; and

(4) To persons who are payees (or beneficiaries of payees if the payees are deceased) under structured settlement annuities if the payees are not residents of this State, but only if all of the following conditions are met:

a. The contract owners of the structured settlement annuities are residents of this State or, if not residents of this State, (i) the insurers that issued the structured settlement annuities are domiciled in this State and (ii) the state in which the contract owners reside has an association similar to the Association created by this Article; and

b. Neither the payees (or beneficiaries of payees if the payees are deceased) nor the contract owners of the structured settlement annuities are eligible for coverage by an association of the state in which the payees or contract owners reside.

(b) This Article provides coverage to the persons specified in subsection (a) of this section for direct, nongroup life, health, annuity, and supplemental policies, for certificates under direct group policies and contracts, and for unallocated annuity contracts issued by member insurers, except as limited by this Article. Annuity contracts and certificates under group annuity contracts include guaranteed investment contracts, deposit administration contracts, unallocated funding agreements, allocated funding agreements, structured settlement agreements, lottery contracts, and any immediate or deferred annuity contracts.

(c) This Article does not provide coverage for:

(1) Any part of a policy not guaranteed by the insurer, or under which the risk is borne by the policyholder;

(2) Any policy or contract of reinsurance, unless assumption certificates have been issued;

(3) Any part of a policy to the extent that the rate of interest on which it is based, or the interest rate, crediting rate, or similar factor determined by the use of an index or other external reference stated in the policy or contract and employed in calculating returns or changes in value:

a. Averaged over the period of four years before the date on which the Association becomes obligated with respect to the policy, exceeds a rate of interest determined by subtracting two percentage points from Moody's Corporate Bond Yield Average averaged for that same four-year period or for a lesser period if the policy was issued less than four years before the Association became obligated; and

b. On and after the date on which the Association becomes obligated with respect to the policy, exceeds the rate of interest determined by subtracting three percentage points from Moody's Corporate Bond Yield Average as most recently available;

(4) Any plan or program of an employer, association, or similar entity to provide life, health, or annuity benefits to its employees or members to the extent that the plan or program is self-funded or uninsured, including benefits payable by an employer, association, or similar entity under:

a. A multiple employer welfare arrangement as defined in section 514 of the Employee Retirement Income Security Act of 1974 as amended;

b. A minimum premium group insurance plan;

c. A stop-loss group insurance plan; or

d. An administrative services only contract;

(5) Any part of a policy to the extent that it provides dividends or experience-rating credits, or provides that any fees or allowances be paid to any person, including the policyholder, in connection with the service to or administration of the policy;

(6) Any policy issued in this State by a member insurer at a time when it was not licensed to issue the policy in this State;

(7) Any unallocated annuity contract issued to an employee benefit plan protected under the federal Pension Benefit Guaranty Corporation; and

(8) Any part of any unallocated annuity contract that is not issued to or in connection with a specific employee, union, or association of natural persons benefit plan or a government lottery.

(9) A policy or contract providing any hospital, medical, prescription drug, or other health care benefits pursuant to Part C or Part D of Subchapter XVIII, Chapter 7 of Title 42 of the United States Code (commonly known as Medicare Parts C & D) or any regulations issued pursuant thereto.

(10) A portion of a policy or contract to the extent it provides for interest or other changes in value to be determined by the use of an index or other external reference stated in the policy or contract, but which have not been credited to the policy or contract or as to which the policy or contract owner's rights are subject to forfeiture, as of the date the member insurer becomes an impaired or insolvent insurer under this Act, whichever is earlier. If a policy's or contract's interest or changes in value are credited less frequently than annually, then for

purposes of determining the values that have been credited and are not subject to forfeiture under this subdivision, the interest or change in value determined by using the procedures defined in the policy or contract will be credited as if the contractual date of crediting interest or changing values was the date of impairment or insolvency, whichever is earlier, and will not be subject to forfeiture.

(d) The benefits for which the Association is liable do not, in any event, exceed the lesser of:

(1) The contractual obligations for which the insurer is liable or would have been liable if it were not a delinquent insurer; or

(2) With respect to any one individual, regardless of the number of policies, three hundred thousand dollars ($300,000) for all benefits, including cash values; or

(2a) With respect to health insurance benefits for any one individual, regardless of the number of policies:

a. Three hundred thousand dollars ($300,000) for coverages not defined as basic hospital, medical, and surgical insurance or major medical insurance as defined in this Chapter and regulations adopted pursuant to this Chapter, including disability insurance and long-term care insurance; or

b. Five hundred thousand dollars ($500,000) for basic hospital, medical, and surgical insurance or major medical insurance as defined in this Chapter and regulations adopted pursuant to this Chapter;

(3) With respect to each individual participating in a governmental retirement plan established under section 401, 403(b), or 457 of the Internal Revenue Code covered by an unallocated annuity contract, or the beneficiaries of each individual if deceased, in the aggregate, three hundred thousand dollars ($300,000) in present value annuity benefits, including net cash surrender and net cash withdrawal values; or

(4) With respect to any one contract holder covered by any unallocated annuity contract not included in subdivision (3) of this subsection, five million dollars ($5,000,000) in benefits, regardless of the number of such contracts held by that contract holder; or

(5)　With respect to any one payee (or beneficiaries of one payee if the payee is deceased) of a structured settlement annuity, one million dollars ($1,000,000) for all benefits, including cash values.

(6)　However, in no event shall the Association be obligated to cover more than (i) an aggregate of three hundred thousand dollars ($300,000) in benefits with respect to any one individual under subdivisions (2) and (3) and sub-subdivision (2a)a. except with respect to benefits for basic hospital, medical, and surgical and major medical insurance under sub-subdivision (2a)b. of this subsection, in which case the aggregate liability of the Association shall not exceed five hundred thousand dollars ($500,000) with respect to any one individual.

(e)　Repealed by Session Laws 2010-11, s. 2, effective June 23, 2010, and applicable to claims submitted to the North Carolina Life and Health Insurance Guaranty Association on or after August 7, 2009. (1991, c. 681, s. 56; c. 720, s. 93; 1993, c. 452, s. 61; 2009-448, ss. 2, 3, 4; 2010-11, ss. 1, 2; 2013-136, s. 1.)

§ 58-62-25: Repealed by Session Laws 1991, c. 681, s. 57.

§ 58-62-26. Creation of the Association.

(a)　There is created a nonprofit legal entity to be known as the North Carolina Life and Health Insurance Guaranty Association. All member insurers shall be and remain members of the Association as a condition of their authority to transact insurance in this State. The Association shall perform its functions under the Plan established and approved under G.S. 58-62-46 and shall exercise its powers through the Board established under G.S. 58-62-31. For purposes of administration and assessment, the Association shall maintain two accounts:

(1)　The life insurance and annuity account, which includes the following subaccounts:

a.　Life insurance account;

b.　Annuity account.

(2) The health insurance account.

(b) The Association is under the immediate supervision of the Commissioner and is subject to the applicable provisions of this Chapter. Meetings or records of the Association may be opened to the public upon majority vote of the Board. (1991, c. 681, s. 56.)

§ 58-62-30: Repealed by Session Laws 1991, c. 681, s. 57.

§ 58-62-31. Board of directors.

(a) The Board shall consist of not less than five nor more than nine member insurers serving terms as established in the Plan. The members of the Board shall be selected by member insurers, subject to the Commissioner's approval. Vacancies on the Board shall be filled for the remaining period of the term by a majority vote of the remaining Board members, subject to the Commissioner's approval. To select the initial Board, and initially organize the Association, the Board's predecessor shall notify all member insurers of the time and place of the organizational meeting. In determining voting rights at the organizational meeting, each member insurer is entitled to one vote in person or by proxy. If the Board is not selected within 60 days after notice of the organizational meeting, the Commissioner may appoint the initial members.

(b) In approving selections or in appointing members to the Board, the Commissioner shall consider, among other things, whether all member insurers are fairly represented.

(c) Members of the Board may be reimbursed from the assets of the Association for expenses they incur as members of the Board, but they shall not otherwise be compensated by the Association for their services. (1991, c. 681, s. 56.)

§ 58-62-35: Repealed by Session Laws 1991, c. 681, s. 57.

§ 58-62-36. Powers and duties of the Association.

(a) If a member insurer is an impaired domestic insurer, the Association may, subject to any conditions imposed by the Association and approved by the Commissioner that do not impair the contractual obligations of the impaired insurer and that are, except in cases of court-ordered conservation or rehabilitation, also approved by the impaired insurer:

(1) Guarantee, assume, or reinsure, or cause to be guaranteed, assumed, or reinsured, any or all of the policies of the impaired insurer;

(2) Provide such monies, pledges, notes, guarantees, or other means as are proper to carry out subdivision (1) of this subsection and assure payment of the contractual obligations of the impaired insurer pending action under subdivision (1) of this subsection; or

(3) Lend money to the impaired insurer.

(b), (c) Repealed by Session Laws 2013-136, s. 2, effective July 1, 2013.

(d) If a member insurer is an insolvent insurer, the Association shall, in its discretion, either:

(1) Guarantee, assume or reinsure, or cause to be guaranteed, assumed, or reinsured, the policies of the insolvent insurer; or

(2) Assure payment of the contractual obligations of the insolvent insurer; and

(3) Provide such monies, pledges, guarantees, or other means as are reasonably necessary to discharge those duties; or

(4) With respect only to life and health insurance policies, provide benefits and coverages in accordance with subsection (e) of this section.

(d1) In carrying out its duties in connection with guaranteeing, assuming, or reinsuring policies or contracts under subsections (a) and (d) of this section, the Association may, subject to approval of the receivership court, issue substitute coverage for a policy or contract that provides an interest rate, crediting rate, or similar factor determined by use of an index or other external reference stated in the policy or contract employed in calculating returns or changes in value by issuing an alternative policy or contract in accordance with the following provisions:

(1) In lieu of the index or other external reference provided for in the original policy or contract, the alternative policy or contract provides for (i) a fixed interest rate, (ii) payment of dividends with minimum guarantees, or (iii) a different method for calculating interest or changes in value;

(2) There is no requirement for evidence of insurability, waiting period, or other exclusion that would not have applied under the replaced policy or contract; and

(3) The alternative policy or contract is substantially similar to the replaced policy or contract in all other material terms.

(e) When proceeding under subdivision (b)(2) or (d)(4) of this section, the Association shall, with respect to only life and health insurance policies:

(1) Assure payment of benefits for premiums identical to the premiums and benefits (except for terms of conversion and renewability) that would have been payable under the policies of the insolvent insurer, for claims incurred:

a. With respect to group policies, not later than the earlier of the next renewal date under the policies or 45 days, but in no event less than 30 days after the date on which the Association becomes obligated with respect to the policies;

b. With respect to individual policies, not later than the earlier of the next renewal date (if any) under the policies or one year, but in no event less than 30 days from the date on which the Association becomes obligated with respect to the policies;

(2) Make diligent efforts to provide all known insureds or group policyholders with respect to group policies 30 days' notice of the termination of the benefits provided; and

(3) With respect to individual policies, make available to each known insured, or owner if other than the insured, and with respect to an individual formerly insured under a group policy who is not eligible for replacement group

coverage, make available substitute coverage on an individual basis in accordance with the provisions of subsection (f) of this section, if the insured had a right under law or the terminated policy to convert coverage to individual coverage or to continue an individual policy in force until a specified age or for a specified time, during which the insurer had no right unilaterally to make changes in any provision of the policy or had a right only to make changes in premium by class.

(f) In providing the substitute coverage required under subdivision (e)(3) of this section, the Association may offer either to reissue the terminated coverage or to issue an alternative policy. An alternative or reissued policy shall be offered without requiring evidence of insurability, and shall not provide for any waiting period or exclusion that would not have applied under the terminated policy. The Association may reinsure any alternative or reissued policy.

(g) Alternative life or health insurance policies adopted by the Association are subject to the Commissioner's approval. The Association may adopt alternative policies of various types for future issuance without regard to any particular delinquency. Alternative policies shall contain at least the minimum statutory provisions required in this State and provide benefits that are not unreasonable in relation to the premium charged. The Association shall set the premium in accordance with a table of rates, which it shall adopt. The premium shall reflect the amount of insurance to be provided and the age and class of risk of each insured, but it shall not reflect any changes in the health of the insured after the original policy was last underwritten. Any alternative policy issued by the Association shall provide coverage of a type similar to that of the policy issued by the delinquent insurer, as determined by the Association.

(h) If the Association elects to reissue terminated coverage at a premium rate different from that charged under the terminated life or health insurance policy, the premium shall be set by the Association in accordance with the amount of insurance provided and the age and class of risk, subject to the approval of the Commissioner or by a court of competent jurisdiction.

(i) The Association's obligations with respect to coverage under any life or health insurance policy of the delinquent insurer or under any reissued or alternative policy cease on the date the coverage or policy is replaced by another similar policy by the policyholder, the insured, or the Association.

(j) When proceeding under subdivision (b)(2) of this section or under subsection (c) of this section with respect to any policy carrying guaranteed minimum interest rates, the Association shall assure the payment or crediting of a rate of interest consistent with G.S. 58-62-21(c)(3).

(k) Nonpayment of premiums within 31 days after the date required under the terms of any guaranteed, assumed, alternative, or reissued policy or substitute coverage terminates the Association's obligations under the policy or coverage under this Article with respect to the policy or coverage, except with respect to any claims incurred or any net cash surrender value that may be due under this Article.

(l) Premiums due for coverage after an entry of an order of liquidation of an insolvent insurer belong to and are payable at the direction of the Association; and the Association is liable for unearned premiums owed to policyowners arising after the entry of the order.

(m) The protection provided by this Article does not apply where any similar guaranty protection is provided to residents of this State by the laws of the domiciliary state or jurisdiction of a delinquent foreign or alien insurer.

(n) In carrying out its duties under subsections (b) through (d) of this section, the Association may, subject to approval by the court:

(1) Impose permanent policy liens in connection with any guarantee, assumption, or reinsurance agreement, if the Association finds that the amounts that can be assessed under this Article are less than the amounts needed to assure full and prompt performance of the Association's duties under this Article, or that the economic or financial conditions as they affect member insurers are sufficiently adverse to render the imposition of the permanent policy liens to be in the public interest;

(2) Impose temporary moratoria or liens on payments of cash values and policy loans, or any other right to withdraw funds held in conjunction with policies, in addition to any contractual provisions for deferral of cash or policy loan value.

(o) If the Association fails to act within a reasonable period of time as provided in subdivision (b)(2) of this section and subsections (d) and (e) of this section, the Commissioner has the powers and duties of the Association under this Article with respect to delinquent insurers.

(p) The Association may render assistance and advice to the Commissioner, upon the Commissioner's request concerning rehabilitation, payment of claims, continuance of coverage, or the performance of other contractual obligations of any delinquent insurer.

(q) The Association has standing to appear before any court in this State with jurisdiction over a delinquent insurer for which the Association is or may become obligated under this Article. This standing extends to all matters germane to the powers and duties of the Association including, but not limited to, proposals for reinsuring, modifying, or guaranteeing the policies of the delinquent insurer and the determination of the policies and contractual obligations. The Association also has the right to appear or intervene before a court in another state with jurisdiction over a delinquent insurer for which the Association is or may become obligated or with jurisdiction over a third party against whom the Association may have rights through subrogation of the insurer's policyholders.

(r) Any person receiving benefits under this Article is considered to have been assigned the rights under, and any causes of action relating to, the covered policy to the Association to the extent of the benefits received because of this Article, whether the benefits are payments of or on account of contractual obligations, continuation of coverage, or provision of substitute or alternative coverages. The Association may require an assignment to it of such rights and cause of action by any payee, policyowner, beneficiary, insured or annuitant as a condition precedent to the receipt of any right or benefits conferred by this Article upon the person. The subrogation rights of the Association under this subsection have the same priority against the delinquent insurer's assets as that possessed by the person entitled to receive benefits under this Article. In addition to other provisions of this subsection, the Association has all common-law rights of subrogation and any other equitable or legal remedy that would have been available to the delinquent insurer or holder of a policy with respect to the policy.

(s) The Association may:

(1) Enter into contracts that are necessary or proper to carry out the provisions and purposes of this Article;

(2) Sue or be sued, including taking any legal actions necessary or proper to recover any unpaid assessments under G.S. 58-62-41 and to settle claims or potential claims against it;

(3) Borrow money to effect the purposes of this Article; any notes or other evidence of indebtedness of the Association not in default shall be legal investments for domestic insurers and may be carried as admitted assets;

(4) Employ or retain persons that are necessary to handle the financial transactions of the Association, and to perform other functions that become necessary or proper under this Article;

(5) Take legal action that may be necessary to avoid payment of improper claims;

(6) Exercise, for the purposes of this Article and to the extent approved by the Commissioner, the powers of a domestic life or health insurer, but in no case may the Association issue insurance policies or annuity contracts other than those issued to perform its obligations under this Article.

(t) The Association may join an organization of one or more other state associations of similar purposes, in order to further the purposes of this Article and administer the powers and duties of the Association. (1991, c. 681, s. 56; c. 720, s. 94; 2013-136, s. 2.)

§ 58-62-40: Repealed by Session Laws 1991, c. 681, s. 57.

§ 58-62-41. Assessments.

(a) To provide the funds necessary to carry out the powers and duties of the Association, the Board shall assess the member insurers, separately for each account, at such time and for such amounts as the Board finds necessary. Assessments are due not less than 30 days after prior written notice to the member insurers and shall accrue interest at the rate of one percent (1%) per month, or any part thereof, after the due date.

(b) There shall be two classes of assessments, as follows:

(1) Class A assessments shall be made for the purpose of meeting administrative and legal costs and other expenses and examinations conducted

under the authority of G.S. 58-62-56(e). Class A assessments may be made whether or not they are related to a particular delinquent insurer.

(2) Class B assessments shall be made to the extent necessary to carry out the powers and duties of the Association under G.S. 58-62-36 with regard to a delinquent insurer.

(c) The amount of any Class A assessment shall be determined by the Board and may or may not be prorated. If prorated, the Board may provide that it be credited against future Class B assessments. If not prorated, the assessment shall not exceed five hundred dollars ($500.00) per member insurer in any one calendar year. The amount of any Class B assessment shall be allocated for assessment purposes among the accounts pursuant to an allocation formula, which may be based on the premiums or reserves of the delinquent insurer or any other standard considered by the Board in its sole discretion to be fair and reasonable under the circumstances.

(d) Class B assessments against member insurers for each account and subaccount shall be in the proportion that the premiums received on business in this State by each assessed member insurer or policies covered by each account for the three most recent calendar years for which information is available preceding the year in which the insurer became delinquent, as the case may be, bears to the premiums received on business in this State for those calendar years by all assessed member insurers.

(e) Assessments for funds to meet the requirements of the Association with respect to a delinquent insurer shall not be made until necessary to implement the purposes of this Article. Classification of assessments under subsection (b) of this section and computation of assessments under this subsection shall be made with a reasonable degree of accuracy, recognizing that exact determinations may not always be possible.

(f) The Association may abate or defer, in whole or in part, the assessment of a member insurer if, in the Board's opinion, payment of the assessment would endanger the member insurer's ability to fulfill its contractual obligations. If an assessment against a member insurer is abated, or deferred in whole or in part, the amount by which the assessment is abated or deferred may be assessed against the other member insurers in a manner consistent with the basis for assessments set forth in this section.

(g) The total of all assessments upon a member insurer for the life and annuity account and for each subaccount thereunder shall not in any one calendar year exceed two percent (2%) and for the health account shall not in any one calendar year exceed two percent (2%) of the insurer's average premiums received in this State on the policies and contracts covered by the account during the three calendar years preceding the year in which an insurer became a delinquent insurer. If the maximum assessment, together with the other assets of the Association in any account, does not provide in any one year in either account an amount sufficient to carry out the Association's responsibilities, the necessary additional funds shall be assessed as soon thereafter as permitted by this Article.

(h) The Board may provide in the Plan a method of allocating funds among claims, whether relating to one or more delinquent insurers, when the maximum assessment will be insufficient to cover anticipated claims.

(i) If a one percent (1%) assessment for any subaccount of the life and annuity account in any one year does not provide an amount sufficient to carry out the Association's responsibilities, then under subsection (d) of this section, the Board shall assess all subaccounts of the life and annuity account for the necessary additional amount, subject to the maximum stated in subsection (g) of this section.

(j) The Board may, by an equitable method as established in the Plan, refund to member insurers, in proportion to the contribution of each insurer to that account, the amount by which the assets of the account exceed the amount the Board finds is necessary to carry out during the coming year the obligations of the Association with regard to that account, including assets accruing from assignment, subrogation, net realized gains, and income from investments. A reasonable amount may be retained in any account to provide funds for the continuing expenses of the Association and for future losses.

(k) It is proper for any member insurer, in determining its premium rates and policyowner dividends as to any kind of insurance within the scope of this Article, to consider the amount reasonably necessary to meet its assessment obligations under this Article.

(l) The Association shall issue to each insurer paying an assessment under this Article, other than a Class A assessment, a certificate of contribution, in a form prescribed by the Commissioner, for the amount of the assessment so paid All outstanding certificates shall be of equal dignity and priority without reference to amounts or dates of issue. (1991, c. 681, s. 56; 1993, c. 452, ss. 61.1, 62; 1995, c. 193, ss. 47, 48; 2013-136, s. 3.)

§ 58-62-45: Repealed by Session Laws 1991, c. 681, s. 57.

§ 58-62-46. Plan of operation.

(a) The Association shall submit to the Commissioner a Plan and any amendments necessary or suitable to assure the fair, reasonable, and equitable administration of the Association. The Plan and any amendments shall become effective upon the Commissioner's written approval or unless the Commissioner has not disapproved it within 30 days.

(b) If the Association fails to submit a suitable Plan within 120 days after the effective date of this Article or if at any time thereafter the Association fails to submit suitable amendments to the Plan, the Commissioner shall, after notice and hearing, adopt rules that are necessary or advisable to carry out the provisions of this Article. The rules shall continue in force until modified by the Commissioner or superseded by a Plan submitted by the Association and approved by the Commissioner.

(c) All member insurers shall comply with the Plan.

(d) The Plan shall, in addition to other requirements specified in this Article, establish:

(1) Procedures for handling the assets of the Association;

(2) The amount and method of reimbursing members of the Board under G.S. 58-62-31;

(3) Regular places and times for meetings, including telephone conference calls, of the Board;

(4) Procedures for records to be kept of all financial transactions of the Association, its agents, and the Board;

(5) The procedures whereby selections for the Board will be made and submitted to the Commissioner;

(6) Any additional procedures for assessments under G.S. 58-62-41;

(7) Additional provisions necessary or proper for the execution of the powers and duties of the Association.

(e) The Plan may provide that any or all powers and duties of the Association, except those under G.S. 58-62-36(r) and G.S. 58-62-41, may be delegated to a corporation, association, or other organization that performs or will perform functions similar to those of the Association, or its equivalent, in two or more states. Such a corporation, association, or organization shall be reimbursed for any payments made on behalf of the Association and shall be paid for its performance of any function of the Association. A delegation under this subsection is effective only with the approval of both the Board and the Commissioner, and may be made only to a corporation, association, or organization that extends protection not substantially less favorable and effective than that provided by this Article. (1991, c. 681, s. 56.)

§ 58-62-50: Repealed by Session Laws 1991, c. 681, s. 57.

§ 58-62-51. Duties and powers of the Commissioner.

(a) In addition to other duties and powers specified in this Article, the Commissioner shall:

(1) Upon request of the Board, provide the Association with a statement of the premiums in this State and any other appropriate states for each member insurer;

(2) When an impairment is declared and the amount of the impairment is determined, serve a demand upon the impaired insurer to make good the impairment within a reasonable time; notice to the impaired insurer shall constitute notice to its shareholders, if any; the failure of the insurer to comply promptly with the demand does not excuse the Association from the performance of its powers and duties under this Article; and

(3) In any liquidation or rehabilitation proceeding involving a domestic insurer, be appointed as the liquidator or rehabilitator as provided in Article 30 of this Chapter.

(b) The Commissioner may suspend or revoke, after notice and hearing, the license to transact insurance in this State of any member insurer that fails to pay an assessment when due or fails to comply with the Plan. As an alternative the Commissioner may levy a forfeiture on any member insurer that fails to pay an assessment when due. The forfeiture shall not exceed five percent (5%) of the unpaid assessment per month, but no forfeiture shall be less than one hundred dollars ($100.00) per month.

(c) Any action of the Board or the Association may be appealed to the Commissioner by any member insurer if the appeal is taken within 60 days of the final action being appealed. If a member company is appealing an assessment, the amount assessed shall be paid to the Association and available to meet Association obligations during the pendency of an appeal. If the appeal on the assessment is upheld, the amount paid in error or excess shall be returned to the member company. No later than 20 days before each hearing, the appellant shall file with the Commissioner or the Commissioner's designated hearing officer and shall serve on the appellee a written statement of the appellant's case and any evidence the appellant intends to offer at the hearing. No later than five days before the hearing, the appellee shall file with the Commissioner or the Commissioner's designated hearing officer and shall serve on the appellant a written statement of the appellee's case and any evidence the appellee intends to offer at the hearing. Each hearing shall be recorded and transcribed. The cost of the recording and transcribing shall be borne equally by the appellant and appellee; however, upon any final adjudication the prevailing party shall be reimbursed for that party's share of the costs by the other party. Each party shall, on a date determined by the Commissioner or the Commissioner's designated hearing officer, but not sooner than 15 days after delivery of the completed transcript to the party, submit to the Commissioner or the Commissioner's designated hearing officer and serve on the other party, a proposed order. The Commissioner or the Commissioner's designated hearing officer shall then issue an order Any final action or order of the Commissioner or the Commissioner's designated hearing officer is subject to judicial review under G.S. 58-2-75.

(d) The liquidator, rehabilitator, or conservator of any impaired insurer may notify all interested persons of the effect of this Article. (1991, c. 681, s. 56.)

§ 58-62-55: Repealed by Session Laws 1991, c. 681, s. 57.

§ 58-62-56. Prevention of delinquencies.

(a) To aid in the detection and prevention of insurer delinquencies, it is the Commissioner's duty to:

(1) Notify insurance regulators when revoking or suspending the license of a member insurer, or making any formal order that the insurer restrict its premium writing, obtain additional contributions to surplus, withdraw from this State, reinsure all or any part of its business, or increase capital, surplus, or any other account for the security of policyholders or creditors. That notice shall be sent electronically through the NAIC headquarters and mailed to all insurance regulators within 30 days following the action taken or the date on which the action occurs.

(2) Report to the Board when the Commissioner has taken any of the actions in subdivision (1) of this subsection or has received a report from another insurance regulator indicating that any such action has been taken in another state. The report to the Board shall contain all significant details of the action taken or the report received from another insurance regulator.

(3) Report to the Board when the Commissioner has reasonable cause to believe from any examination, whether completed or in process, of any member insurer that the insurer may be delinquent.

(4) Furnish the Board with the NAIC Insurance Regulatory Information System financial test ratios and a listing of companies that are not included in the ratios developed by the NAIC; and the Board may use that data in carrying out its duties and responsibilities under this section. The data shall be kept confidential by the Board until it is made public by the Commissioner or another lawful authority.

(b) The Commissioner may seek the advice and recommendations of the Board concerning any matter affecting the Commissioner's duties and responsibilities regarding the financial condition of member insurers and other entities seeking admission to transact insurance business in this State.

(c) The Board may, upon majority vote, make reports and recommendations to the Commissioner upon any matter germane to the solvency, liquidation, rehabilitation, or conservation of any member insurer or germane to the solvency of any company seeking to do an insurance business in this State. The reports and recommendations are not public records.

(d) The Board shall, upon majority vote, notify the Commissioner of any information indicating that any member insurer may be delinquent.

(e) The Board may, upon majority vote, request that the Commissioner order an examination of any member insurer that the Board in good faith believes may be delinquent. Within 30 days of the receipt of the request, the Commissioner shall begin the examination. The examination may be conducted as an NAIC examination or may be conducted by persons the Commissioner designates. The examination report shall be treated as are other examination reports. In no event shall the examination report be released to the Board before its release to the public; but this does not preclude the Commissioner from complying with subsection (a) of this section. The Commissioner shall notify the Board when the examination is completed. The request for an examination shall be kept on file by the Commissioner, but shall not be open to public inspection before the release of the examination report to the public.

(f) The Board may, upon majority vote, make recommendations to the Commissioner for the detection and prevention of insurer delinquencies.

(g) The Board shall, at the conclusion of any insurer insolvency in which the Association was obligated to pay covered claims, prepare a report to the Commissioner containing any information that it has in its possession bearing on the history and causes of the insolvency. The Board shall cooperate with the boards of directors of guaranty associations in other states in preparing a report on the history and causes of insolvency of a particular insurer, and the Board may adopt by reference any report prepared by such other associations. (1991, c. 681, s. 56; 1995, c. 360, s. 2(k).)

§ 58-62-60: Repealed by Session Laws 1991, c. 681, s. 57.

§ 58-62-61. Miscellaneous provisions.

(a)   Nothing in this Article reduces the liability for unpaid assessments of the insureds of a delinquent insurer operating under an insurance plan with assessment liability.

(b)   Records shall be kept of all negotiations and meetings in which the Association or its representatives are involved and in which the activities of the Association in carrying out its powers and duties under G.S. 58-62-36 are discussed. Records of those negotiations or meetings shall be made public only upon the termination of a liquidation, rehabilitation, or conservation proceeding involving the delinquent insurer, upon the termination of the delinquency of the insurer, or upon the order of a court of competent jurisdiction. Nothing in this subsection limits the duty of the Association to render a report of its activities under G.S. 58-62-66.

(c)   For the purpose of carrying out its obligations under this Article, the Association is a creditor of the delinquent insurer to the extent of assets attributable to covered policies reduced by any amounts to which the Association is entitled as subrogee under G.S. 58-62-36(r). Assets of the delinquent insurer attributable to covered policies shall be used to continue all covered policies and pay all contractual obligations of the delinquent insurer as required by this Article. Assets attributable to covered policies, as used in this subsection, are that proportion of the assets that the reserves that should have been established for the policies bear to the reserves that should have been established for all policies of insurance written by the delinquent insurer.

(d)   Before the termination of any liquidation, rehabilitation, or conservation proceeding, the court may take into consideration the contributions of the respective parties, including the Association, the shareholders, and policyowners of the insolvent insurer, and any other party with a bona fide interest, in making an equitable distribution of the ownership rights of the insolvent insurer. In making such a determination, consideration shall be given to the welfare of the policyholders of the continuing or successor insurer.

(e)   No distribution to stockholders, if any, of a delinquent insurer shall be made until and unless the Association has fully recovered the total amount of its valid claims with interest thereon for funds expended in carrying out its powers and duties under G.S. 58-62-36 with respect to the insurer.

(f) If an order for liquidation or rehabilitation of an insurer domiciled in this State has been entered, the receiver appointed under the order has a right to recover on behalf of the insurer, from any affiliate that controlled it, the amount of distributions, other than stock dividends paid by the insurer on its capital stock, made at any time during the five years preceding the petition for liquidation or rehabilitation subject to the limitations of subsections (g) through (i) of this section.

(g) No such distribution is recoverable if the insurer shows that when paid the distribution was lawful and reasonable, and that the insurer did not know and could not reasonably have known that the distribution might adversely affect the insurer's ability to fulfill its contractual obligations.

(h) Any person who was an affiliate that controlled the insurer when the distributions were paid is liable up to the amount of distributions it received. Any person who was an affiliate that controlled the insurer when the distributions were declared is liable up to the amount of distributions it would have received if they had been paid immediately. If two or more persons are liable with respect to the same distributions, they are jointly and severally liable.

(i) The maximum amount recoverable under this subsection is the amount needed in excess of all other available assets of the insolvent insurer to pay the insolvent insurer's contractual obligations.

(j) If any person liable under subsection (h) of this section is insolvent, all of its affiliates that controlled it when the distribution was paid are jointly and severally liable for any resulting deficiency in the amount recovered from the insolvent affiliate. (1991, c. 681, s. 56.)

§ 58-62-65: Repealed by Session Laws 1991, c. 681, s. 57.

§ 58-62-66. Examination of the Association; annual report.

The Association is subject to examination and regulation by the Commissioner. The Board shall submit to the Commissioner each year, not later than 120 days after the Association's fiscal year, a financial report in a form approved by the

Commissioner and a report of its activities during the preceding fiscal year. (1991, c. 681, s. 56.)

§ 58-62-70: Repealed by Session Laws 1991, c. 681, s. 57.

§ 58-62-75. Tax exemptions.

The Association shall be exempt from payment of all fees and all taxes levied by this State or any of its subdivisions, except taxes levied on real property. (1973, c. 1438, s. 1.)

§ 58-62-76. Immunity.

There is no liability by, and no cause of action of any nature arises against, any member insurer or its agents or employees, the Association or its agents or employees, members of the Board, the Commissioner or the Commissioner's representatives, or insurance regulators or their representatives, for any act or omission by them in the performance of their powers and duties under this Article. This immunity extends to the participation in any organization of one or more other state associations of similar purposes and to any such organization and its agents or employees. (1991, c. 681, s. 56.)

§ 58-62-77. Actions not precluded.

Nothing in this Article precludes any resident from bringing any action against the Association in any court of competent jurisdiction with respect to any contractual obligation arising under covered policies. (1993 (Reg. Sess., 1994), c. 678, s. 26.)

§ 58-62-80: Repealed by Session Laws 1991, c. 681, s. 57.

§ 58-62-81. Stay of proceedings; reopening default judgments.

All proceedings in which the insolvent insurer is a party in any court in this State shall be stayed 60 days from the date an order of liquidation, rehabilitation, or conservation is final to permit proper legal action by the Association on any matters germane to its powers or duties. As to a judgment under any decision, order, verdict or finding based on default, the Association may apply to have the judgment set aside by the same court that made the judgment and may defend against such suit on the merits. (1991, c. 681, s. 56.)

§ 58-62-85: Repealed by Session Laws 1991, c. 681, s. 57.

§ 58-62-86. Prohibited advertisement of Article in insurance sales; notice to policyholders.

(a) No person shall make, publish, disseminate, circulate, or place before the public, or cause directly or indirectly to be made, published, disseminated, circulated, or placed before the public, in any newspaper, magazine, or other publication, or in the form of a notice, circular, pamphlet, letter, or poster, or over any radio station or television station, or in any other way, any oral or written advertisement, announcement, or statement that uses the existence of the Association or this Article for the purpose of sale or solicitation of or inducement to purchase any kind of insurance covered by this Article. However, this subsection does not apply to the Association or any other person who does not sell or solicit insurance.

(b) Within 180 days after the effective date of this Article, the Association shall prepare a summary document that describes the general purposes and current limitations of this Article and that complies with subsection (c) of this section. This document shall be submitted to the Commissioner for the Commissioner's approval. Sixty days after receiving approval, no insurer may deliver a policy described in G.S. 58-62-21(b) to any person unless the document is delivered to that person before or at the time of delivery of the policy, unless subsection (d) of this section applies. The document shall also be available upon request by a policyholder. The distribution, delivery, contents, or interpretation of this document does not mean that either the policy or the policyholder would be covered in the event of the delinquency of a member insurer. The document shall be revised by the Association as amendments to this Article require. Failure to receive this document does not give any person greater rights than those stated in this Article.

(c)   The document prepared under subsection (b) of this section shall contain a clear and conspicuous disclaimer on its face. The Commissioner shall prescribe the form and content of the disclaimer. The disclaimer shall:

(1)   State the name and addresses of the Association and Department;

(2)   Prominently warn the policyholder that the Association may not cover the policy or, if coverage is available, it will be subject to substantial limitations and exclusions and conditioned on continued residence in this State;

(3)   State that the insurer and its agents are prohibited by law from using the existence of the Association for the purpose of sale or solicitation of or inducement to purchase any kind of insurance;

(4)   Emphasize that the applicant or policyholder should not rely on coverage under the Association when selecting an insurer; and

(5)   Provide other information as directed by the Commissioner.

(d)   No insurer or agent may deliver a policy described in G.S. 58-62-21(b) and excluded under G.S. 58-62-21(c) from coverage under this Article unless the insurer or agent, before or at the time of delivery, gives the policyholder a separate written notice that clearly and conspicuously discloses that the policy is not covered by the Association. The Commissioner shall prescribe the form and content of the notice. (1991, c. 681, s. 56.)

§ 58-62-90: Repealed by Session Laws 1991, c. 681, s. 57.

§ 58-62-92: Repealed by Session Laws 1993 (Reg. Sess., 1994), c. 678, s. 27.

§ 58-62-95. Use of deposits made by impaired insurer.

Notwithstanding any other provision of this Chapter pertaining to the use of deposits made by insurance companies for the protection of policyholders, the Association shall receive, upon its request, from the Commissioner and may expend, any deposit or deposits made, whether or not made pursuant to statute, by an insurer determined to be impaired under this Article to the extent those deposits are needed by the Association to pay contractual obligations of that impaired insurer owed under covered policies as required by this Article, and to the extent those deposits are needed to pay all expenses of the Association relating to the impaired insurer: Provided that the Commissioner may retain and use an amount of the deposit up to ten thousand dollars ($10,000) to defray administrative costs to be incurred by the Commissioner in carrying out his powers and duties with respect to the insolvent insurer, notwithstanding G.S. 58-5-70. The Association shall account to the Commissioner and the impaired insurer for all deposits received from the Commissioner under this section. After the deposits of the impaired insurer received by the Association under this section have been expended by the Association for the purposes set out in this section, the member insurers shall be assessed as provided by this Article to pay any remaining liabilities of the Association arising under this Article. (1979, c. 418; 1985, c. 666, s. 42; 1989, c. 452, s. 6; 1993 (Reg. Sess., 1994), c. 678, s. 28.)

Article 63.

Unfair Trade Practices.

§ 58-63-1. Declaration of purpose.

The purpose of this Article is to regulate trade practices in the business of insurance in accordance with the intent of Congress as expressed in the Act of Congress of March 9, 1945 (Public Law 15, 79th Congress), by defining, or providing for the determination of, all such practices in this State which constitute unfair methods of competition or unfair or deceptive acts or practices and by prohibiting the trade practices so defined or determined. (1949, c. 1112.)

§ 58-63-5. Definitions.

When used in this Article:

(1)	Repealed by Session Laws 1991, c. 720, s. 6.

(2)	"Person" means any individual, corporation, association, partnership, reciprocal exchange, interinsurer, Lloyds insurer, fraternal benefit society, and any other legal entity engaged in the business of insurance under this Chapter; and includes agents, brokers, limited representatives, and adjusters. (1949, c. 1112; 1987, c. 629, s. 10; 1991, c. 720, s. 6; 1999-244, s. 13.)

§ 58-63-10. Unfair methods of competition or unfair and deceptive acts or practices prohibited.

No person shall engage in this State in any trade practice which is defined in this Article as or determined pursuant to this Article to be an unfair method of competition or an unfair or deceptive act or practice in the business of insurance. (1949, c. 1112.)

§ 58-63-15. Unfair methods of competition and unfair or deceptive acts or practices defined.

The following are hereby defined as unfair methods of competition and unfair and deceptive acts or practices in the business of insurance:

(1)	Misrepresentations and False Advertising of Policy Contracts. - Making, issuing, circulating, or causing to be made, issued or circulated, any estimate, illustration, circular or statement misrepresenting the terms of any policy issued or to be issued or the benefits or advantages promised thereby or the dividends or share of the surplus to be received thereon, or making any false or misleading statement as to the dividends or share or surplus previously paid on similar policies, or making any misleading representation or any misrepresentation as to the financial condition of any insurer, or as to the legal reserve system upon which any life insurer operates, or using any name or title of any policy or class of policies misrepresenting the true nature thereof, or making any misrepresentation to any policyholder insured in any company for the purpose of inducing or tending to induce such policyholder to lapse, forfeit, or surrender his insurance.

(2)   False Information and Advertising Generally. - Making, publishing, disseminating, circulating, or placing before the public, or causing, directly or indirectly, to be made, published, disseminated, circulated, or placed before the public, in a newspaper, magazine or other publication, or in the form of a notice, circular, pamphlet, letter or poster, or over any radio station, or in any other way, an advertisement, announcement or statement containing any assertion, representation or statement with respect to the business of insurance or with respect to any person in the conduct of his insurance business, which is untrue, deceptive or misleading.

(3)   Defamation. - Making, publishing, disseminating, or circulating, directly or indirectly, or aiding, abetting or encouraging the making, publishing, disseminating or circulating of any oral or written statement or any pamphlet, circular, article or literature which is false, or maliciously critical of or derogatory to the financial condition of an insurer, and which is calculated to injure any person engaged in the business of insurance.

(4)   Boycott, Coercion and Intimidation. - Entering into any agreement to commit, or by any concerted action committing, any act of boycott, coercion or intimidation resulting in or tending to result in unreasonable restraint of, or monopoly in, the business of insurance.

(5)   False Financial Statements. - Filing with any supervisory or other public official, or making, publishing, disseminating, circulating or delivering to any person, or placing before the public, or causing directly or indirectly, to be made, published, disseminated, circulated, delivered to any person, or placed before the public, any false statement of financial condition of an insurer with intent to deceive.

Making any false entry in any book, report or statement of any insurer with intent to deceive any agent or examiner lawfully appointed to examine into its condition or into any of its affairs, or any public official to whom such insurer is required by law to report, or who has authority by law to examine into its condition or into any of its affairs, or, with like intent, willfully omitting to make a true entry of any material fact pertaining to the business of such insurer in any book, report or statement of such insurer.

(6) Stock Operations and Insurance Company Advisory Board Contracts. - Issuing or delivering or permitting agents, officers, or employees to issue or deliver, agency company stock or other capital stock, or benefit certificates or shares in any common-law corporation, or securities or any special or any insurance company advisory board contracts or other contracts of any kind promising returns and profit as an inducement to insurance.

(7) Unfair Discrimination.

a Making or permitting any unfair discrimination between individuals of the same class and equal expectation of life in the rates charged for any contract of life insurance or of life annuity or in the dividends or other benefits payable thereon, or in any other of the terms and conditions of such contract.

b. Making or permitting any unfair discrimination between individuals of the same class and of essentially the same hazard in the amount of premium, policy fees, or rates charged for any policy or contract of accident or health insurance or in the benefits payable thereunder, or in any of the terms or conditions of such contract, or in any other manner whatever.

c. Making or permitting any unfair discrimination between or among individuals or risks of the same class and of essentially the same hazard by refusing to issue, refusing to renew, cancelling, or limiting the amount of insurance coverage on a property or casualty risk because of the geographic location of the risk, unless:

1. The refusal or limitation is for the purpose of preserving the solvency of the insurer and is not a mere pretext for unfair discrimination, or

2. The refusal, cancellation, or limitation is required by law.

d. Making or permitting any unfair discrimination between or among individuals or risks of the same class and of essentially the same hazard by refusing to issue, refusing to renew, cancelling, or limiting the amount of insurance coverage on a residential property risk, or the personal property contained therein, because of the age of the residential property, unless:

1. The refusal or limitation is for the purpose of preserving the solvency of the insurer and is not a mere pretext for unfair discrimination, or

2. The refusal, cancellation, or limitation is required by law.

(8) Rebates.

a. Except as otherwise expressly provided by law, knowingly permitting or offering to make or making any contract of life insurance, life annuity or accident and health insurance, or agreement as to such contract other than as plainly expressed in the contract issued thereon, or paying cr allowing, or giving or offering to pay, allow, or give, directly or indirectly, as inducement to such insurance, or annuity, any rebate of premiums payable on the contract, or any special favor or advantage in the dividends or other benefits thereon, or any valuable consideration or inducement whatever not specified in the contract; or giving, or selling, or purchasing or offering to give, sell, or purchase as inducement to such insurance or annuity or in connection therewith, any stocks, bonds, or other securities of any insurance company or other corporation, association, or partnership, or any dividends or profits accrued thereon, or anything of value whatsoever not specified in the contract.

b. Nothing in subdivision (7) or paragraph a of subdivision (8) of this section shall be construed as including within the definition of discrimination or rebates any of the following practices:

1. In the case of any contract of life insurance or life annuity, paying bonuses to policyholders or otherwise abating their premiums in whole or in part out of surplus accumulated from nonparticipating insurance, provided, that any such bonuses or abatement of premiums shall be fa r and equitable to policyholders and for the best interests of the company and its policyholders;

2. In the case of life insurance policies issued cn the industrial debit plan, making allowance to policyholders who have continuously for a specified period made premium payments directly to an office of the insurer in an amount which fairly represents the saving in collection expense;

3. Readjustment of the rate of premium for a group insurance policy based on the loss or expense experienced thereunder, at the end of the first or any subsequent policy year of insurance thereunder, which may be made retroactive only for such policy year.

c. No insurer or employee thereof, and no broker or agent shall pay, allow, or give, or offer to pay, allow, or give, directly or indirectly, as an inducement to insurance, or after insurance has been effected, any rebate, discount, abatement, credit or reduction of the premium named in a policy of insurance, or any special favor or advantage in the dividends or other benefits to accrue thereon, or any valuable consideration or inducement whatever, not specified in the policy of insurance. Nothing herein contained shall be construed as prohibiting the payment of commissions or other compensation to regularly appointed and licensed agents and to brokers duly licensed by this State; nor as prohibiting any participating insurer from distributing to its policyholders dividends, savings or the unused or unabsorbed portion of premiums and premium deposits.

(9)   Advertising of Health, Accident or Hospitalization Insurance. - In all advertising of policies, certificates or service plans of health, accident or hospitalization insurance, except those providing group coverage, where details of benefits provided by a particular policy, certificate or plan are set forth in any advertising material, such advertising material shall contain reference to the major exceptions or major clauses limiting or voiding liability contained in the policy, certificate or plan so advertised. The references to such exceptions or clauses shall be printed in a type no smaller than that used to set forth the benefits of the policy, certificate or plan. In all advertising of such policies, certificates or plans which contain a cancellation provision or a provision that the policies, certificates or plans may be renewed at the option of the company or medical service corporation only, such advertising material shall contain clear and definite reference to the fact that the policies, certificates or plans are cancellable or that the same may be renewed at the option of the company only.

In advertising, sale, or solicitation for sale of any insurance policy represented or advertised to afford coverages and benefits supplemental to or in addition to Medicare coverage, all such advertising materials, except for advertisements which have as their objective the creation of a desire to inquire further about an insurance product and do nothing more than generally describe the product and invite inquiries for costs and further details of the coverage, including limitations, exclusions, reductions or limitations and terms under which the policy may be continued in force, in whatever medium, and all solicitation and presentations for the sale of such policies, shall contain specific references to major exclusions or major exceptions that may result in voiding liability or in a reduction of benefits below those primarily advertised. When such policies contain a coordination of benefits clause whereby benefits are limited by or prorated with other outstanding coverages, such provision shall be called to the attention of the prospective purchaser by conspicuously printed type no smaller than 10 point type. When such policies are advertised to provide coverage above Medicare payments, but contain provisions limiting benefits to those approved for payment by Medicare under Part B, such limitation in benefits shall be called to the attention of the prospective purchaser regardless of the advertising medium; and when policies containing such provisions are delivered, there shall be incorporated therein the language or affixed thereto a sticker in conspicuously printed type no smaller than 10 point type stating: CAUTION: POLICY BENEFITS ARE LIMITED TO THOSE APPROVED BY MEDICARE FOR PAYMENT. Any person engaged in the solicitation or sale of such supplemental Medicare policies in this State shall, as a part of the application, determine and list on the application all policies of Medicare supplement or other health insurance currently in force that cover the prospective insured. In compiling such information, the person is entitled to rely upon information furnished by the prospective purchaser or insured.

(10) Soliciting, etc., Unauthorized Insurance Contracts in Other States. - Soliciting, advertising or entering into insurance contracts in foreign states and any other jurisdiction in which such domestic insurer is not licensed in accordance with the laws of such state or jurisdiction, except as provided in G.S. 58-14-5.

(11) Unfair Claim Settlement Practices. - Committing or performing with such frequency as to indicate a general business practice of any of the following: Provided, however, that no violation of this subsection shall of itself create any cause of action in favor of any person other than the Commissioner:

a. Misrepresenting pertinent facts or insurance policy provisions relating to coverages at issue;

b. Failing to acknowledge and act reasonably promptly upon communications with respect to claims arising under insurance policies;

c. Failing to adopt and implement reasonable standards for the prompt investigation of claims arising under insurance policies;

d. Refusing to pay claims without conducting a reasonable investigation based upon all available information;

e. Failing to affirm or deny coverage of claims within a reasonable time after proof-of-loss statements have been completed;

f. Not attempting in good faith to effectuate prompt, fair and equitable settlements of claims in which liability has become reasonably clear;

g. Compelling [the] insured to institute litigation to recover amounts due under an insurance policy by offering substantially less than the amounts ultimately recovered in actions brought by such insured;

h. Attempting to settle a claim for less than the amount to which a reasonable man would have believed he was entitled;

i. Attempting to settle claims on the basis of an application which was altered without notice to, or knowledge or consent of, the insured;

j. Making claims payments to insureds or beneficiaries not accompanied by [a] statement setting forth the coverage under which the payments are being made;

k. Making known to insureds or claimants a policy of appealing from arbitration awards in favor of insureds or claimants for the purpose of compelling them to accept settlements or compromises less than the amount awarded in arbitration;

l. Delaying the investigation or payment of claims by requiring an insured claimant, or the physician, of [or] either, to submit a preliminary claim report and then requiring the subsequent submission of formal proof-of-loss forms, both of which submissions contain substantially the same information;

m. Failing to promptly settle claims where liability has become reasonably clear, under one portion of the insurance policy coverage in order to influence settlements under other portions of the insurance policy coverage; and

n. Failing to promptly provide a reasonable explanation of the basis in the insurance policy in relation to the facts or applicable law for denial of a claim or for the offer of a compromise settlement.

(12) Misuse of Borrowers' Confidential Information. - Soliciting, accepting, or using any information from a lender concerning policies of insurance held by such lender as a mortgagee of real property, except from a lender who is an insurer where the loan has been made by or sold or held for sale to such insurer. Provided, however, this subdivision shall not apply to the use of such information by a lender for the solicitation of life or accident and health insurance.

(13) Overinsurance in Credit or Loan Transactions. - In connection with a loan or extension of credit secured by real or personal property or both, requiring the applicant to procure property and casualty insurance against any one risk which results in coverage which exceeds the replacement value of the secured property at the time of the loan or extension of credit. In connection with a secured or unsecured loan or extension of credit, requiring the applicant to procure life or health insurance against any one risk which exceeds the amount of the loan. In connection with a loan secured by both real and personal property, requiring credit property insurance, as defined in G.S. 58-57-90, on the personal property. For the purposes of this subsection "amount of loan" shall be deemed to be the amount of principal and accrued interest to be paid by the debtor including other allowable charges. (1949, c. 1112; 1955, c. 850, s. 3; 1967, c. 935, s. 2; 1975, c. 668; 1983, c. 831; 1985 (Reg. Sess., 1986), c. 1027, ss. 18, 20; 1987, c. 787, ss. 1, 3.)

§ 58-63-20. Power of Commissioner.

The Commissioner shall have power to examine and investigate into the affairs of every person engaged in the business of insurance in this State in order to determine whether such person has been or is engaged in any unfair method of competition or in any unfair or deceptive act or practice prohibited by G.S. 58-63-10. (1949, c. 1112; 1991, c. 720, s. 62.)

§ 58-63-25. Hearings, witnesses, appearances, production of books and service of process.

(a) When the Commissioner has reason to believe that any person has been engaged or is engaging in this State in any unfair method of competition or any unfair or deceptive act or practice defined in G.S. 58-63-15 or under G.S. 58-63-65, and that a proceeding by the Commissioner on the matter would be in the interest of the public, the Commissioner shall issue and serve upon the person a statement of the charges in that respect and a notice of the hearing on the matter to be held at the time and place fixed in the notice, which shall not be less than 10 days after the date of the service of the notice.

(b) At the time and place fixed for such hearing, such person shall have an opportunity to be heard and to show cause why an order should not be made by the Commissioner requiring such person to cease and desist from the acts, methods or practices so complained of. Upon good cause shown, the Commissioner shall permit any person to intervene, appear and be heard at such hearing by counsel or in person.

(c) Nothing contained in this Article shall require the observance at any such hearing of formal rules of pleading or evidence.

(d) The Commissioner, upon such hearing, may administer oaths, examine and cross-examine witnesses, receive oral and documentary evidence, and shall have the power to subpoena witnesses, compel their attendance, and require the production of books, papers, records, correspondence, or other documents which he deems relevant to the inquiry. The Commissioner, upon such hearing, may, and upon the request of any party shall, cause to be made a stenographic record of all the evidence and all the proceedings had at such hearing. If no stenographic record is made and if a judicial review is sought, the Commissioner shall prepare a statement of the evidence and proceeding for use on review. In case of a refusal of any person to comply with any subpoena issued hereunder or to testify with respect to any matter concerning which he may be lawfully interrogated, the Superior Court of Wake County, on application of the Commissioner, may issue an order requiring such person to comply with such subpoena and to testify; and any failure to obey any such order of the court may be punished by the court as a contempt thereof.

(e) Statements of charges, notices, orders, and other processes of the Commissioner under this Article may be served by anyone duly authorized by the Commissioner, either in the manner provided by law for service of process in civil actions, or by registering and mailing a copy thereof to the person affected by such statement, notice, order, or other process at his or its residence or principal office or place of business. The verified return by the person so serving such statement, notice, order, or other process, setting forth the manner of such service, shall be proof of the same, and the return postcard receipt for such statement, notice, order, or other process, registered and mailed as aforesaid, shall be proof of the service of the same. (1949, c. 1112; 1995, c. 193, s. 49.)

§ 58-63-30: Repealed by Session Laws 1991, c. 644, s. 29.

§ 58-63-32. Cease and desist order.

(a) If, after a hearing under G.S. 58-63-25, the Commissioner determines that the method of competition or the act or practice in question is defined in G.S. 58-63-15 and that the person complained of has engaged in the method of competition, act, or practice in violation of this Article, the Commissioner shall reduce his finding to writing and shall issue and cause to be served upon the person charged with the violation an order requiring the person to cease and desist from engaging in the method, act, or practice.

(b) Until the expiration of the time allowed under G.S. 58-63-35(a) for filing a petition for review, if no such petition has been duly filed within that time, then until the transcript of the record in the proceeding has been filed in court, the Commissioner may at any time, upon such notice and in such manner as the Commissioner considers proper, modify or set aside in whole or in part any order issued by the Commissioner under this section.

(c) After the expiration of the time allowed for filing a petition for review, if no such petition has been duly filed within that time, the Commissioner may at any time, after notice and opportunity for hearing, reopen and alter, modify, or set aside, in whole or in part, any order issued by the Commissioner under this section, whenever in the Commissioner's opinion conditions of fact or of law have so changed as to require the action or if the public interest requires. (1991, c. 644, s. 28.)

§ 58-63-35. Judicial review of cease and desist orders.

(a) Any person required by an order of the Commissioner under G.S. 58-63-32 to cease and desist from engaging in any unfair method of competition or any unfair or deceptive act or practice defined in G.S. 58-63-15 may obtain a review of the order by filing in the Superior Court of Wake County, within 30 days from the date of the service of such order, a written petition praying that the order of the Commissioner be set aside. A copy of the petition shall be immediately served upon the Commissioner, and at that time the Commissioner immediately shall certify and file in the court a transcript of the entire record in the proceeding, including all the evidence taken and the report and order of the Commissioner. Upon the filing of the petition and transcript, the court has jurisdiction of the proceeding and of the question determined therein, shall determine whether the filing of the petition shall operate as a stay of the Commissioner's order, and has power to make and enter upon the pleadings, evidence, and proceedings set forth in the transcript a decree modifying, affirming or reversing the order of the Commissioner, in whole or in part. The findings of the Commissioner as to the facts, if supported by substantial evidence, are conclusive.

(b) To the extent that the order of the Commissioner is affirmed, the court shall thereupon issue its own order commanding obedience to the terms of such order of the Commissioner. If either party shall apply to the court for leave to adduce additional evidence, and shall show to the satisfaction of the court that such additional evidence is material and that there were reasonable grounds for the failure to adduce such evidence in the proceeding before the Commissioner, the court may order such additional evidence to be taken before the Commissioner and to be adduced upon the hearing in such manner and upon such terms and conditions as to the court may seem proper. The Commissioner may modify his findings of fact, or make new findings by reason of the additional evidence so taken, and he shall file such modified or new findings which, if supported by substantial evidence shall be conclusive, and his recommendations, if any, for the modification or setting aside of his original order, with the return of such additional evidence.

(c) A cease and desist order issued by the Commissioner under G.S. 58-63-30 shall become final:

(1) Upon the expiration of the time allowed for filing a petition for review if no such petition has been duly filed within such time; except that the Commissioner may thereafter modify or set aside his order to the extent provided in G.S. 58-63-30(b); or

(2) Upon the final decision of the court if the court directs that the order of the Commissioner be affirmed or the petition for review dismissed.

(d) No order of the Commissioner under this Article or order of a court to enforce the same shall in any way relieve or absolve any person affected by such order from any liability under any other laws of this State. (1949, c. 1112; 1995, c. 193, s. 50.)

§ 58-63-40. Procedure as to unfair methods of competition and unfair or deceptive acts or practices which are not defined.

(a) Whenever the Commissioner shall have reason to believe that any person engaged in the business of insurance is engaging in this State in any method of competition or in any act or practice in the conduct of such business which is not defined in G.S. 58-63-15, that such method of competition is unfair or that such act or practice is unfair or deceptive and that a proceeding by him in respect thereto would be to the interest of the public, he may issue and serve upon such person a statement of the charges in that respect and a notice of a hearing thereon to be held at a time and place fixed in the notice, which shall not be less than 10 days after the date of the service thereof. Each such hearing shall be conducted in the same manner as the hearings provided for in G.S. 58-63-25. The Commissioner shall, after such hearing, make a report in writing in which he shall state his findings as to the facts, and he shall serve a copy thereof upon such person.

(b) If such report charges a violation of this Article and if such method of competition, act or practice has not been discontinued, the Commissioner may, through the Attorney General of this State, at any time after 10 days after the service of such report cause a petition to be filed in the superior court of this State of the county wherein the person resides or has his principal place of business, to enjoin and restrain such person from engaging in such method, act or practice. The court shall have jurisdiction of the proceeding and shall have power to make and enter appropriate orders in connection therewith and to issue such writs as are ancillary to its jurisdiction or are necessary in its judgment to prevent injury to the public pendente lite. To the extent that the order of the Commissioner is affirmed, the court shall thereupon issue its order commanding obedience to the terms of such order of the Commissioner.

(c) A transcript of the proceedings before the Commissioner including all evidence taken and the report and findings shall be filed with such petition. If either party shall apply to the court for leave to adduce additional evidence and shall show, to the satisfaction of the court, that such additional evidence is material and there were reasonable grounds for the failure to adduce such evidence in the proceeding before the Commissioner, the court may order such additional evidence to be taken before the Commissioner and to be adduced upon the hearing in such manner and upon such terms and conditions as to the court may seem proper. The Commissioner may modify his findings of fact or make new findings by reason of the additional evidence so taken, and he shall file such modified or new findings with the return of such additional evidence.

(d) If the court finds that the method of competition complained of is unfair or that the act or practice complained of is unfair or deceptive, that the proceeding by the Commissioner with respect thereto is to the interest of the public and that the findings of the Commissioner are supported by the weight of the evidence, it shall issue its order enjoining and restraining the continuance of such method of competition, act or practice. (1949, c. 1112.)

§ 58-63-45. Judicial review by intervenor.

If the report of the Commissioner does not charge a violation of this Article, then any intervenor in the proceedings may within 10 days after the service of such report, cause a notice of appeal to be filed in the Superior Court of Wake County for a review of such report. Upon such review, the court shall have authority to issue appropriate orders and decrees in connection therewith, including, if the court finds that it is to the interest of the public, orders enjoining and restraining the continuance of any method of competition, act or practice which it finds, notwithstanding such report of the Commissioner, constitutes a violation of this Article. (1949, c. 1112.)

§ 58-63-50. Penalty.

Any person who willfully violates a cease and desist order of the Commissioner under G.S. 58-63-32, after it has become final, and while the order is in effect, shall forfeit and pay to the Commissioner the sum of not less than one thousand dollars ($1,000) nor more than five thousand dollars ($5,000) for each violation, which if not paid shall be recovered in a civil action instituted in the name of the Commissioner in the Superior Court of Wake County. The clear proceeds of forfeitures provided for in this section shall be remitted to the Civil Penalty and Forfeiture Fund in accordance with G.S. 115C-457.2. (1949, c. 1112; 1985, c. 666 s. 21; 1991, c. 720, ss. 33, 63; 1995, c. 193, s. 51; 1998-215, s. 88.)

§ 58-63-55. Provisions of Article additional to existing law.

The powers vested in the Commissioner by this Article shall be additional to any other powers to enforce any penalties, fines or forfeitures authorized by law with respect to the methods, acts and practices hereby declared to be unfair or deceptive. (1949, c. 1112.)

§ 58-63-60. Immunity from prosecution.

If any person shall ask to be excused from attending and testifying or from producing any books, papers, records, correspondence or other documents at any hearing on the ground that the testimony or evidence required of him may tend to incriminate him or subject him to a penalty or forfeiture, and shall notwithstanding be directed to give such testimony or produce such evidence, he must nonetheless comply with such direction, but he shall not thereafter be prosecuted or subjected to any penalty or forfeiture for or on account of any transaction, matter or thing concerning which he may testify or produce evidence pursuant thereto, and no testimony so given or evidence produced shall be received against him upon any criminal action, investigation or proceeding, provided, however, that no such individual so testifying shall be exempt from prosecution or punishment for any perjury committed by him while so testifying and the testimony or evidence so given or produced shall be admissible against him upon any criminal action, investigation or proceeding concerning such perjury, nor shall he be exempt from the refusal, revocation or suspension of any license, permission or authority conferred, or to be conferred, pursuant to the insurance law of this State. Any such individual may execute, acknowledge and file in the office of the Commissioner a statement expressly waiving such immunity or privilege in respect to any transaction, matter or thing specified in such statement and thereupon the testimony of such person or such evidence in relation to such transaction, matter or thing may be received or produced before any judge or justice, court, tribunal, grand jury or otherwise, and if so received or produced such individual shall not be entitled to any immunity or privilege on account of any testimony he may so give or evidence so produced. (1949, c. 1112.)

§ 58-63-65. Rule-making authority.

The Commissioner may adopt rules to carry out the provisions of this Article, including rules that define unfair methods of competition or unfair or deceptive acts or practices in the business of insurance, in addition to those defined in G.S. 58-63-15 and determined under G.S. 58-63-40. (1993, c. 409, s. 15.)

§§ 58-63-66 through 58-63-69. Reserved for future codification purposes.

§ 58-63-70. Health care service discount practices by insurers and service corporations.

(a) It is an unfair trade practice for any insurer or service corporation subject to this Chapter to make an intentional misrepresentation to a health care provider to the effect that the insurer or service corporation is entitled to a certain preferred provider or other discount off the fees charged for medical services, procedures, or supplies provided by the health care provider, when the insurer or service corporation is not entitled to any discount or is entitled to a lesser discount from the provider on those fees.

(b) It is an unfair trade practice for any person with knowledge that an insurer or service corporation intends to make the type of misrepresentation prohibited in subsection (a) of this section to provide substantial assistance to that insurer or service corporation in accomplishing that misrepresentation. (1997-519, s. 3.2.)

§ 58-63-75. Senior-specific certifications and professional designations; rules.

The Commissioner may adopt rules to set forth standards to protect consumers from misleading and fraudulent marketing practices with respect to the use of senior-specific certifications and professional designations in the solicitation, sale, or purchase of, or advice made in connection with, a life insurance or annuity product. These rules shall be substantially similar to the NAIC Model Regulation on the Use of Senior-Specific Certifications and Professional Designations in the Sale of Life Insurance and Annuities, as amended. The Commissioner may adopt, amend, or repeal provisions of these rules under G.S. 150B-21.1 in order to keep these rules current with the NAIC model rule. (2009-382, s. 15.)

Article 64.

Continuing Care Retirement Communities.

§ 58-64-1. Definitions.

As used in this Article, unless otherwise specified:

(1) Continuing care. - The furnishing to an individual other than an individual related by blood, marriage, or adoption to the person furnishing the care, of lodging together with nursing services, medical services, or other health related services, under a contract approved by the Department in accordance with this Article effective for the life of the individual or for a period longer than one year. "Continuing care" may also include home care services provided or arranged by a provider of lodging at a facility to an individual who has entered into a continuing care contract with the provider but is not yet receiving lodging.

(2) Entrance fee. - A payment that assures a resident a place in a facility for a term of years or for life.

(3) Facility. - The retirement community or communities in which a provider undertakes to provide continuing care to an individual.

(4) Health-related services. - At a minimum, nursing home admission or assistance in the activities of daily living, exclusive of the provision of meals or cleaning services.

(4a) Home care services. - Defined in G.S. 131E-136.

(5) Living unit. - A room, apartment, cottage, or other area within a facility set aside for the exclusive use or control of one or more identified residents.

(5a) Lodging. - A living unit as set forth in a contract approved by the Department in accordance with this Article.

(6) Provider. - The promoter, developer, or owner of a facility, whether a natural person, partnership, or other unincorporated association, however

organized, trust, or corporation, of an institution, building, residence, or other place, whether operated for profit or not, or any other person, that solicits or undertakes to provide continuing care under a continuing care facility contract, or that represents himself, herself, or itself as providing continuing care or "life care."

(7) Resident. - A purchaser of, a nominee of, or a subscriber to, a continuing care contract.

(8) Hazardous financial condition. - A provider is insolvent or in eminent danger of becoming insolvent. (1989, c. 758, s. 1; 1989 (Reg. Sess., 1990), c. 1024, s. 45; 1991, c. 720, ss. 2, 39; 1999-132, ss. 2.2, 2.3; 2010-128, s. 2.)

§ 58-64-5. License.

(a) No provider shall engage in the business of offering or providing continuing care in this State without a license to do so obtained from the Commissioner as provided in this Article. It is a Class 1 misdemeanor for any person, other than a provider licensed under this Article, to advertise or market to the general public any product similar to continuing care through the use of such terms as "life care", "continuing care", or "guaranteed care for life", or similar terms, words, or phrases. The licensing process may involve a series of steps pursuant to rules adopted by the Commissioner under this Article.

(b) The application for a license shall be filed with the Department by the provider on forms prescribed by the Department and within a period of time prescribed by the Department; and shall include all information required by the Department pursuant to rules adopted by it under this Article including, but not limited to, the disclosure statement meeting the requirements of this Article and other financial and facility development information required by the Department. The application for a license must be accompanied by an application fee of one thousand dollars ($1,000).

(c) Upon receipt of the complete application for a license in proper form, the Department shall, within 10 business days, issue a notice of filing to the applicant. Within 90 days of the notice of filing, the Department shall enter an order issuing the license or rejecting the application.

(d) If the Commissioner determines that any of the requirements of this Article have not been met, the Commissioner shall notify the applicant that the application must be corrected within 30 days in such particulars as designated by the Commissioner. If the requirements are not met within the time allowed, the Commissioner may enter an order rejecting the application, which order shall include the findings of fact upon which the order is based and which shall not become effective until 20 days after the end of the 30-day period. During the 20-day period, the applicant may petition for reconsideration and is entitled to a hearing.

(e) Repealed by Session Laws 2003-193, s. 1, effective June 12, 2003.

(f) The Commissioner may, on an annual basis or on a more frequent basis if he deems it to be necessary, in addition to the annual disclosure statement revision required by G.S. 58-64-30, require every licensed provider to file with the Department any of the information provided by G.S. 58-64-5(b) for new licensure that the Commissioner, pursuant to rules adopted by him under this Article, determines is needed for review of licensed providers.

(g) The Commissioner may require a provider to: (i) provide the report of an actuary that estimates the capacity of the provider to meet its contractual obligation to the resident, or (ii) give consideration to expected rates of mortality and morbidity, expected refunds, and expected capital expenditures in accordance with standards promulgated by the American Academy of Actuaries, within the five-year forecast statements, as required by G.S. 58-64-20(a)(12). (1989, c. 758, s. 1; 1991, c. 196, ss. 1, 2; 2001-223, s. 22.1; 2003-193, ss. 1, 2; 2009-451, s. 21.9(a); 2010-128, s. 1.)

§ 58-64-7. Continuing care services without lodging.

(a) A provider of continuing care who has obtained a license pursuant to this Article and desires to provide or arrange for continuing care services, including home care services, to an individual who has entered into a continuing care contract with the provider but is not yet receiving lodging must submit the following to the Commissioner:

(1) An application to offer continuing care services without providing lodging.

(2) An amended disclosure statement containing a description of the proposed continuing care services that will be provided without lodging, including the target market, the types of services to be provided, and the fees to be charged.

(3) A copy of the written service agreement, which must contain those provisions as prescribed in G.S. 58-64-25(b).

(4) A summary of an actuarial report that presents the impact of providing continuing care services without lodging on the overall operation of the continuing care retirement community.

(5) A financial feasibility study prepared by a certified public accountant that shows the financial impact of providing continuing care services without lodging on the applicant and the continuing care retirement facility or facilities. The financial feasibility study shall include a statement of activities reporting the revenue and expense details for providing continuing care services without lodging, as well as any impact the provision of these services will have on operating reserves.

(6) Evidence of the license required under Part 3 of Article 6 of Chapter 131E of the General Statutes to provide home care services, or a contract with a licensed home care agency for the provision of home care services to the individuals under the continuing care services without lodging program.

(b) A provider issued a start-up certificate for the provision of continuing care services without lodging must enter into binding written service agreements with subscribers to provide continuing care services without lodging.

(c) When providing the financial statements and five-year forecasts required by G.S. 58-64-20, a provider offering continuing care services without lodging must account for the related revenue and expenses generated from the provision of these services separate from the facility's on-site operation. (2010-128, s. 4.)

§ 58-64-10. Revocation of license.

(a) The license of a provider shall remain in effect until revoked after notice and hearing, upon written findings of fact by the Commissioner, that the provider has:

(1) Willfully violated any provision of this Article or of any rule or order of the Commissioner;

(2) Failed to file an annual disclosure statement or standard form of contract as required by this Article;

(3) Failed to deliver to prospective residents the disclosure statements required by this Article;

(4) Delivered to prospective residents a disclosure statement that makes an untrue statement or omits a material fact and the provider, at the time of the delivery of the disclosure statement, had actual knowledge of the misstatement or omission;

(5) Failed to comply with the terms of a cease and desist order; or

(6) Has been determined by the Commissioner to be in a hazardous financial condition.

(b) Findings of fact in support of revocation shall be accompanied by an explicit statement of the underlying facts supporting the findings.

(c) If the Commissioner has good cause to believe that the provider is guilty of a violation for which revocation could be ordered, the Commissioner may first issue a cease and desist order. If the cease and desist order is not or cannot be effective in remedying the violation, the Commissioner may, after notice and hearing, order that the license be revoked and surrendered. Such a cease and desist order may be appealed to the Superior Court of Wake County in the manner provided by G.S. 58-63-35. The provider shall accept no new applicant funds while the revocation order is under appeal. (1989, c. 758, s. 1.)

§ 58-64-15. Sale or transfer of ownership.

No license is transferable, and no license issued pursuant to this Article has value for sale or exchange as property. No provider or other owning entity shall sell or transfer ownership of the facility, or enter into a contract with a third-party provider for management of the facility, unless the Commissioner approves such transfer or contract. (1989, c. 758, s. 1.)

§ 58-64-20. Disclosure statement.

(a) At the time of, or prior to, the execution of a contract to provide continuing care, or at the time of, or prior to, the transfer of any money or other property to a provider by or on behalf of a prospective resident, whichever occurs first, the provider shall deliver a current disclosure statement to the person with whom the contract is to be entered into, the text of which shall contain at least:

(1) The name and business address of the provider and a statement of whether the provider is a partnership, corporation, or other type of legal entity.

(2) The names and business addresses of the officers, directors, trustees, managing or general partners, any person having a ten percent (10%) or greater equity or beneficial interest in the provider, and any person who will be managing the facility on a day-to-day basis, and a description of these persons' interests in or occupations with the provider.

(3) The following information on all persons named in response to subdivision (2) of this section:

a. A description of the business experience of this person, if any, in the operation or management of similar facilities;

b. The name and address of any professional service firm, association, trust, partnership, or corporation in which this person has, or which has in this person, a ten percent (10%) or greater interest and which it is presently intended shall currently or in the future provide goods, leases, or services to the facility, or to residents of the facility, of an aggregate value of five hundred dollars ($500.00) or more within any year, including a description of the goods, leases, or services and the probable or anticipated cost thereof to the facility, provider, or residents or a statement that this cost cannot presently be estimated; and

c. A description of any matter in which the person (i) has been convicted of a felony or pleaded nolo contendere to a felony charge, or been held liable or enjoined in a civil action by final judgment, if the felony or civil action involved fraud, embezzlement, fraudulent conversion, or misappropriation of property; or (ii) is subject to a currently effective injunctive or restrictive court order, or within the past five years, had any State or federal license or permit suspended or revoked as a result of an action brought by a governmental agency or department, if the order or action arose out of or related to business activity of health care, including actions affecting a license to operate a foster care facility, nursing home, retirement home, home for aged, or facility subject to this Article or a similar law in another state.

(4) A statement as to whether the provider is, or is not affiliated with, a religious, charitable, or other nonprofit organization, the extent of the affiliation, if any, the extent to which the affiliate organization will be responsible for the financial and contract obligations of the provider, and the provision of the Federal Internal Revenue Code, if any, under which the provider or affiliate is exempt from the payment of income tax.

(5) The location and description of the physical property or properties of the facility, existing or proposed, and to the extent proposed, the estimated completion date or dates, whether construction has begun, and the contingencies subject to which construction may be deferred.

(6) The services provided or proposed to be provided pursuant to contracts for continuing care at the facility, including the extent to which medical care is furnished, and a clear statement of which services are included for specified basic fees for continuing care and which services are made available at or by the facility at extra charge.

(7) A description of all fees required of residents, including the entrance fee and periodic charges, if any. The description shall include:

a. A statement of the fees that will be charged if the resident marries while at the facility, and a statement of the terms concerning the entry of a spouse to the facility and the consequences if the spouse does not meet the requirements for entry;

b. The circumstances under which the resident will be permitted to remain in the facility in the event of possible financial difficulties of the resident;

c. The terms and conditions under which a contract for continuing care at the facility may be canceled by the provider or by the resident, and the conditions, if any, under which all or any portion of the entrance fee or any other fee will be refunded in the event of cancellation of the contract by the provider or by the resident or in the event of the death of the resident prior to or following occupancy of a living unit;

d. The conditions under which a living unit occupied by a resident may be made available by the provider to a different or new resident other than on the death of the prior resident; and

e. The manner by which the provider may adjust periodic charges or other recurring fees and the limitations on these adjustments, if any; and, if the facility is already in operation, or if the provider or manager operates one or more similar continuing care locations within this State, tables shall be included showing the frequency and average dollar amount of each increase in periodic charges, or other recurring fees at each facility or location for the previous five years, or such shorter period as the facility or location may have been operated by the provider or manager.

(8) The health and financial condition required for an individual to be accepted as a resident and to continue as a resident once accepted, including the effect of any change in the health or financial condition of a person between the date of entering into a contract for continuing care and the date of initial occupancy of a living unit by that person.

(9) The provisions that have been made or will be made, including, but not limited to, the requirements of G.S. 58-64-33 and G.S. 58-64-35, to provide reserve funding or security to enable the provider to perform its obligations fully under contracts to provide continuing care at the facility, including the establishment of escrow accounts, trusts, or reserve funds, together with the manner in which these funds will be invested, and the names and experience of any individuals in the direct employment of the provider who will make the investment decisions.

(10) Financial statements of the provider certified to by an independent public accountant as of the end of the most recent fiscal year or such shorter period of time as the provider shall have been in existence. If the provider's fiscal year ended more than 120 days prior to the date the disclosure statement is recorded, interim financial statements as of a date not more than 90 days

prior to the date of recording the statement shall also be included, but need not be certified to by an independent certified public accountant.

(11) In the event the provider has had an actuarial report prepared within the prior two years, the summary of a report of an actuary that estimates the capacity of the provider to meet its contractual obligations to the residents.

(12) Forecasted financial statements for the provider of the next five years, including a balance sheet, a statement of operations, a statement of cash flows, and a statement detailing all significant assumptions, compiled by an independent certified public accountant. Reporting routine, categories, and structure may be further defined by regulations or forms adopted by the Commissioner.

(13) The estimated number of residents of the facility to be provided services by the provider pursuant to the contract for continuing care.

(14) Proposed or development stage facilities shall additionally provide:

a. The summary of the report of an actuary estimating the capacity of the provider to meet its contractual obligation to the residents;

b. Narrative disclosure detailing all significant assumptions used in the preparation of the forecasted financial statements, including:

1. Details of any long-term financing for the purchase or construction of the facility including interest rate, repayment terms, loan covenants, and assets pledged;

2. Details of any other funding sources that the provider anticipates using to fund any start-up losses or to provide reserve funds to assure full performance of the obligations of the provider under contracts for the provision of continuing care;

3. The total life occupancy fees to be received from or on behalf of, residents at, or prior to, commencement of operations along with anticipated accounting methods used in the recognition of revenues from and expected refunds of life occupancy fees;

4. A description of any equity capital to be received by the facility;

5. The cost of the acquisition of the facility or, if the facility is to be constructed, the estimated cost of the acquisition of the land and construction cost of the facility;

6. Related costs, such as financing any development costs that the provider expects to incur or become obligated for prior to the commencement of operations;

7. The marketing and resident acquisition costs to be incurred prior to commencement of operations; and

8. A description of the assumptions used for calculating the estimated occupancy rate of the facility and the effect on the income of the facility of government subsidies for health care services.

(15) Any other material information concerning the facility or the provider which, if omitted, would lead a reasonable person not to enter into this contract.

(b) The cover page of the disclosure statement shall state, in a prominent location and in boldface type, the date of the disclosure statement, the last date through which that disclosure statement may be delivered if not earlier revised, and that the delivery of the disclosure statement to a contracting party before the execution of a contract for the provision of continuing care is required by this Article but that the disclosure statement has not been reviewed or approved by any government agency or representative to ensure accuracy or completeness of the information set out.

(c) A copy of the standard form of contract for continuing care used by the provider shall be attached to each disclosure statement.

(d) The Commissioner, by rules adopted by him under this Article, may prescribe a standardized format for the disclosure statement required by this section.

(e) The disclosure statement shall be in plain English and in language understandable by a layperson and combine simplicity and accuracy to fully advise residents of the items required by this section.

(f) The Department may require a provider to alter or amend its disclosure statement in order to provide full and fair disclosure to prospective residents. The Department may also require the revision of a disclosure statement which it finds to be unnecessarily complex, confusing or illegible. (1989, c. 758, s. 1; 1991, c. 196, s. 3; c. 720, s. 89; 1993, c. 452, s. 63; 2001-223, s. 22.2; 2003-193, ss. 3, 4, 5, 6.)

§ 58-64-25. Contract for continuing care; specifications.

(a) Each contract for continuing care shall provide that:

(1) The party contracting with the provider may rescind the contract within 30 days following the later of the execution of the contract or the receipt of a disclosure statement that meets the requirements of this section, and the resident to whom the contract pertains is not required to move into the facility before the expiration of the 30-day period; and

(2) If a resident dies before occupying a living unit in the facility, or if, on account of illness, injury, or incapacity, a resident would be precluded from occupying a living unit in the facility under the terms of the contract for continuing care, the contract is automatically canceled; and

(3) For rescinded or canceled contracts under this section, the resident or the resident's legal representative shall receive a refund of all money or property transferred to the provider, less (i) periodic charges specified in the contract and applicable only to the period a living unit was actually occupied by the resident; (ii) those nonstandard costs specifically incurred by the provider or facility at the request of the resident and described in the contract or any contract amendment signed by the resident; (iii) nonrefundable fees, if set out in the contract; and (iv) a reasonable service charge, if set out in the contract, not to exceed the greater of one thousand dollars ($1,000) or two percent (2%) of the entrance fee.

(b) Each contract shall include provisions that specify the following:

(1) The total consideration to be paid.

(2) Services to be provided.

(3) The procedures the provider shall follow to change the resident's accommodation if necessary for the protection of the health or safety of the resident or the general and economic welfare of the residents.

(4) The policies to be implemented if the resident cannot pay the periodic fees.

(5) The terms governing the refund of any portion of the entrance fee in the event of discharge by the provider or cancellation by the resident.

(6) The policy regarding increasing the periodic fees.

(7) The description of the living quarters.

(8) Any religious or charitable affiliations of the provider and the extent, if any, to which the affiliate organization will be responsible for the financial and contractual obligations of the provider.

(9) Any property rights of the resident.

(10) The policy, if any, regarding fee adjustments if the resident is voluntarily absent from the facility; and

(11) Any requirement, if any, that the resident apply for Medicaid, public assistance, or any public benefit program.

(12) The procedures for determining when the individual will transition to receiving lodging and health-related services in the event that a contract allows for the provision or arrangement of continuing care without lodging. (1989, c. 758, s. 1; 1991, c. 196, s. 4; 2010-128, s. 3.)

§ 58-64-30. Annual disclosure statement revision.

(a) Within 150 days following the end of each fiscal year, the provider shall file with the Commissioner a revised disclosure statement setting forth current information required pursuant to G.S. 58-64-20. The provider shall also make this revised disclosure statement available to all the residents of the facility. This revised disclosure statement shall include a narrative describing any material differences between (i) the forecasted statements of revenues and expenses and cash flows or other forecasted financial data filed pursuant to G.S. 58-64-20 as a part of the disclosure statement recorded most immediately subsequent to the start of the provider's most recently completed fiscal year and (ii) the actual results of operations during that fiscal year, together with the revised forecasted statements of revenues and expenses and cash flows or other forecasted financial data being filed as a part of the revised disclosure statement. A provider may also revise its disclosure statement and have the revised disclosure statement recorded at any other time if, in the opinion of the provider, revision is necessary to prevent an otherwise current disclosure statement from containing a material misstatement of fact or omitting a material fact required to be stated therein. Only the most recently recorded disclosure statement, with respect to a facility, and in any event, only a disclosure statement dated within one year plus 150 days prior to the date of delivery, shall be considered current for purposes of this Article or delivered pursuant to G.S. 58-64-20.

(b) The annual disclosure statement required to be filed with the Commissioner under this section shall be accompanied by an annual filing fee of one thousand dollars ($1,000). (1989, c. 758, s. 1; 2003-193, s. 7; 2009-451, s. 21.9(b).)

§ 58-64-33. Operating reserves.

(a) A provider shall maintain after the opening of a facility: an operating reserve equal to fifty percent (50%) of the total operating costs of the facility forecasted for the 12-month period following the period covered by the most recent disclosure statement filed with the Department. The forecast statements as required by G.S. 58-64-20(a)(12) shall serve as the basis for computing the operating reserve. In addition to total operating expenses, total operating costs will include debt service, consisting of principal and interest payments along with taxes and insurance on any mortgage loan or other long-term financing, but will exclude depreciation, amortized expenses, and extraordinary items as approved by the Commissioner. If the debt service portion is accounted for by way of another reserve account, the debt service portion may be excluded. If a facility maintains an occupancy level in excess of ninety percent (90%), a provider shall only be required to maintain a twenty-five percent (25%) operating reserve upon approval of the Commissioner, unless otherwise instructed by the Commissioner. The operating reserve may be funded by cash, by invested cash, or by investment grade securities, including bonds, stocks, U.S. Treasury obligations, or obligations of U.S. government agencies.

(b) A provider that has begun construction or has permanent financing in place or is in operation on the effective date of this section has up to five years to meet the operating reserve requirements.

(c)   An operating reserve shall only be released upon the submittal of a detailed request from the provider or facility and must be approved by the Commissioner. Such requests must be submitted in writing for the Commissioner to review at least 10 business days prior to the date of withdrawal. (1991, c. 196, s. 5; c. 720, s. 89; 1993, c. 452, s. 64; 1993 (Reg. Sess., 1994), c. 678, s. 29; 1995, c. 193, s. 52; 2003-193, s. 8; 2004-203, s. 36.)

§ 58-64-35. Escrow, collection of deposits.

(a)   Where escrow accounts are required by this Article, a provider shall establish an escrow account with (i) a bank, (ii) a trust company, or (iii) another independent person or entity agreed upon by the provider and the resident, unless such account arrangement is prohibited by the Commissioner. The terms of this escrow account shall provide that the total amount of any entrance fee, or any other fee or deposit that may be applied toward the entrance fee, received by the provider be placed in this escrow account. These funds may be released only as follows:

(1)   The first twenty-five percent (25%) of escrowed monies can be released when: (i) the provider has presold at least fifty percent (50%) of the independent living units, having received a minimum ten percent (10%) deposit on the presold units; (ii) the provider has received a commitment for any permanent mortgage loan or other long-term financing, and any conditions of the commitment prior to disbursement of funds thereunder have been substantially satisfied; and (iii) aggregate entrance fees received or receivable by the provider pursuant to binding continuing care contracts, plus the anticipated proceeds of any first mortgage loan or other long-term financing commitment are equal to not less than ninety percent (90%) of the aggregate cost of constructing or purchasing, equipping, and furnishing the facility plus not less than ninety percent (90%) of the funds estimated in the statement of cash flows submitted by the provider as that part of the disclosure statement required by G.S. 58-64-20, to be necessary to fund start-up losses and assure full performance of the obligations of the provider pursuant to continuing care contracts.

(2)   The remaining seventy-five percent (75%) of escrowed monies can be released when:

a. (i) the provider has presold a minimum of seventy-five percent (75%) of the independent living units, having received a minimum ten percent (10%) deposit on the presold units, or has maintained an independent living unit occupancy minimum of seventy-five percent (75%) for at least 60 days; (ii) construction or purchase of the independent living unit has been completed and an occupancy permit, if applicable, has been issued by the local government having authority to issue such permits; and (iii) the living unit becomes available for occupancy by the new resident; or

b. the provider submits a plan of reorganization that is accepted and approved by the Commissioner.

(b) Upon receipt by the escrow agent of a request by the provider for the release of these escrow funds, the escrow agent shall approve release of the funds within five working days unless the escrow agent finds that the requirements of subsection (a) of this section have not been met and notifies the provider of the basis for this finding. The request for release of the escrow funds shall be accompanied by any documentation the fiduciary requires.

(b1) Release of any escrowed funds that may be due to the subscriber or resident shall occur upon: five working days' notice of death, nonacceptance by the facility, or voluntary cancellation. If voluntary cancellation occurs after construction has begun, the refund may be delayed until a new subscriber is obtained for that specific unit, provided it does not exceed a period of two years.

(c) If the provider fails to meet the requirements for release of funds held in this escrow account within a time period the escrow agent considers reasonable, these funds shall be returned by the escrow agent to the persons who have made payment to the provider. The escrow agent shall notify the provider of the length of this time period when the provider requests release of the funds.

(d) Facilities that currently meet the seventy-five percent (75%) presales or the seventy-five percent (75%) occupancy requirements, as outlined in subdivision (a)(2) of this section, are not required to escrow entrance fees, unless otherwise required by the Commissioner. (1989, c. 758, s. 1; 1991, c. 196, s. 6, c. 720, s. 8, c. 761, ss. 11, 12.)

§ 58-64-40. Right to organization.

(a) A resident living in a facility operated by a provider licensed under this Article has the right of self-organization, the right to be represented by an individual of the resident's own choosing, and the right to engage in concerted activities to keep informed on the operation of the facility in which the resident resides or for other mutual aid or protection.

(b) The board of directors or other governing body of a provider or its designated representative shall hold semiannual meetings with the residents of each facility operated by the provider for free discussions of subjects including, but not limited to, income, expenditures, and financial trends and problems as they apply to the facility and discussions of proposed changes in policies, programs, and services. Upon request of the most representative residents' organization, a member of the governing body of the provider, such as a board member, a general partner, or a principal owner shall attend such meetings. Residents shall be entitled to at least seven days advance notice of each meeting. An agenda and any materials that will be distributed by the governing body at the meetings shall remain available upon request to residents. (1989, c. 758, s. 1; 1999-132, s. 2.4; 2001-223, s. 22.3; 2003-193, s. 9.)

§ 58-64-45. Supervision, rehabilitation, and liquidation.

(a) If, at any time, the Commissioner determines, after notice and an opportunity for the provider to be heard, that:

(1) A portion of an entrance fee escrow account required to be maintained under this Article has been or is proposed to be released in violation of this Article;

(2) A provider has been or will be unable, in such a manner as may endanger the ability of the provider, to fully perform its obligations pursuant to contracts for continuing care, to meet the forecasted financial data previously filed by the provider;

(3) A provider has failed to maintain the escrow account required under this Article; or

(4) A provider is bankrupt or insolvent, or in imminent danger of becoming bankrupt or insolvent;

the Commissioner may commence a supervision proceeding pursuant to Article 30 of this Chapter or may apply to the Superior Court of Wake County or to the federal bankruptcy court that may have previously taken jurisdiction over the provider or facility for an order directing the Commissioner or authorizing the Commissioner to rehabilitate or to liquidate a facility in accordance with Article 30 of this Chapter.

(b) The definition of "insolvency" or "insolvent" in G.S. 58-30-10(13) shall not apply to providers under this Article. Rules adopted by the Commissioner shall define and describe "insolvency" or "hazardous financial condition" for providers under this Article. G.S. 58-30-12 shall not apply to facilities under this Article.

(c) If, at any time, the Court finds, upon petition of the Commissioner or provider, or on its own motion, that the objectives of an order to rehabilitate a provider have been accomplished and that the facility or facilities owned by, or operated by, the provider can be returned to the provider's management without further jeopardy to the residents of the facility or facilities, the Court may, upon a full report and accounting of the conduct of the provider's affairs during the rehabilitation and of the provider's current financial condition, terminate the rehabilitation and, by order, return the facility or facilities owned by, or operated by, the provider, along with the assets and affairs of the provider, to the provider's management.

(d), (e) Repealed by Session Laws 1995 (Regular Session, 1996), c. 582, s. 3.

(f) In applying for an order to rehabilitate or liquidate a provider, the Commissioner shall give due consideration in the application to the manner in which the welfare of persons who have previously contracted with the provider for continuing care may be best served.

(g) An order for rehabilitation shall be refused or vacated if the provider posts a bond, by a recognized surety authorized to do business in this State and executed in favor of the Commissioner on behalf of persons who may be found entitled to a refund of entrance fees from the provider or other damages in the event the provider is unable to fulfill its contracts to provide continuing care at the facility or facilities, in an amount determined by the Court to be equal to the reserve funding that would otherwise need to be available to fulfill such obligations. (1989, c. 758, s. 1; 1995 (Reg. Sess., 1996), c. 582, s. 3; 2003-193, s. 10.)

§ 58-64-46. Receiverships; exception for facility beds.

When the Commissioner has been appointed as a receiver under Article 30 of this Chapter for a provider or facility subject to this Article, the Department of Health and Human Services may, notwithstanding any other provision of law, accept and approve the addition of adult care home beds for a facility owned by, or operated by, the provider, if it appears to the court, upon petition of the Commissioner or the provider, or on the court's own motion, that (i) the best interests of the provider or (ii) the welfare of persons who have previously contracted with the provider or may contract with the provider, may be best served by the addition of adult care home beds. (1999-219, s. 2; 2003-193, s. 11.)

§ 58-64-50. Investigations and subpoenas.

(a) The Commissioner may make such public or private investigations within or outside of this State as necessary (i) to determine whether any person has violated or is about to violate any provision of this Article, (ii) to aid in the enforcement of this Article, or (iii) to verify statements contained in any disclosure statement filed or delivered under this Article.

(b) For the purpose of any investigation or proceeding under this Article, the Commissioner may require or permit any person to file a statement in writing, under oath or otherwise, as to any of the facts and circumstances concerning the matter to be investigated.

(c) For the purpose of any investigation or proceeding under this Article, the Commissioner or his designee has all the powers given to him for insurance companies. He may administer oaths and affirmations, subpoena witnesses, compel their attendance, take evidence, and require the production of any books, papers, correspondence, memoranda, agreements, or other documents or records deemed relevant or material to the inquiry, all of which may be enforced in the Superior Court of Wake County. (1989, c. 758, s. 1.)

§ 58-64-55. Examinations; financial statements.

The Commissioner or the Commissioner's designee may, in the Commissioner's discretion, visit a provider offering continuing care in this State to examine its books and records. Expenses incurred by the Commissioner in conducting examinations under this section shall be paid by the provider examined. The provisions of G.S. 58-2-131, 58-2-132, 58-2-133, 58-2-134, 58-2-155, 58-2-165, 58-2-180, 58-2-185, 58-2-190, and 58-6-5 apply to this Article and are hereby incorporated by reference. (1989, c. 758, s. 1; 1995, c. 193, s. 53; 1999-132, s. 11.9; 2003-193, s. 12.)

§ 58-64-60. Contracts as preferred claims on liquidation.

In the event of liquidation of a provider, all contracts for continuing care executed by the provider shall be deemed preferred claims against all assets owned by the provider; provided, however, such claims shall be subordinate to the liquidator's cost of administration or any secured claim. (1989, c. 758, s. 1; 1995 (Reg. Sess., 1996), c. 582, s. 4; 2003-193, s. 13.)

§ 58-64-65. Rule-making authority; reasonable time to comply with rules.

(a) The Commissioner is authorized to promulgate rules to carry out and enforce the provisions of this Article.

(b) Any provider who is offering continuing care may be given a reasonable time, not to exceed one year from the date of publication of any applicable rules promulgated pursuant to this Article, within which to comply with the rules. (1989, c. 758, s. 1; 2003-193, s. 14.)

§ 58-64-70. Civil liability.

(a) A provider who enters into a contract for continuing care at a facility without having first delivered a disclosure statement meeting the requirements of G.S. 58-64-20 to the person contracting for this continuing care, or enters into a contract for continuing care at a facility with a person who has relied on a disclosure statement that omits to state a material fact required to be stated therein or necessary in order to make the statements made therein, in light of the circumstances under which they are made, not misleading, shall be liable to the person contracting for this continuing care for actual damages and repayment of all fees paid to the provider violating this Article, less the reasonable value of care and lodging provided to the resident by or on whose behalf the contract for continuing care was entered into prior to discovery of the violation, misstatement, or omission or the time the violation, misstatement, or omission should reasonably have been discovered, together with interest thereon at the legal rate for judgments, and court costs and reasonable attorney fees.

(b)   Liability under this section exists regardless of whether the provider had actual knowledge of the misstatement or omission.

(c)   A person may not file or maintain an action under this section if the person, before filing the action, received a written offer of a refund of all amounts paid the provider, together with interest at the rate established monthly by the Commissioner of Banks pursuant to G.S. 24-1.1(c), less the current contractual value of care and lodging provided prior to receipt of the offer, and if the offer recited the provisions of this section and the recipient of the offer failed to accept it within 30 days of actual receipt.

(d)   An action may not be maintained to enforce a liability created under this Article unless brought before the expiration of three years after the execution of the contract for continuing care that gave rise to the violation. (1989, c. 758, s. 1; 1995, c. 193, s. 54; 2003-193, s. 15.)

§ 58-64-75. Criminal penalties.

Any person who willfully and knowingly violates any provision of this Article is guilty of a Class 1 misdemeanor. The Commissioner may refer such evidence as is available concerning violation of the Article or of any rule or order hereunder to the Attorney General or a district attorney who may, with or without such reference institute the appropriate criminal proceedings under this Article. Nothing in this Article limits the power of the State to punish any person for any conduct that constitutes a crime under any other statute. (1989, c. 758, s. 1; 1993, c. 539, s. 469; 1994, Ex. Sess., c. 24, s. 14(c).)

§ 58-64-80. Advisory Committee.

There shall be a nine member Continuing Care Advisory Committee appointed by the Commissioner. The Committee shall consist of at least two residents of facilities, two representatives of the North Carolina Association of Nonprofit Homes for the Aging, one individual who is a certified public accountant and is licensed to practice in this State, one individual skilled in the field of architecture or engineering, and one individual who is a health care professional. (1989, c. 758, s. 1; 1999-132, s. 2.5.)

§ 58-64-85. Other licensing or regulation.

(a) Nothing in this Article affects the authority of the Department of Health and Human Services or any successor agency otherwise provided by law to license or regulate any health service facility or domiciliary service facility.

(b) Facilities and providers licensed under this Article that also are subject to the provisions of the North Carolina Condominium Act under Chapter 47C of the General Statutes shall not be subject to the provisions of Chapter 39A of the General Statutes, provided that the facility's declaration of condominium does not require the payment of any fee or charge not otherwise provided for in a resident's contract for continuing care, or other separate contract for the provisions of membership or services. (1991, c. 720, s. 1; 1997-443, s. 11A.118(a); 2011-196, s. 13.)

Article 65.

Hospital, Medical and Dental Service Corporations.

Part 1. In General.

§ 58-65-1. Regulation and definitions; application of other laws; profit and foreign corporations prohibited.

(a) Any corporation organized under the general corporation laws of the State of North Carolina for the purpose of maintaining and operating a nonprofit hospital or medical or dental service plan whereby hospital care or medical or dental service may be provided in whole or in part by the corporation or by hospitals, physicians, or dentists participating in the plan, or plans, shall be governed by this Article and Article 66 of this Chapter and shall be exempt from all other provisions of the insurance laws of this State, unless otherwise provided.

The term "hospital service plan" as used in this Article includes the contracting for certain fees for, or furnishing of, hospital care, laboratory facilities, X-ray facilities, drugs, appliances, anesthesia, nursing care, operating and obstetrical equipment, accommodations or any other services authorized or permitted to be furnished by a hospital under the laws of the State of North Carolina and approved by the North Carolina Hospital Association or the American Medical Association.

The term "medical service plan" as used in this Article includes the contracting for the payment of fees toward, or furnishing of, medical, obstetrical, surgical or any other professional services authorized or permitted to be furnished by a duly licensed physician or other provider listed in G.S. 58-50-30. The term "medical services plan" also includes the contracting for the payment of fees toward, or furnishing of, professional medical services authorized or permitted to be furnished by a duly licensed provider of health services licensed under Chapter 90 of the General Statutes.

The term "dental service plan" as used in this Article includes contracting for the payment of fees toward, or furnishing of dental or any other professional services authorized or permitted to be furnished by a duly licensed dentist.

The term "hospital service corporation" as used in this Article is intended to mean any nonprofit corporation operating a hospital or medical or dental service plan, as defined in this section. Any corporation organized and subject to the provisions of this Article, the certificate of incorporation of which authorizes the operation of either a hospital or medical or dental service plan, or any or all of them, may, with the approval of the Commissioner, issue subscribers' contracts or certificates approved by the Commissioner of Insurance, for the payment of either hospital or medical or dental fees, or the furnishing of such services, or any or all of them, and may enter into contracts with hospitals for physicians or dentists, or any or all of them, for the furnishing of fees or services respectively under a hospital or medical or dental service plan, or any or all of them.

The term "preferred provider" as used in this Article with respect to contracts, organizations, policies or otherwise means a health care service provider who has agreed to accept, from a corporation organized for the purposes authorized by this Article or other applicable law, special reimbursement terms in exchange for providing services to beneficiaries of a plan administered pursuant to this Article. Except to the extent prohibited either by G.S. 58-65-140 or by rules adopted by the Commissioner not inconsistent with this Article, the contractual terms and conditions for special reimbursement shall be those which the corporation and preferred provider find to be mutually agreeable.

The term "full service corporation" as used in this Article means any corporation organized under the provisions of this Article that offers a medical service plan or a hospital service plan.

The term "single service corporation" as used in this Article means any corporation organized under the provisions of this Article that offers only a dental service plan.

(b) through (c) Repealed by Session Laws 2001-297.

(d) No foreign or alien hospital or medical or dental service corporation as herein defined shall be authorized to do business in this State. (1941, c. 338, s. 1; 1943, c. 537, s. 1; 1953, c. 1124, s. 1; 1961, c. 1149; 1965, c. 396, s. 1; c. 1169, s. 1; 1967, c. 690, s. 1; 1973, c. 642; 1977, c. 601, ss. 1, 31/2; 1985, c. 735, s. 2; 1993, c. 347, s. 3; c. 375, s. 4; 464, s. 3.1; 1995, c. 223, s. 2; c. 406, s. 4; 1997-197, ss. 1, 2; 1999-186, s. 1; 1999-199, s. 2; 1999-210, ss. 5, 6; 2001-297, s. 2; 2001-487, ss. 40(h), 105(a), 105(b); 2003-212, s. 17; 2009-451, s. 21.13(a).)

§ 58-65-2. Other laws applicable to service corporations.

The following provisions of this Chapter are applicable to service corporations that are subject to this Article:

G.S. 58-2-125.	Authority over all insurance companies; no exemptions from license.
G.S. 58-2-150.	Oath required for compliance with law.
G.S. 58-2-155.	Investigation of charges.
G.S. 58-2-160.	Reporting and investigation of insurance and reinsurance fraud and the financial condition of licensees; immunity from liability.
G.S. 58-2-162.	Embezzlement by insurance agents, brokers, or administrators.
G.S. 58-2-185.	Record of business kept by companies and agents; Commissioner may inspect.
G.S. 58-2-190.	Commissioner may require special reports.
G.S. 58-2-195.	Commissioner may require records, reports, etc., for agencies, agents, and others.
G.S. 58-2-200.	Books and papers required to be exhibited.
G.S. 58-3-50.	Companies must do business in own name; emblems, insignias, etc.
G.S. 58-3-100(c),(e).	Insurance company licensing provisions.
G.S. 58-3-115.	Twisting with respect to insurance policies; penalties.
G.S. 58-7-46.	Notification to Commissioner for president or chief executive officer changes.
Part 7 of Article 10.	Annual Financial Reporting.
G.S. 58-50-35.	Notice of nonpayment of premium required before forfeiture.

G.S. 58-50-290. Health benefit plans or insurers contracting for the provision of dental services; no limitation on fees for noncovered services.
G.S. 58-51-15(a)(2)b. Accident and health policy provisions.

G.S. 58-51-17 Portability for accident and health insurance.

G.S. 58-51-25. Policy coverage to continue as to mentally retarded or physically handicapped children.

G.S. 58-51-95(h),(i),(j). Approval by Commissioner of forms, classification and rates; hearings; exceptions. (1999-244, s. 1; 2005-215, s. 17; 2005-412, s. 3; 2009-382, s. 6; 2009-384, s. 3; 2010-138, s. 2.)

§ 58-65-5. Contract for joint assumption or underwriting of risks.

Any corporation organized or regulated by the provisions of this Article and Article 66 of this Chapter is authorized to enter into such contracts with any other firm or corporation for joint assumption or underwriting of any part or all of any risks undertaken upon such terms and conditions as are approved by the Commissioner of Insurance. (1955, c. 894, s. 1.)

§ 58-65-10. Premium or dues paid by employer, employee, principal or agent or jointly and severally.

Any premium or dues charged by a corporation regulated under the provisions of this Article and Article 66 of this Chapter may be paid by the employer, employee, principal, or agent, or jointly and severally. The term "employer" as used herein includes counties, municipal corporations, and all departments or subdivisions of the State, county, municipal corporation, and official boards including city and county boards of alcoholic control, together with all others occupying the status of employer and employee, principal and agent. (1955, c. 894, s. 2.)

§ 58-65-15. Incorporation.

Any number of persons not less than seven, desiring to form a nonprofit hospital service corporation, shall incorporate under the provisions of the general laws of the State of North Carolina governing corporations, but subject to the following provisions:

(1) The certificate of incorporation of each such corporation shall have endorsed thereon or attached thereto, the consent of the Commissioner of Insurance, if he shall find the same to be in accordance with the provisions of this Article and Article 66 of this Chapter.

(2) A statement of the services to be rendered by the corporation and the rates currently to be charged therefor which said statement shall be accompanied by two copies of each contract for services which the corporation proposes to make with its subscribers, and two copies of the type of contract which said corporation proposes to make with participating hospitals, shall have been furnished the Commissioner of Insurance; provided, however, that if the articles of incorporation of any such corporation within the meaning of this Article and Article 66 of this Chapter shall have been filed with the Secretary of State prior to March 15, 1941, the approval thereof by the Commissioner of Insurance shall be evidenced by a separate instrument in writing filed with the Secretary of State. (1941, c. 338, s. 2.)

§ 58-65-20. Members of governing boards.

(a) For the purpose of this section the words "board of directors" includes the board of directors, trustees, or other governing board.

(b) The board of directors of each hospital service corporation subject to the provisions of this Article shall include persons who are representative of its subscribers and the general public. Less than one half of the directors of any such corporation shall be persons who are licensed to practice medicine in this State or who are paid directors or employees of a corporation organized for hospital purposes. (1979, c. 538, s. 1.)

§ 58-65-25. Hospital, physician and dentist contracts.

(a) Any corporation organized under this Article may enter into contracts for the rendering of hospital service to any of its subscribers by hospitals approved by the American Medical Association and/or the North Carolina Hospital Association, and may enter into contracts for the furnishing of, or the payment in whole or in part for, medical and/or dental services rendered to any of its subscribers by duly licensed physicians and/or dentists. All obligations arising under contracts issued by such corporations to its subscribers shall be satisfied by payments made directly to the hospitals or hospitals and/or physicians and/or dentists rendering such service, or direct to the subscriber or his, her, or their legal representatives upon the receipt by the corporation from the subscriber of a statement marked paid by the hospital(s) and/or physician(s) and/or dentist(s) or both rendering such service, and all such payments heretofore made are hereby ratified. Nothing in this section shall be construed to discriminate against hospitals conducted by other schools of medical practice.

(b) All certificates, plans or contracts issued to subscribers or other persons by hospital and medical and/or dental service corporations operating under this Article shall contain in substance a provision as follows: "After two years from the date of issue of this certificate, contract or plan no misstatements, except fraudulent misstatements made by the applicant in the application for such certificate, contract or plan, shall be used to void said certificate, contract or plan, or to deny a claim for loss incurred or disability (as therein defined) commencing after the expiration of such two-year period." (1941, c. 338, s. 3; 1943, c. 537, s. 2; 1947, c. 820, s. 1; 1955, c. 850, s. 7; 1961, c. 1149; 1979, c. 755, s. 17; 1997-259, s. 16.)

§ 58-65-30. Dentists' services.

Any corporation organized under the provisions of this Article and Article 66 of this Chapter may, in addition to its authority to contract under G.S. 58-65-25, enter into contracts to pay duly licensed dentists for treatment of fractures and dislocations of the jaw, and cutting procedures in the oral cavity other than extractions, repairs and care of the teeth and gums. (1957, c. 987.)

§ 58-65-35. Nurses' services.

No agency, institution or physician providing a service for which payment or reimbursement is required to be made under a contract governed by this Article and Article 66 of this Chapter shall be denied such payment or reimbursement on account of the fact that the service was rendered through a registered nurse acting under authority of rules and regulations adopted by the North Carolina Medical Board and the Board of Nursing pursuant to G.S. 90-6 and 90-171.23. (1973, c. 436; 1991, c. 720, s. 37; 1993, c. 347, s. 4; 1995, c. 94, s. 4; 1997-197, s. 1.)

§ 58-65-36. Physician services provided by physician assistants.

No agency, institution, or physician providing a service for which payment or reimbursement is required to be made under a contract governed by this Article or Article 66 of this Chapter shall be denied the payment or reimbursement on account of the fact that the service was rendered through a physician assistant acting under authority of rules adopted by the North Carolina Medical Board pursuant to G.S. 90-18.1. (1999-210, s. 4.)

§ 58-65-40. Supervision of Commissioner of Insurance; form of contract with subscribers; schedule of rates.

No hospital service corporation shall enter into any contract with subscribers unless and until it shall have filed with the Commissioner of Insurance a specimen copy of the contract or certificate and of all applications, riders, and endorsements for use in connection with the issuance or renewal thereof to be formally approved by him as conforming to the section of this Article entitled "Subscribers' contracts," and conforms to all rules and regulations promulgated by the Commissioner of Insurance under the provisions of this Article and Article 66 of this Chapter. The Commissioner of Insurance shall, within a reasonable time after the filing of any such form, notify the corporation filing the same either of his approval or of his disapproval of such form.

No corporation subject to the provisions of this Article and Article 66 of this Chapter shall enter into any contract with a subscriber after the enactment hereof unless and until it shall have filed with the Commissioner of Insurance a full schedule of rates to be paid by the subscribers to such contracts and shall have obtained the Commissioner's approval thereof. The Commissioner may refuse approval if he finds that such rates are excessive, inadequate, or unfairly discriminatory; or do not exhibit a reasonable relationship to the benefits provided by such contracts. At all times such rates and form of subscribers' contracts shall be subject to modification and approval of the Commissioner of Insurance under rules and regulations adopted by the Commissioner, in conformity to this Article and Article 66 of this Chapter. (1941, c. 338, s. 4; 1989, c. 485, s. 57.)

§ 58-65-45. Public hearings on revision of existing schedule or establishment of new schedule; publication of notice.

Whenever any hospital service corporation licensed under this Article and Article 66 of this Chapter makes a rate filing or any proposal to revise an existing rate schedule or contract form, the effect of which is to increase or decrease the charge for its contracts, or to set up a new rate schedule, and such rate schedule is subject to the approval of the Commissioner, such hospital service corporation shall file its proposed rate change or contract form and supporting data with the commissioner, who shall review the filing in accordance with the standards in G.S. 58-65-40. Such rate revision or new rate schedule with respect to individual subscriber contracts shall be guaranteed by the insurer, as to the contract and certificate holders thereby affected, for a period of not less than 12 months; or with respect to individual subscriber contracts as an alternative to giving such guarantee, such rate revision or new rate schedule may be made applicable to all individual contracts at one time if the corporation chooses to apply for such relief with respect to such contracts no more frequently than once in any 12-month period. Such rate revision or new rate schedule shall be applicable to all contracts of the same type; provided that no rate revision or new rate schedule may become effective for any contract holder unless the corporation has given written notice of the rate revision or new rate schedule not less than 30 days prior to the effective date of such revision or new rate schedule. The contract holder thereafter must pay the revised rate or new rate schedule in order to continue the contract in force. The Commissioner may promulgate reasonable rules, after notice and hearing, to require the submission of supporting data and such information as is deemed necessary to determine whether such rate revisions meet these standards. At any time within 60 days after the date of any filing under this section or G.S. 58-65-40, the Commissioner may give written notice to the corporation of a fixed time and place for a hearing on the filing, which time shall be no less than 20 days after notice is given. In the event no notice of hearing is issued within 60 days from the date of any filing, the filing shall be deemed to be approved, subject to modification by the Commissioner as authorized by G.S. 58-65-40. In the event the Commissioner gives notice of a hearing, the corporation making the filing shall, not less than 10 days before the time of the hearing, cause to be published in a daily newspaper or newspapers published in North Carolina, and in accordance with the rules and regulations of the Commissioner of Insurance, a notice, in the form and content approved by the Commissioner, setting forth the nature and effect of such proposal and the time and place of the public hearing to be held. If the Commissioner does not issue an order within 45 days after the day on which the hearing began, the filing shall be deemed to be approved, subject to modification by the Commissioner as authorized by G.S. 58-65-40. (1953, c. 1118; 1985, c. 666, s. 60; 1989, c. 485, s. 58.)

§ 58-65-50. Application for certificate of authority or license.

No corporation subject to the provisions of this Article and Article 66 of this Chapter shall issue contracts for the rendering of hospital or medical and/or dental service to subscribers, until the Commissioner of Insurance has, by formal certificate or license, authorized it to do so. Application for such certificate of authority or license shall be made on forms to be supplied by the Commissioner of Insurance, containing such information as he shall deem necessary. Each application for such certificate of authority or license, as a part thereof shall be accompanied by duplicate copies of the following documents duly certified by at least two of the executive officers of such corporation:

(1) Certificate of incorporation with all amendments thereto.

(2) Bylaws with all amendments thereto.

(3) Each contract executed or proposed to be executed by and between the corporation and any participating hospital, and/or physicians under the terms of which hospital and/or medical and/or dental service is to be furnished to subscribers to the plan.

(4) Each form of contract, application, rider, and endorsement, issued or proposed to be issued to subscribers to the plan, or in renewal of any of contracts with subscribers to the plan, together with a table of rates charged or proposed to be charged to subscribers for each form of such contract.

(5) Financial statement of the corporation which shall include the amounts of each contribution paid or agreed to be paid to the corporation for working capital, the name or names of each contributor and the terms or each contribution. (1941, c. 338, s. 5; 1943, c. 537, s. 3; 1961, c. 1149.)

§ 58-65-55. Issuance and continuation of license.

(a) Every corporation subject to this Article shall pay to the Commissioner a fee of two hundred fifty dollars ($250.00) for filing an application for a license. Fee payment shall be contemporaneous with the filing. Before issuing or continuing any such license or certificate the Commissioner may make such an examination or investigation as the Commissioner deems expedient. The Commissioner shall issue a license upon the payment of a fee of one thousand five hundred dollars ($1,500) for a single service corporation or two thousand five hundred dollars ($2,500) for a full service corporation and upon being satisfied on the following points:

(1) The applicant is established as a bona fide nonprofit hospital service corporation as defined by this Article and Article 66 of this Chapter.

(2) The rates charged and benefits to be provided are fair and reasonable.

(3) The amounts provided as working capital of the corporation are repayable only out of earned income in excess of amounts paid and payable for operating expenses and hospital and medical and/or dental expenses and such reserve as the Department deems adequate, as provided hereinafter.

(4) That the amount of money actually available for working capital be sufficient to carry all acquisition costs and operating expenses for a reasonable period of time from the date of the issuance of the certificate.

(b) The license shall continue in full force and effect, subject to payment of an annual license continuation fee of one thousand five hundred dollars ($1,500) for a single service corporation or two thousand five hundred dollars ($2,500), subject to all other provisions of subsection (a) of this section and subject to any other applicable provisions of the insurance laws of this State. (1941, c. 338, s. 6; 1943, c. 537, s. 4; 1947, c. 820, s. 2; 1961, c. 1149; 1989 (Reg. Sess., 1990), c. 1069, s. 5; 1995, c. 507, s. 11A(c); 1999-435, s. 5; 2003-212, s. 26(j); 2005-424, s. 1.5; 2009-451, s. 21.13(b).)

§ 58-65-60. Subscribers' contracts; required and prohibited provisions.

(a)   Every contract made by a corporation subject to the provisions of this Article and Article 66 of this Chapter shall be for a period not to exceed 12 months, and no contract shall be made providing for the inception of benefits at a date later than one year from the date of the contract. Any such contract may provide that it shall be automatically renewed for a similar period unless there shall have been one month's prior written notice of termination by either the subscriber or the corporation.

(b)   Contracts may be issued that entitle one or more persons to benefits under those contracts. Persons entitled to benefits under those contracts, other than the certificate holder, may only be the certificate holder's spouse, lawful or legally adopted child of the certificate holder or the certificate holder's spouse, or any other person who resides in the same household with the certificate holder and is dependent upon the certificate holder.

(c)   Every contract entered into by any such corporation with any subscriber thereof shall be in writing and a certificate stating the terms and conditions thereof shall be furnished to the subscriber to be kept by him. No such certificate form, other than to group subscribers of groups of 10 or more certificate holders or those issued pursuant to a master group contract covering 10 or more certificate holders shall be made, issued or delivered in this State unless it contains the following provisions, provided, however, groups between five and 10 certificate holders complying with and maintaining eligibility status under regulations approved by the Commissioner of Insurance for group enrollment may be cancelled if such participation falls below the minimum participation of five certificate holders; or if the group takes other group hospital, medical or surgical coverage:

(1)   A statement of the amount payable to the corporation by the subscriber and the times at which and manner in which such amount is to be paid; this provision may be inserted in the application rather than in the certificate. Application need not be attached to certificate.

(2)   A statement of the nature of the benefits to be furnished and the period during which they will be furnished.

(3) A statement of the terms and conditions, if any, upon which the contract may be cancelled or otherwise terminated at the option of either party. The statement shall be in the following language:

a. "Renewability": Any contract subject to the provisions of this subdivision is renewable at the option of the subscriber unless sufficient notice in writing of nonrenewal is mailed to the subscriber by the corporation addressed to the last address recorded with the corporation.

b. "Sufficient notice" shall be as follows:

1. During the first year of any such contract, or during the first year following any lapse and reinstatement, or reenrollment, a period of 30 days.

2. During the second and subsequent years of continuous coverage, a number of full calendar months most nearly equivalent to one fourth the number of months of continuous coverage from the first anniversary of the date of issue or reinstatement or reenrollment, whichever date is more recent, to the date of mailing of such notice.

3. No period of required notice shall exceed two years, and no renewal hereunder shall renew any such contract for any period beyond the required period of notice except by written agreement of the subscriber and corporation.

The contract may be modified, terminated or cancelled by the corporation at any time at its option, upon:

a. Nonpayment by the subscriber of fees or dues as required.

b. Failure or refusal by the subscriber to comply with rate or benefit changes approved by the Commissioner under G.S. 58-65-45.

c. Failure or refusal by the subscriber after 30 days' written notice to subscriber to transfer into hospital, medical, or dental service plan serving the area to which the subscriber has changed residence and is eligible for or to which corporation is required to transfer by interplan agreement of transfer.

(4) A statement that the contract includes the endorsement thereon and attached papers, if any, and together with the applications contains the entire contract.

(5) A statement that if the subscriber defaults in making any payment, under the contract, the subsequent acceptance of a payment by the corporation at its home office shall reinstate the contract, but with respect to sickness and injury, only to cover such sickness as may be first manifested more than 10 days after the date of such acceptance.

(d) In every such contract made, issued or delivered in this State:

(1) All printed portions shall be plainly printed;

(2) The exceptions from the contract shall appear with the same prominence as the benefits to which they apply; and

(3) If the contract contains any provision purporting to make any portion of the articles, constitution or bylaws of the corporation a part of the contract, such portion shall be set forth in full.

(e) A service corporation may issue a master group contract with the approval of the Commissioner if the contract and the individual certificates issued to members of the group comply in substance to the other provisions of this Article and Article 66 of this Chapter. The contract may provide for the adjustment of the rate of the premium or benefits conferred as provided in the contract, and in accordance with an adjustment schedule filed with and approved by the Commissioner. If the contract is issued, altered or modified, the subscribers' contracts issued under that contract are altered or modified accordingly, all laws and clauses in subscribers' contracts to the contrary notwithstanding. Nothing in this Article and Article 66 of this Chapter shall be construed to prohibit or prevent the same. Forms of such contract shall at all times be furnished upon request of subscribers thereto.

(e1) Employees shall be added to the master group coverage no later than 90 days after their first day of employment. Employment shall be considered continuous and not be considered broken except for unexcused absences from work for reasons other than illness or injury. The term "employee" is defined as a nonseasonal person who works on a full-time basis, with a normal work week of 30 or more hours and who is otherwise eligible for coverage, but does not include a person who works on a part-time, temporary, or substitute basis.

(e2) Whenever an employer master group contract replaces another group contract, whether this contract was issued by a corporation under Articles 1 through 67 of this Chapter, the liability of the succeeding corporation for insuring persons covered under the previous group contract is (i) each person is eligible for coverage in accordance with the succeeding corporation's plan of benefits with respect to classes eligible and activity at work and nonconfinement rules must be covered by the succeeding corporation's plan of benefits; and (ii) each person not covered under the succeeding corporation's plan of benefits in accordance with (i) above must nevertheless be covered by the succeeding corporation if that person was validly covered, including benefit extension, under the prior plan on the date of discontinuance and if the person is a member of the class of persons eligible for coverage under the succeeding corporation's plan.

(e3) When determining employee eligibility for a large employer, as defined in G.S. 58-68-25(10), an individual proprietor, owner, or operator shall be defined as an "employee" for the purpose of obtaining coverage under the employee group health plan and shall not be held to a minimum workweek requirement as imposed on other eligible employees.

(f) Any hospitalization contract renewed in the name of the subscriber during the grace period shall be construed to be a continuation of the contract first issued. (1941, c. 338, s. 7; 1947, c. 820, ss. 3, 4; 1955, c. 679, ss. 1-3; 1957, c. 1085, s. 1; 1961, c. 1149; 1989, c. 775, s. 4; 1991, c. 720, ss. 38, 88; 1991 (Reg. Sess., 1992), c. 837, s. 4; 1993, c. 408, s. 4; c. 409, s. 24; 1995, c. 507, s. 23A.1(e); 1997-259, s. 17; 2001-417, s. 12; 2005-223, s. 2(a).)

§ 58-65-65. Coverage for active medical treatment in tax-supported institutions.

(a) No hospital or medical or dental service plan, contract or certificate governed by the provisions of this Article and Article 66 of this Chapter shall be delivered, issued, executed or renewed in this State, or approved for issuance or renewal in this State by the Commissioner of Insurance, after May 21, 1975, unless such plan, contract or certificate provides for the payment of benefits for charges made for medical care rendered in or by duly licensed state tax-supported institutions, including charges for medical care of cerebral palsy, other orthopedic and crippling disabilities, mental and nervous diseases and disorders, mental retardation, alcoholism and drug or chemical dependency, and respiratory illness, on a basis no less favorable than the basis which would apply had the medical care been rendered in or by any other public or private institution or provider. The term "state tax-supported institutions" shall include community mental health centers and other health clinics which are certified as Medicaid providers.

(b)   No plan, contract, or certificate shall exclude payment for charges of a duly licensed state tax-supported institution because of its being a specialty facility for one particular type of illness nor because it does not have an operating room and related equipment for the performance of surgery, but it is not required that benefits be payable for domiciliary or custodial care, rehabilitation, training, schooling, or occupational therapy.

(c)   The restrictions and requirements of this section shall not apply to any plan, contract, or certificate which is individually underwritten or provided for a specific individual and the members of his family as a nongroup policy, but shall apply only to those hospital service and medical service subscriber plans, contracts, or certificates delivered, issued for delivery, reissued or renewed in th s State on and after July 1, 1975. (1975, c. 345, s. 2.)

§ 58-65-70. Contracts to cover any person possessing the sickle cell trait or hemoglobin C trait.

No hospital, medical, dental, or any health service governed by this Article and Article 66 of this Chapter shall refuse to issue or deliver any individual or group hospital, dental, medical, or health service contract in this State which it is currently issuing for delivery in this State, and which affords benefits or coverage for any medical treatment or service authorized or permitted to be furnished by a hospital, clinic, family health clinic, neighborhood health clinic, health maintenance organization, physician, physician's assistant, nurse practitioner or any medical service facility or personnel, on account of the fact that the person who is to be insured possesses sickle cell trait or hemoglobin C tra t; nor shall any such policy issued and delivered in this State carry a higher premium rate or charge on account of the fact that the person who is to be insured possesses sickle cell trait. (1975, c. 599, s. 2.)

§ 58-65-75. Coverage for chemical dependency treatment.

(a)   As used in this section, the term "chemical dependency" means the pathological use or abuse of alcohol or other drugs in a manner or to a degree that produces an impairment in personal, social, or occupational functioning and which may, but need not, include a pattern of tolerance and withdrawal.

(b) Every group insurance certificate or group subscriber contract under any hospital or medical plan governed by this Article and Article 66 of this Chapter that is issued, renewed, or amended on or after January 1, 1985, shall offer to its insureds benefits for the necessary care and treatment of chemical dependency that are not less favorable than benefits for physical illness generally. Except as provided in subsection (c) of this section, benefits for chemical dependency shall be subject to the same durational limits, dollar limits, deductibles, and coinsurance factors as are benefits for physical illness generally.

(c) Every group insurance certificate or group subscriber contract that provides benefits for chemical dependency treatment and that provides total annual benefits for all illnesses in excess of eight thousand dollars ($8,000) is subject to the following conditions:

(1) The certificate or contract shall provide, for each 12-month period, a minimum benefit of eight thousand dollars ($8,000) for the necessary care and treatment of chemical dependency.

(2) The certificate or contract shall provide a minimum benefit of sixteen thousand dollars ($16,000) for the necessary care and treatment of chemical dependency for the life of the certificate or contract.

(d) Provisions for benefits for necessary care and treatment of chemical dependency in group certificates or group contracts shall provide for benefit payments for the following providers of necessary care and treatment of chemical dependency:

(1) The following units of a general hospital licensed under Article 5 of General Statutes Chapter 131E:

a. Chemical dependency units in facilities licensed after October 1, 1984;

b. Medical units;

c. Psychiatric units; and

(2) The following facilities or programs licensed after July 1, 1984, under Article 2 of General Statutes Chapter 122C:

a. Chemical dependency units in psychiatric hospitals;

b. Chemical dependency hospitals;

c. Residential chemical dependency treatment facilities;

d. Social setting detoxification facilities or programs;

e. Medical detoxification facilities or programs; and

(3) Duly licensed physicians and duly licensed psychologists and certified professionals working under the direct supervision of such physicians or psychologists in facilities described in (1) and (2) above and in day/night programs or outpatient treatment facilities licensed after July 1, 1984, under Article 2 of General Statutes Chapter 122C. After January 1, 1995, "duly licensed psychologists" shall be defined as licensed psychologists who hold permanent licensure and certification as health services provider psychologist issued by the North Carolina Psychology Board.

Provided, however, that nothing in this subsection shall prohibit any certificate or contract from requiring the most cost effective treatment setting to be utilized by the person undergoing necessary care and treatment for chemical dependency.

(e) Coverage for chemical dependency treatment as described in this section shall not be applicable to any group certificate holder or group subscriber contract holder who rejects the coverage in writing.

(f) Notwithstanding any other provisions of this section, a group health benefit plan that covers both medical and surgical benefits and chemical dependency treatment benefits shall, with respect to the chemical dependency treatment benefits, comply with all applicable standards of Subtitle B of Title V of Public Law 110-343, known as the Paul Wellstone and Pete Domenici Mental Health Parity and Addiction Equity Act of 2008.

(g) Subsection (f) of this section applies only to a group health benefit plan covering a large employer as defined in G.S. 58-68-25(a)(10). (1983 (Reg. Sess., 1984), c. 1110, s. 8; 1985, c. 589, s. 43(a), (b); 1989, c. 175, s. 2; 1991, c. 720, s. 64; 1993, c. 375, s. 5; 2009-382, s. 21.)

§ 58-65-80. Meaning of terms "accident", "accidental injury", and "accidental means".

(a)   This section applies to the provisions of all subscriber contracts under this Article and Article 66 of this Chapter that are issued on or after October 1, 1989, and preferred provider arrangements under this Article and Article 66 of this Chapter that are entered into on or after October 1, 1989.

(b)   "Accident", "accidental injury", and "accidental means" shall be defined to imply "result" language and shall not include words that establish an accidental means test. (1989, c. 485, s. 11.)

§ 58-65-85. Discriminatory practices prohibited.

No person subject to this Article and Article 66 of this Chapter shall refuse to issue or refuse to reissue to an individual any certificate, plan, or contract governed by this Article and Article 66 of this Chapter; limit the amount, extent, or kind of services available to an individual; or charge an individual a different rate for the same services, because of the race, color, or national or ethnic origin of that individual. (1989, c. 485, s. 23.)

§ 58-65-90. No discrimination against mentally ill or chemically dependent individuals.

(a)   Definitions. - As used in this section, the term:

(1)   "Mental illness" has the same meaning as defined in G.S. 122C-3(21), with a mental disorder defined in the Diagnostic and Statistical Manual of Mental Disorders, DSM-IV, or subsequent editions published by the American Psychiatric Association, except those mental disorders coded in the DSM-IV or subsequent editions as substance-related disorders (291.0 through 292.9 and 303.0 through 305.9), those coded as sexual dysfunctions not due to organic disease (302.70 through 302.79), and those coded as "V" codes.

(2)   "Chemical dependency" has the same meaning as defined in G.S. 58-65-75, with a mental disorder defined in the Diagnostic and Statistical Manual of

Mental Disorders, DSM-IV, or subsequent editions published by the American Psychiatric Association.

(b) Coverage of Physical Illness. - No service corporation governed by this Chapter shall, solely because an individual to be insured has or had a mental illness or chemical dependency:

(1) Refuse to issue or deliver to that individual any individual or group subscriber contract in this State that affords benefits or coverage for medical treatment or service for physical illness or injury;

(2) Have a higher premium rate or charge for physical illness or injury coverages or benefits for that individual; or

(3) Reduce physical illness or injury coverages or benefits for that individual.

(b1) [Expired October 1, 2001.]

(c) Chemical Dependency Coverage Not Required. - Nothing in this section requires a service corporation to offer coverage for chemical dependency, except as provided in G.S. 58-65-75.

(d) Applicability. - This section applies only to group health insurance contracts, other than excepted benefits as defined in G.S. 58-68-25. For purposes of this section, "group health insurance contracts" include MEWAs, as defined in G.S. 58-49-30(a).

(e) Nothing in this section requires an insurer to cover treatment or studies leading to or in connection with sex changes or modifications and related care. (1989, c. 369, s. 1; 1991, c. 720, s. 82; 1997-259, s. 22; 1999-132, s. 4.3; 2007-268, s. 3.)

§ 58-65-91. Coverage for certain treatment of diabetes.

(a) Every insurance certificate or subscriber contract under any hospital service plan or medical service plan governed by this Article and Article 66 of this Chapter, and every preferred provider plan under G.S. 58-50-56 that is issued, renewed, or amended on or after October 1, 1997, shall provide coverage for medically appropriate and necessary services, including diabetes outpatient self-management training and educational services, and equipment, supplies, medications, and laboratory procedures used to treat diabetes. Diabetes outpatient self-management training and educational services shall be provided by a physician or a health care professional designated by the physician. The hospital or medical service plan shall determine who shall provide and be reimbursed for the diabetes outpatient self-management training and educational services. The same deductibles, coinsurance, and other limitations as apply to similar services covered under the policy, contract, or plan shall apply to the diabetes coverage required under this section.

(b)   For the purposes of this section, "physician" is a person licensed to practice in this State under Article 1 or Article 7 of Chapter 90 of the General Statutes. (1997-225, s. 2; 1997-519, s. 3.12.)

§ 58-65-92. Coverage for mammograms and cervical cancer screening.

(a)   Every insurance certificate or subscriber contract under any hospital service plan or medical service plan governed by this Article and Article 66 of this Chapter, and every preferred provider benefit plan under G.S. 58-50-56, that is issued, renewed, or amended on or after January 1, 1992, shall provide coverage for examinations and laboratory tests for the screening for the early detection of cervical cancer and for low-dose screening mammography. The same deductibles, coinsurance, and other limitations as apply to similar services covered under the certificate or contract shall apply to coverage for examinations and laboratory tests for the screening for the early detection of cervical cancer and low-dose screening mammography.

(a1)   As used in this section, "examinations and laboratory tests for the screening for the early detection of cervical cancer" means conventional PAP smear screening, liquid-based cytology, and human papilloma virus (HPV) detection methods for women with equivocal findings on cervical cytologic analysis that are subject to the approval of and have been approved by the United States Food and Drug Administration.

(b)   As used in this section, "low-dose screening mammography" means a radiologic procedure for the early detection of breast cancer provided to an asymptomatic woman using equipment dedicated specifically for mammography, including a physician's interpretation of the results of the procedure.

(c) Coverage for low-dose screening mammography shall be provided as follows:

(1) One or more mammograms a year, as recommended by a physician, for any woman who is at risk for breast cancer. For purposes of this subdivision, a woman is at risk for breast cancer if any one or more of the following is true:

a. The woman has a personal history of breast cancer;

b. The woman has a personal history of biopsy-proven benign breast disease;

c. The woman's mother, sister, or daughter has or has had breast cancer; or

d. The woman has not given birth prior to the age of 30;

(2) One baseline mammogram for any woman 35 through 39 years of age, inclusive;

(3) A mammogram every other year for any woman 40 through 49 years of age, inclusive, or more frequently upon recommendation of a physician; and

(4) A mammogram every year for any woman 50 years of age or older.

(d) Reimbursement for a mammogram authorized under this section shall be made only if the facility in which the mammogram was performed meets mammography accreditation standards established by the North Carolina Medical Care Commission.

(e) Coverage for the screening for the early detection of cervical cancer shall be in accordance with the most recently published American Cancer Society guidelines or guidelines adopted by the North Carolina Advisory Committee on Cancer Coordination and Control. Coverage shall include the examination, the laboratory fee, and the physician's interpretation of the laboratory results. Reimbursements for laboratory fees shall be made only if the laboratory meets accreditation standards adopted by the North Carolina Medical Care Commission. (1991, c. 490, s. 2; 1997-519, s. 3.6; 2003-186, s. 3.)

§ 58-65-93. Coverage for prostate-specific antigen (PSA) tests.

(a) Every insurance certificate or subscriber contract under any hospital service plan or medical service plan governed by this Article and Article 66 of this Chapter, and every preferred provider benefit plan under G.S. 58-50-56, that is issued, renewed, or amended on or after January 1, 1994, shall provide coverage for prostate-specific antigen (PSA) tests or equivalent tests for the presence of prostate cancer. The same deductibles, coinsurance, and other limitations as apply to similar services covered under the certificate or contract shall apply to coverage for prostate-specific antigen (PSA) tests or equivalent tests for the presence of prostate cancer.

(b) As used in this section, "prostate-specific antigen (PSA) tests or equivalent tests for the presence of prostate cancer" means serological tests for determining the presence of prostate cytoplasmic protein (PSA) and the generation of antibodies to it, as a novel marker for prostatic disease.

(c) Coverage for prostate-specific antigen (PSA) tests or equivalent tests for the presence of prostate cancer shall be provided when recommended by a physician. (1993, c. 269, s. 2; 1997-519, s. 3.7.)

§ 58-65-94. Coverage of certain prescribed drugs for cancer treatment.

(a) No insurance certificate or subscriber contract under any hospital service plan or medical service plan governed by this Article and Article 66 of this Chapter, and no preferred provider benefit plan under G.S. 58-50-56, that is issued, renewed, or amended on or after January 1, 1994, and that provides coverage for prescribed drugs approved by the federal Food and Drug Administration for the treatment of certain types of cancer shall exclude coverage of any drug on the basis that the drug has been prescribed for the treatment of a type of cancer for which the drug has not been approved by the federal Food and Drug Administration. The drug, however, must be approved by the federal Food and Drug Administration and must have been proven effective and accepted for the treatment of the specific type of cancer for which the drug has been prescribed in any one of the following established reference compendia:

(1) The National Comprehensive Cancer Network Drugs & Biologics Compendium;

(2) The ThomsonMicromedex DrugDex;

(3) The Elsevier Gold Standard's Clinical Pharmacology; or

(4) Any other authoritative compendia as recognized periodically by the United States Secretary of Health and Human Services.

(b) Notwithstanding subsection (a) of this section, coverage shall not be required for any experimental or investigational drugs or any drug that the federal Food and Drug Administration has determined to be contraindicated for treatment of the specific type of cancer for which the drug has been prescribed.

(c) This section shall apply only to cancer drugs and nothing in this section shall be construed, expressly or by implication, to create, impair, alter, limit, notify, enlarge, abrogate, or prohibit reimbursement for drugs used in the treatment of any other disease or condition. (1993, c. 506, s. 4.2; 1997-519, s. 3.8; 2009-170, s. 2.)

§ 58-65-95. Investments and reserves.

(a) Corporations subject to this Article shall invest in or hold only those assets permitted by Article 7 of this Chapter for life and health insurance companies.

(b) Every such corporation shall accumulate and maintain, in addition to proper reserves for current administrative liabilities and whatever reserves are deemed to be adequate and proper by the Commissioner for unpaid hospital, medical, or dental bills, and unearned membership dues, a special contingent surplus or reserve at the following rates annually of its gross annual collections from membership dues, exclusive of receipts from cost plus plans, until the reserve equals an amount that is three times its average monthly expenditures for claims and administrative and selling expenses:

(1) First $200,000   4%

(2) Next $200,000   2%

(3) All above $400,000   1%

(c) Any such corporation may accumulate and maintain a contingent reserve in excess of the reserve required in subsection (b) of this section, not to exceed an amount equal to six times the average monthly expenditures for claims and administrative and selling expenses.

(d) If the Commissioner finds that special conditions exist warranting an increase or decrease in the reserves or schedule of reserves in subsection (b) of this section, the Commissioner may modify them accordingly. Provided, however, when special conditions exist warranting an increase in the schedule of reserves, the schedule shall not be increased by the Commissioner until a reasonable length of time has elapsed after the Commissioner gives notice of the increase. (1941, c. 338, s. 8; 1943, c. 537, s. 5; 1947, c. 820, s. 5; 1961, c. 1149; 1991, c. 720, s. 79; 1999-244, s. 6; 2003-212, s. 18.)

§ 58-65-96. Coverage for reconstructive breast surgery following mastectomy.

(a) Every insurance certificate or subscriber contract under any hospital service plan or medical service plan governed by this Article and Article 66 of this Chapter, and every preferred provider benefit plan under G.S. 58-50-56 that provides coverage for mastectomy shall provide coverage for reconstructive breast surgery following a mastectomy. The coverage shall include coverage for all stages and revisions of reconstructive breast surgery performed on a nondiseased breast to establish symmetry if reconstructive surgery on a diseased breast is performed, as well as coverage for prostheses and physical complications in all stages of mastectomy, including lymphademas. The same deductibles, coinsurance, and other limitations as apply to similar services covered under the policy, contract, or plan shall apply to coverage for reconstructive breast surgery. Reconstruction of the nipple/areolar complex following a mastectomy is covered without regard to the lapse of time between the mastectomy and the reconstruction, subject to the approval of the treating physician.

(b) As used in this section, the following terms have the meanings indicated:

(1) "Mastectomy" means the surgical removal of all or part of a breast as a result of breast cancer or breast disease.

(2) "Reconstructive breast surgery" means surgery performed as a result of a mastectomy to reestablish symmetry between the two breasts, and includes reconstruction of the mastectomy site, creation of a new breast mound, and creation of a new nipple/areolar complex. "Reconstructive breast surgery" also includes augmentation mammoplasty, reduction mammoplasty, and mastopexy of the nondiseased breast.

(c) A policy, contract, or plan subject to this section shall not:

(1) Deny coverage described in subsection (a) of this section on the basis that the coverage is for cosmetic surgery;

(2) Deny to a woman eligibility or continued eligibility to enroll or to renew coverage under the terms of the contract, policy, or plan, solely for the purpose of avoiding the requirements of this section;

(3) Provide monetary payments or rebates to a woman to encourage her to accept less than the minimum protections available under this section;

(4) Penalize or otherwise reduce or limit the reimbursement of an attending provider because the provider provided care to an individual participant or beneficiary in accordance with this section; or

(5) Provide incentives, monetary or otherwise, to an attending provider to induce the provider to provide care to an individual participant or beneficiary in a manner inconsistent with this section.

(d) Written notice of the availability of the coverage provided by this section shall be delivered to every subscriber under an individual certificate, contract, or plan and to every certificate holder under a group policy, contract, or plan upon initial coverage under the certificate, contract, or plan and annually thereafter. The notice required by this subsection may be included as a part of any yearly informational packet sent to the subscriber or certificate holder. (1997-312, s. 2; 1997-519, s. 3.10; 1999-351, s. 3.2; 2001-334, s. 13.2.)

§ 58-65-100. Statements filed with Commissioner.

Every service corporation subject to this Article is subject to G.S. 58-2-165. (1941, c. 338, s. 9; 1999-244, s. 11.)

§ 58-65-105. Visitations and examinations.

Service corporations subject to this Article shall be examined under G.S. 58-2-131, 58-2-132, 58-2-133, and 58-2-134. (1941, c. 338, s. 10; 1995, c. 360, s. 2(l); 1999-244, s. 5.)

§ 58-65-110. Expenses.

All acquisition expenses in connection with the solicitation of subscribers to such hospital and/or medical and/or dental service plan and administration costs including salaries paid to officers of the corporations, if any, shall at all times be subject to inspection by the Commissioner of Insurance. (1941, c. 338, s. 11; 1943, c. 537, s. 6; 1961, c. 1149.)

§ 58-65-115. Licensing and regulation of agents.

Every agent of any service corporation authorized to do business in this State under this Article is subject to the licensing provisions of Article 33 of this Chapter and all other provisions in this Chapter applicable to life and health insurance agents. (1941, c. 338, s. 12; 1943, c. 537, s. 7; 1947, c. 1023, s. 1; 1961, c. 1149; 1971, c. 1080, s. 2; 1983, c. 790, s. 5; 1985 (Reg. Sess., 1986), c. 928, s. 4; 1987, c. 629, s. 2; 1999-244, s. 7.)

§ 58-65-120. Medical, dental and hospital service associations and agent to transact business through licensed agents only.

No medical and/or dental or hospital service association; nor any agent of any association shall on behalf of such association or agent, knowingly permit any person not licensed as an agent as provided by law, to solicit, negotiate for, collect or transmit a premium for a new contract of medical and/or dental or hospital service certificate or to act in any way in the negotiation for any contract or policy; provided, no license shall be required of the following:

(1) Persons designated by the association or subscriber to collect or deduct or transmit premiums or other charges for medical and/or dental care or hospital contracts, or to perform such acts as may be required for providing coverage for additional persons who are eligible under a master contract.

(2) An agency office employee acting in the confines of the agent's office, under the direction and supervision of the duly licensed agent and within the scope of such agent's license, in the acceptance of request for insurance and payment of premiums, and the performance of clerical, stenographic, and similar office duties. (1955, c. 1268; 1961, c. 1149.)

§ 58-65-125. Revocation and suspension of license; unfair trade practices.

(a) The Commissioner may revoke or suspend the license of any service corporation if:

(1) The service corporation fails or refuses to comply with any law, order, or rule applicable to the service corporation.

(2) The service corporation's financial condition is unsound.

(3) The service corporation has published or made to the Department or to the public any false statement or report.

(4) The service corporation refuses to submit to any examination authorized by law.

(5) The service corporation is found to make a practice of unduly engaging in litigation or of delaying the investigation of claims or the adjustment or payment of valid claims.

(b) Any suspension or revocation of a service corporation's license under this section may also be made applicable to the license or registration of any natural person regulated under this Chapter who is a party to any of the causes for licensing sanctions listed in subsection (a) of this section.

(c) Article 63 of this Chapter applies to service corporations and their agents and representatives. (1941, c. 338, s. 13; 1943, c. 537, s. 8; 1971, c. 1080, s. 3; 1999-244, s. 3; 1999-351, s. 8; 2003-212, s. 26(k).)

§ 58-65-130. Amendments to certificate of incorporation.

Any corporation subject to the provisions of this Article and Article 66 of this Chapter may hereafter amend its charter in the following manner only:

(1) a. A meeting of the board of directors, trustees or other governing authority shall be called in accordance with the bylaws specifying the amendment to be voted upon at such meeting.

b. If at such meeting two thirds of the directors, trustees or other governing authority present vote in favor of the proposed amendment, then the president and secretary shall under oath make a certificate to this effect, which certificate shall set forth the call for such meeting, a statement showing service of such call upon all directors, and a certified copy of so much of the minutes of the meeting as relate to the adoption of the proposed amendment.

c. Said officers shall cause said certificate to be published once a week for two consecutive weeks in a newspaper in Raleigh and in the county where the corporation's principal office is located, or posted at the courthouse door if no newspaper be published within the county. Said printed or posted notices shall be in such form and of such size as the Commissioner may approve, and in addition to setting forth in full the certificate required in paragraph b shall state that application for amending the corporation's charter in the manner specified has been proposed by the board of directors, trustees, or other governing authority, and shall also state the time set for the meeting of certificate holders thereby called to be held at the principal office of the corporation to take action on the proposed amendment. A true copy of such notice shall be filed with the Commissioner. Such publication and filing of notice shall be completed at least 30 days prior to the date set therein for the meeting of the certificate holders and due proof thereof shall be filed with the Commissioner at least 15 days prior to the date of such meeting. If the meeting at which the proposed amendment is to be considered is a special meeting, rather than a regular annual meeting of certificate holders, such special meeting can be called only after the Commissioner has given his approval in writing, and the published notice shall show the fact of such approval. At said meeting those present in person or represented by proxy shall constitute a quorum.

d. If at such certificate holders' meeting two thirds of those present in person or by proxy shall vote in favor of any proposed amendment, the president and secretary shall make a certificate under oath setting forth such fact together with the full text of the amendment thus approved. Said certificate shall, within 30 days after such meeting, be submitted to the Commissioner for his approval as conforming to the requirement of law, and it shall be the duty of the Commissioner to act upon all proposed amendments within 10 days after filing of such certificates with him. Should the Commissioner approve the proposed amendment or amendments, he shall certify this fact, together with the full text of such amendments as are approved by him, to the Secretary of State who shall thereupon issue the charter amendment in the usual form. Should the Commissioner disapprove of any amendment, then the same shall not be allowed.

(2) All charters and charter amendments heretofore issued upon application of the board of directors, trustees or other governing authority of any corporations subject to the provisions of this Article and Article 66 of this Chapter are hereby validated.

(3) The charter of any corporation subject to the provisions of this Article and Article 66 of this Chapter may be amended to convert that corporation, so amending its charter, into a stock accident and health insurance company or stock life insurance company subject to the provisions of Articles 1 through 64 of this Chapter provided the contractual rights of the subscribers and certificate holders of the corporation are adequately protected. The proposed amendment shall be considered pursuant to G.S. 58-65-131, 58-65-132, and 58-65-133. Other provisions of this section and this Article relating to the procedure for amending the charter shall not apply. (1941, c. 338, s. 15; 1947, c. 820, s. 6; 1953, c. 1124, s. 2; 1998-3, s. 1.)

§ 58-65-131. Findings; definitions; conversion plan.

(a) Intent and Findings. - It is the intent of the General Assembly by the enactment of this section, G.S. 58-65-132, and G.S. 58-65-133 to create a procedure for a medical, hospital, or dental service corporation to convert to a stock accident and health insurance company or stock life insurance company that is subject to the applicable provisions of Articles 1 through 64 of this Chapter. Except as provided herein, it is not the intent of the General Assembly to supplant, modify, or repeal other provisions of this Article and Article 66 of this Chapter or the provisions of Chapter 55A of the General Statutes (the Nonprofit Corporation Act) that govern other transactions and the procedures relating to such transactions that apply to corporations governed by the provisions of this Article and Article 66 of this Chapter.

The General Assembly recognizes the substantial and recent changes in market and health care conditions that are affecting these corporations and the benefit of equal regulatory treatment and competitive equality for health care insurers. The General Assembly finds that a procedure for conversion is in the best interest of policyholders because it will provide greater financial stability for these corporations and a greater opportunity for the corporations to remain financially independent. The General Assembly also finds that if a medical, hospital, or dental service corporation converts to a stock accident and health insurance company or stock life insurance company, the conversion plan must provide a benefit to the people of North Carolina equal to one hundred percent (100%) of the fair market value of the corporation.

(b) Definitions. - As used in this section, G.S. 58-65-132, and G.S. 58-65-133:

(1) "Certificate holder" includes an enrollee, as defined in Article 67 of this Chapter, in a health maintenance plan provided by the corporation or a subsidiary or by the new corporation or a subsidiary.

(2) "Code" means Title 26 of the United States Code, the United States Internal Revenue Code of 1986, as amended.

(3) "Conversion" means the conversion of a hospital, medical, or dental service corporation to a stock accident and health insurance company or stock life insurance company subject to the applicable provisions of Articles 1 through 64 of this Chapter.

(4) "Corporation" means a hospital, medical, or dental service corporation governed by this Article that files or is required to file a plan of conversion with the Commissioner under subsection (d) of this section to convert from a hospital, medical, or dental service corporation to a stock accident and health insurance company or stock life insurance company.

(5) "Foundation" means a newly formed tax-exempt charitable social welfare organization formed and operating under section 501(c)(4) of the Code and Chapter 55A of the General Statutes.

(6) "New corporation" means a corporation originally governed by this Article that has had its plan of conversion approved by the Commissioner under G.S. 58-65-132 and that has converted to a stock accident and health insurance company or stock life insurance company.

(c) Compliance Required in Certain Events. - A corporation governed by this Article shall comply with the provisions of this section, G.S. 58-65-132, and G.S. 58-65-133 before it may do any of the following:

(1) Sell, lease, convey, exchange, transfer, or make other disposition, either directly or indirectly in a single transaction or related series of transactions, of ten percent (10%) of the corporation's assets, as determined by statutory accounting principles, to, or merge or consolidate or liquidate with or into, any business corporation or other business entity, except a business corporation or other business entity that is a wholly owned subsidiary of the corporation. The ten percent (10%) asset limitation in this subdivision does not apply to:

a. The purchase, acquisition by assignment or otherwise by the corporation of individual accident and health policies or contracts insuring North Carolina residents, or with respect to accident and health group master policies or contracts, only the percentage portion of those policies or contracts covering North Carolina resident certificate holders, and that are issued by a company domiciled or licensed to do business in North Carolina, if the purchase is first approved by the Commissioner after notice to the Attorney General, no profit will inure to the benefit of any officer, director, or employee of the corporation or its subsidiaries, the purchase is transacted at arm's length and for fair value, and the purchase will further the corporation's ability to fulfill its purposes;

b. In the case of a purchase by the corporation of all the common stock of a company domiciled or licensed to do business in North Carolina, that portion of the value of the company which is determined by the Commissioner to be attributable to individual accident and health policies or contracts insuring North Carolina residents or, in the case of accident and health group master policies or contracts, the percentage portion of those policies or contracts covering North Carolina resident certificate holders, if the purchase is first approved by the Commissioner after notice to the Attorney General, no profit will inure to the benefit of any officer, director, or employee of the corporation or its subsidiaries, the purchase is transacted at arm's length and for fair value, and the purchase will further the corporation's ability to fulfill its purposes;

c.   Granting encumbrances such as security interests or deeds of trust with respect to assets owned by the corporation or any wholly owned subsidiary to secure indebtedness for borrowed money, the proceeds of which are paid solely to the corporation or its wholly owned subsidiaries and remain subject to the provisions of this section; and

d.   Sales or other transfers in the ordinary course of business for fair value of any interest in real property or stocks, bonds, or other securities within the investment portfolio owned by the corporation or any wholly owned subsidiary, the proceeds of which are paid solely to the corporation or any wholly owned subsidiary and remain subject to the provisions of this section.

(2)   Directly or indirectly issue, sell, convey, exchange, transfer, or make other disposition to any party of any equity or ownership interest in the corporation or in any business entity that is owned by or is a subsidiary of the corporation, including stock, securities, or bonds, debentures, notes or any other debt or similar obligation that is convertible into any equity or ownership interest, stock or securities. This subdivision shall not be construed to prohibit the corporation or a wholly owned subsidiary, with the approval of the Commissioner after notice to the Attorney General, from investing in joint ventures or partnerships with unrelated third parties, if no profit will inure to the benefit of any officer, director, or employee of the corporation or its subsidiaries, the transaction is conducted at arm's length and for fair value, and the transaction furthers the corporation's ability to fulfill its purposes.

(3)   Permit its aggregate annual revenues, determined in accordance with statutory accounting principles, from all for-profit activities or operations, including but not limited to those of the corporation, any wholly owned subsidiaries, and any joint ventures or partnerships, to exceed forty percent (40%) of the aggregate annual revenues, excluding investment income, of the corporation and its subsidiaries and determined in accordance with statutory accounting principles; or

(4)   Permit its aggregate assets for four consecutive quarters, determined in accordance with statutory accounting principles, employed in all for-profit activities or operations, including, but not limited to, those assets owned or controlled by any for-profit wholly owned subsidiaries, to exceed forty percent (40%) of the aggregate admitted assets of the corporation and its subsidiaries

for four consecutive quarters, determined in accordance with statutory accounting principles.

In determining whether the corporation must comply with the provisions of this section, G.S. 58-65-132, and G.S. 58-65-133, the Commissioner may review and consolidate actions of the corporation, its subsidiaries, and other legal entities in which the corporation directly or indirectly owns an interest, and treat the consolidated actions as requiring a conversion. An appeal of the Commissioner's order that consolidated actions require a conversion shall lie directly to the North Carolina Court of Appeals, provided that any party may petition the North Carolina Supreme Court, pursuant to G.S. 7A-31(b), to certify the case for discretionary review by the Supreme Court prior to determination by the Court of Appeals. Appeals under this subsection must be filed within 30 days of the Commissioner's order and shall be considered in the most expeditious manner practical. The corporation must file a plan of conversion within 12 months of the later of the issuance of the Commissioner's order or a final decision on appeal.

(d) Charter Amendment for Conversion. - A corporation may propose to amend its charter pursuant to this Article to convert the corporation to a stock accident and health insurance company or stock life insurance company subject to the applicable provisions of Articles 1 through 64 of this Chapter. The proposed amended charter and a plan for conversion as described in subsection (e) of this section shall be filed with the Commissioner for approval.

(e) Filing Conversion Plan; Costs of Review. - A corporation shall file a plan for conversion with the Commissioner and submit a copy to the Attorney General at least 120 days before the proposed date of conversion. The corporation or the new corporation shall reimburse the Department of Insurance and the office of the Attorney General for the actual costs of reviewing, analyzing, and processing the plan. The Commissioner and the Attorney General may contract with experts, consultants, or other professional advisors to assist in reviewing the plan. These contracts are personal professional service contracts exempt from Articles 3 and 3C of Chapter 143 of the General Statutes. Contract costs for these personal professional services shall not exceed an amount that is reasonable and appropriate for the review of the plan.

(f) Plan Requirements. - A plan of conversion submitted to the Commissioner shall state with specificity the following terms and conditions of the proposed conversion:

(1) The purposes of the conversion.

(2) The proposed articles of incorporation of the new corporation.

(3) The proposed bylaws of the new corporation.

(4) A description of any changes in the new corporation's mode of operations after conversion.

(5) A statement describing the manner in which the plan provides for the protection of all existing contractual rights of the corporation's subscribers and certificate holders to medical or hospital services or the payment of claims for reimbursement for those services. The corporation's subscribers and certificate holders shall have no right to receive any assets, surplus, capital, payment or distribution or to receive any stock or other ownership interest in the new corporation in connection with the conversion.

(6) A statement that the legal existence of the corporation does not terminate and that the new corporation is subject to all liabilities, obligations, and relations of whatever kind of the corporation and succeeds to all property, assets, rights, interests, and relations of the corporation.

(7) Documentation showing that the corporation, acting by its board of directors, trustees, or other governing authority, has approved the plan. It shall not be necessary for the subscribers or certificate holders of the corporation to vote on or approve the plan of conversion, any amendments to the corporation's articles of incorporation or bylaws, or the articles of incorporation or the bylaws of the new corporation, notwithstanding any provision to the contrary in this Article or Article 66 of this Chapter or in the articles of incorporation or bylaws of the corporation.

(8) The business plan of the new corporation, including, but not limited to, a comparative premium rate analysis of the new corporation's major plans and product offerings, that, among other things, compares actual premium rates for the three-year period before the filing of the plan for conversion and forecasted premium rates for a three-year period following the proposed conversion. This rate analysis shall address the forecasted effect, if any, of the proposed conversion on the cost to policyholders or certificate holders of the new corporation and on the new corporation's underwriting profit, investment income, and loss and claim reserves, including the effect, if any, of adverse market or

risk selection upon these reserves. Information provided under this subsection is confidential pursuant to G.S. 58-19-40.

(9) Any conditions, other than approval of the plan of conversion by the Commissioner, to be fulfilled by a proposed date upon which the conversion would become effective.

(10) The proposed articles of incorporation and bylaws of the Foundation, containing the provisions required by G.S. 58-65-133(h).

(11) Any proposed agreement between the Foundation and the new corporation, including, but not limited to, any agreement relating to the voting or registration for sale of any capital stock to be issued by the new corporation to the Foundation.

(g) Public Comment. - Within 20 days of receiving a plan to convert, the Commissioner shall publish a notice in one or more newspapers of general circulation in the corporation's service area describing the name of the corporation, the nature of the plan filed under G.S. 58-65-131(d), and the date of receipt of the plan. The notice shall indicate that the Commissioner will solicit public comments and hold three public hearings on the plan. The public hearings must be completed within 60 days of the filing of the conversion plan. The written public comment period will be held open until 10 days after the last public hearing. For good cause the Commissioner may extend these deadlines once for a maximum of 30 days. The Commissioner shall provide copies of all written public comments to the Attorney General.

(h) Public Access to Records. - All applications, reports, plans, or other documents under this section, G.S. 58-65-132, and G.S. 58-65-133 are public records unless otherwise provided in this Chapter. The Commissioner shall provide the public with prompt and reasonable access to public records relating to the proposed conversion of the corporation. Access to public records covered by this section shall be made available for at least 30 days before the end of the public comment period. (1998-3, s. 2.)

§ 58-65-132. Review and approval of conversion plan; new corporation.

(a) Approval of Plan of Conversion. - The Commissioner shall approve the plan of conversion and issue a certificate of authority to the new corporation to transact business in this State only if the Commissioner finds all of the following:

(1) The plan of conversion meets the requirements of G.S. 58-65-131, this section, and G.S. 58-65-133.

(2) Upon conversion, the new corporation will meet the applicable standards and conditions under this Chapter, including applicable minimum capital and surplus requirements.

(3) The plan of conversion adequately protects the existing contractual rights of the corporation's subscribers and certificate holders to medical or hospital services and payment of claims for reimbursement for those services.

(4) No director, officer, or employee of the corporation will receive:

a. Any fee, commission, compensation, or other valuable consideration for aiding, promoting, or assisting in the conversion of the corporation other than compensation paid to any director, officer, or employee of the corporation in the ordinary course of business; or

b. Any distribution of the assets, surplus, capital, or capital stock of the new corporation as part of a conversion.

(5) The corporation has complied with all material requirements of this Chapter, and disciplinary action is not pending against the corporation.

(6) The plan of conversion is fair and equitable and not prejudicial to the contractual rights of the policyholders and certificate holders of the new corporation.

(7) The plan of conversion is in the public interest. The Commissioner shall find that the plan is in the public interest only if it provides a benefit for the people of North Carolina equal to the value of the corporation at the time of conversion, in accordance with the criteria set out in this subdivision. In determining whether the plan of conversion is in the public interest, the Commissioner may also consider other factors, including, but not limited to, those relating to the accessibility and affordability of health care. The Commissioner must determine that the plan of conversion meets all of the following criteria:

a. Consideration, determined by the Commissioner to be equal to one hundred percent (100%) of the fair market value of the corporation, will be conveyed or issued by the corporation to the Foundation at the time the new corporation files its articles of incorporation. If the consideration to be conveyed is all of the common stock of the new corporation that is then issued and outstanding at the time of conversion, and there is no other capital stock of any type or nature then outstanding, it is conclusively presumed that the Foundation will acquire the fair market value of the corporation.

b. At any time after the conversion, the new corporation may issue, in a public offering or a private placement, additional shares of common stock of the same class and having the same voting, dividend, and other rights as that transferred to the Foundation, subject to the applicable provisions of Chapter 55 of the General Statutes and any voting and registration agreements.

(8) The plan of conversion contains a proposed voting agreement and registration agreement between the Foundation and the proposed new corporation that meets the requirements of G.S. 58-65-133.

(9) The Attorney General has given approval pursuant to G.S. 58-65-133(h).

(b) New Corporation. - After issuance of the certificate of authority as provided in subsection (a) of this section, the new corporation shall no longer be subject to this Article and Article 66 of this Chapter but shall be subject to and comply with all applicable laws and regulations applicable to domestic insurers and Chapter 55 of the General Statutes, except that Articles 9 and 9A of Chapter 55 shall not apply to the new corporation. The new corporation shall file its articles of incorporation, as amended and certified by the Commissioner, with the North Carolina Secretary of State. The legal existence of the corporation does not terminate, and the new corporation is a continuation of the corporation. The conversion shall only be a change in identity and form of organization. Except as provided in subdivision (a)(7) of this subsection, all property, assets, rights, liabilities, obligations, interests, and relations of whatever kind of the corporation shall continue and remain in the new corporation. All actions and legal proceedings to which the corporation was a party prior to conversion shall be unaffected by the conversion.

(c) Final Decision and Order; Procedures. - The Commissioner's final decision and order regarding the plan of conversion shall include findings of fact and conclusions of law. Findings of fact shall be based upon and supported by substantial evidence, including evidence submitted with the plan by the corporation and evidence obtained at hearings held by the Commissioner. A person aggrieved by a final decision of the Commissioner approving or disapproving a conversion may petition the Superior Court of Wake County within 30 days thereafter for judicial review. An appeal from a final decision and order of the Commissioner under this section shall be conducted pursuant to G.S. 58-2-75. Chapter 150B of the General Statutes does not apply to the procedures of G.S. 58-65-131, this section, and G.S. 58-65-133. This subsection does not apply to appeal of an order of the Commissioner issued pursuant to G.S. 58-65-131(c).

(d) Attorney General's Enforcement Authority; Legal Action on Validity of Plan of Conversion. -

(1) Nothing in this Chapter limits the power of the Attorney General to seek a declaratory judgment or to take other legal action to protect or enforce the rights of the public in the corporation.

(2) Any legal action with respect to the conversion must be filed in the Superior Court of Wake County. (1998-3, s. 2.)

§ 58-65-133. Creation and operation of foundation.

(a) Creation. - A Foundation shall be created to receive the fair market value of the corporation as provided in G.S. 58-65-132(a)(7) when the corporation converts.

(b) Purpose. - The charitable purpose of the Foundation shall be to promote the health of the people of North Carolina. For a period of 10 years from the effective date of the conversion, the Foundation may not, without the consent of the Attorney General, establish or operate any entity licensed pursuant to Chapter 58 of the General Statutes that would compete with the new corporation or any of its subsidiaries.

(c) Board of Directors. - The initial board of directors of the foundation shall consist of 11 members appointed by the Attorney General from a list of nominees recommended pursuant to subsection (d) of this section. The Attorney General shall stagger the terms of the initial appointees so that six members serve two-year terms and five members serve four-year terms. The board shall fill a vacancy in an initial term. Their successors shall be chosen by the board of directors of the Foundation in accordance with the bylaws of the Foundation and shall serve four-year terms. No member may serve more than two consecutive full terms nor more than 10 consecutive years. The Foundation may increase or decrease the size of the board in accordance with its bylaws, provided that the board shall have no fewer than nine directors and no more than 15 directors and that a decrease in size does not eliminate the then current term of any director.

(d) Advisory Committee. - An advisory committee shall be formed to (i) develop, subject to the approval of the Attorney General, the criteria for selection of the Foundation's initial board of directors and (ii) nominate candidates for the initial board of directors. The advisory committee shall be comprised of the following 11 members: three representatives of the business community selected by the North Carolina Chamber, three representatives of the public and private medical school community selected by The University of North Carolina Board of Governors, three representatives of private foundations and other nonprofit organizations selected by the North Carolina Center for Nonprofits, a representative of NCHA, Inc., and a representative of the North Carolina Medical Society. After receiving a copy of the proposed plan of conversion, the Attorney General shall immediately notify these organizations, and the advisory committee shall be constituted within 45 days thereafter.

The advisory committee's criteria shall ensure an open recruitment process for the directors. The advisory committee shall nominate 22 residents of North Carolina for the 11 positions to be filled by the Attorney General. The Attorney General shall retain an independent executive recruiting firm or firms to assist the advisory committee in its work.

(e) Foundation and New Corporation Independent. - The Foundation and its directors, officers, and employees shall be and remain independent of the new corporation and its affiliates. No director, officer, or employee of the Foundation shall serve as a director, officer, or employee of the new corporation or any of its affiliates. No director, officer, or employee of the new corporation or any of its affiliates shall serve as a director, officer, or employee of the Foundation. This subsection shall no longer apply after (i) 10 years following the effective date of the conversion or (ii) the divestment by the Foundation of at least ninety-five percent (95%) of the stock of the new corporation received pursuant to G.S. 58-65-132(a)(7)a. and subsection (a) of this section, whichever occurs later.

(f) Voting and Stock Registration Agreement. - The Foundation and the new corporation shall operate under a voting agreement and a stock registration agreement, approved by the Commissioner and the Attorney General, that provides at a minimum for the following:

(1) The Foundation will vote the common stock in the new corporation for directors of the new corporation nominated by the board of directors of the new corporation to the extent provided by the terms of the voting agreement.

(2) The voting restrictions will not apply to common stock of the new corporation sold by the Foundation.

(3) The board of directors of the new corporation will determine the timing of any initial public offering of the new corporation's common stock, either by the new corporation or by the Foundation, and the Foundation shall have demand registration rights and optional "piggy-back" or "incidental" registration rights in connection with any offerings of the new corporation's common stock by the new corporation, on the terms and conditions set forth in a stock registration agreement and agreed upon by the new corporation and the Foundation and approved by the Commissioner and the Attorney General.

(4) The voting agreement may contain additional terms, including (i) voting and ownership restrictions with regard to the common stock of the new corporation and (ii) provisions for the voting or registration for sale of any common stock to be issued to the Foundation by the new corporation.

(g) Costs. - The corporation shall pay the reasonable expenses of the advisory committee and executive search firm and the costs of any consultants, experts, or other professional advisors retained by the Attorney General incident to review under this section.

(h) Attorney General's Approval. - Before the Commissioner approves a plan of conversion pursuant to G.S. 58-65-132, the Attorney General, on behalf of the public and charitable interests in this State, must approve the determination relating to the fair market value of the corporation under G.S. 58-65-132(a)(7), the articles of incorporation and bylaws of the foundation, and all proposed agreements between the new corporation and the Foundation, including stock voting or registration agreements. The Attorney General may seek advice on these matters from consultants, investment bankers, and other professional advisors engaged by the Commissioner or Attorney General incident to review of the plan. The proposed articles of incorporation of the Foundation shall provide for all of the following:

(1) State that the Foundation is organized and operated exclusively for charitable purposes and for the promotion of social welfare.

(2) State that no part of the net earnings of the Foundation shall inure to the benefit of any private shareholder or individual.

(3) State that the Foundation shall not engage in any political campaign activity or the making of political contributions.

(4) Prohibit the Foundation from paying or incurring any amount that, if paid by an organization classified as a "private foundation" under section 509(a) of the Code, would constitute a "taxable expenditure" as defined by sections 4945(d)(1) and (2) of the Code.

(5) Prohibit the Foundation from engaging in any self-dealing for the benefit of its directors, officers, or employees.

(6) Provide for an ongoing community advisory committee to offer broad public input to the Foundation concerning its operations and activities.

(7) Provide that the Foundation, after its first three years of operation, will pay out the lesser of (i) "qualifying distributions" of "distributable amounts," as defined in section 4942 of the Code, as if the Foundation were classified as a private Foundation subject to the distribution requirements, but not the taxes imposed, under that section or (ii) substantially all of its income, less qualifying expenses. In no event shall the Foundation be required to invade its corpus to meet the distribution requirements under this subdivision.

(8) State that provisions in the articles of incorporation that are either required by this subdivision or designated by the Attorney General cannot be amended without the prior written approval of the Attorney General.

Within 120 days of the end of its fiscal year, the Foundation shall provide the Attorney General, the Commissioner, the Speaker of the House of Representatives, and the President Pro Tempore of the Senate its State and federal tax returns for the preceding fiscal year. The tax returns shall be made available for public inspection. (1998-3, s. 2; 1998-217, s. 56; 2009-570, s. 8(b).)

§ 58-65-135. Cost plus plans.

Any corporation organized under the provisions of this Article and Article 66 of this Chapter shall be authorized as agent of any other corporation, firm, group, partnership, or association, or any subsidiary or subsidiaries thereof, municipal corporation, State, federal government, or any agency thereof, to administer on behalf of such corporation, firm, group, partnership, or association, or any subsidiary or subsidiaries thereof, municipal corporation, State, federal government, or any agency thereof, any group hospitalization or medical and/or dental service plan, promulgated by such corporation, firm, group, partnership, or association, or any subsidiary or subsidiaries thereof, municipal corporation, State, federal government, or any agency thereof, on a cost plus administrative expense basis, provided said other corporation, firm, group, partnership, or association, or any subsidiary or subsidiaries thereof, municipal corporation, State, federal government, or any agency thereof shall have had an active existence for at least one year preceding the establishment of such plan, and was formed for purposes other than procuring such group hospitalization and/or medical and/or dental service coverage in a cost plus administrative expense basis, and provided only that administrative costs of such a cost plus plan administered by a corporation organized under the provisions of this Article and Article 66 of this Chapter, acting as an agent as herein provided, shall not exceed the remuneration received therefor, and provided further that the corporation organized under this Article and Article 66 of this Chapter administering such a plan shall have no liability to the subscribers or to the hospitals for the success or failure, liquidation or dissolution of such group hospitalization or medical and/or dental service plan and provided further, that nothing herein contained shall be construed to require of said corporation, firm, group, partnership, or association, or any subsidiary or subsidiaries thereof, municipal corporation, State, federal government, or any agency thereof, conformity to the provisions of this Article and Article 66 of this Chapter if such group hospitalization is administered by a corporation organized under this Article and Article 66 of this Chapter, on a cost plus expense basis. The administration of any cost plus plans as herein provided shall not be subject to regulation or supervision by the Commissioner of Insurance. (1941, c. 338, s. 16; 1943, c. 537, s. 9; 1947, c. 820, s. 7; 1961, c. 1149.)

§ 58-65-140: Repealed by Session Laws 1997-519, s. 3.16.

§ 58-65-145. Preexisting hospital service corporations.

No corporations organized under the laws of this State prior to the ratification of this Article and Article 66 of this Chapter, for the purposes herein provided, shall be required to reincorporate as provided for herein, and the provisions of this Article and Article 66 of this Chapter shall apply to said corporations only with regard to operations by said corporations with respect to subscribers' contracts, participating hospital contracts, reserves, investments, reports, visitations, expenses, taxation, amendments to charters, supervision of Commissioner of Insurance, application for certificate, issuance of certificates, licensing of agents after the date of the passage of this Article and Article 66 of this Chapter, provided, however, as soon as practical hereafter and in accordance with rules and regulations adopted by the Commissioner of Insurance said corporations shall conform to this Article and Article 66 of this Chapter as near as practical with respect to subscribers' contracts, endorsements, riders, and applications entered into prior to the ratification of this Article and Article 66 of this Chapter. (1941, c. 338, s. 17.)

§ 58-65-150. Construction of Chapter as to single employer plans; associations exempt.

Nothing in this Article and Article 66 of this Chapter shall be construed to affect or apply to hospital or medical and/or dental service plans which limit their membership to employees and the immediate members of the families of the employees of a single employer or his or its subsidiary or subsidiaries and which plans are operated by such employer of such limited group of the employees; nor shall this Article and Article 66 of this Chapter be construed to affect or apply to any nonstock, nonprofit medical service association which was, on January 1, 1943, organized solely for the purpose of, and actually engaged in, the administration of any medical service plan in this State upon contracts and participating agreements with physicians, surgeons, or medical societies, whereby such physicians or surgeons underwrite such plan by contributing their services to members of such association upon agreement with such association as to the schedule of fees to apply and the rate and method of payment by the association from the common fund paid in periodically by the members for medical, surgical and obstetrical care; and such hospital service plans, and such medical service associations as are herein specifically described, are hereby exempt from the provisions of this Article and Article 66 of this Chapter. The Commissioner of Insurance may require from any such hospital service plan or medical service association such information as will enable him to determine whether such hospital service plan or medical service association is exempt from the provisions of this Article and Article 66 of this Chapter. (1941, c. 338, s. 18; 1943, c. 537, s. 10; 1947, c. 140; 1961, c. 1149.)

§ 58-65-155. Merger or consolidation, proceedings for.

Any two or more hospital and/or medical and/or dental service corporations organized under and/or subject to the provisions of this Article and Article 66 of this Chapter as determined by the Commissioner of Insurance may, as shall be specified in the agreement hereinafter required, be merged into one of such constituent corporations, herein designated as the surviving corporation, or may be consolidated into a new corporation to be formed by the means of such consolidation of the constituent corporations, which new corporation is herein designated as the resulting or consolidated corporation, and the directors and/or trustees, or a majority of them, of such corporations as desire to consolidate or merge, may enter into an agreement signed by them and under the corporate seals of the respective corporations, prescribing the terms and conditions of consolidation or merger, the mode of carrying the same into effect and stating such other facts as can be stated in the case of a consolidation or merger, stated in such altered form as the circumstances of the case require, and with such other details as to conversion of certificates of the subscribers as are deemed necessary and/or proper.

Said agreement shall be submitted to the certificate holders of each constituent corporation, at a separate meeting thereof, called for the purpose of taking the same into consideration; of the time, place and object of which meeting due notice shall be given by publication once a week for two consecutive weeks in some newspaper published in Raleigh, North Carolina, and in the counties in which the principal offices of the constituent corporations are located, and if no such paper is published in the county of the principal office of such constituent corporations, then said notice shall be posted at the courthouse door of said county or counties for a period of two weeks.

Said printed or posted notices shall be in such form and of such size as the Commissioner of Insurance may approve. A true copy of said notices shall be filed with the Commissioner of Insurance.

Such publication and filing of notices shall be completed at least 15 days prior to the date set therein for the meeting, and due proof thereof shall be filed with the Commissioner of Insurance at least 10 days prior to the date of such meeting.

At this meeting those present in person or represented by proxy shall constitute a quorum and said agreement shall be considered and voted upon by ballot in person or by proxy or both taken for the adoption or rejection of the same; and if the votes of two thirds of those at said meeting voting in person or by proxy shall be for the adoption of the said agreement, then that fact shall be certified on said agreement by the president and secretary of each such corporation, under the seal thereof.

The agreement so adopted and certified shall be signed by the president or vice-president and secretary or assistant secretary of each of such corporations under the corporate seals thereof and acknowledged by the president or vice-president of each such corporation before any officer authorized by the laws of this State to take acknowledgement of deeds to be the respective act, deed, and agreement of each of said corporations.

The said agreement shall be submitted to and approved by the Commissioner of Insurance, in advance of the merger or consolidation and his approval thereof shall be indicated by his signature being affixed thereto under the seal of his office.

The Commissioner shall not approve any such plans, unless, after a hearing, he finds that it is fair, equitable to certificate holders and members, consistent with law, and will not conflict with the public interest.

The agreement so certified and acknowledged with the approval of the Commissioner of Insurance noted thereon, shall be filed in the office of the Secretary of State, and shall thenceforth be taken and deemed to be the agreement and act of consolidation or merger of said corporations; and a copy of said agreement and act of consolidation or merger duly certified by the Secretary of State under the seal of his office shall also be recorded, in the office of the register of deeds of the county of this State in which the principal office of the surviving or consolidated corporation is, or is to be established, and in the office of the registers of deeds of the counties of this State in which the respective corporations so merging or consolidating shall have their original certificates of incorporation recorded, and also in the office of the register of deeds in each county in which either or any of the corporations entering into merger or consolidation owns any real estate; and such record, or a certified copy thereof, shall be evidence of the agreement and act of consolidation or merger of said corporations, and of the observance and performance of all acts and conditions necessary to have been observed and performed precedent to such consolidation or merger. When an agreement shall have been signed, authorized, adopted, acknowledged, approved, and filed and recorded as hereinabove set forth in this section, for all purposes of the laws of this State, the separate existence of all constituent corporations, parties to said agreement, or of all such constituent corporations, except the one into which the other or others of such constituent corporations have been merged, as the case may be, shall cease and the constituent corporations shall become a new corporation, or be merged into one of such corporations, as the case may be, in accordance with the provisions of said agreement, possessing all the rights, privileges, powers and franchises as well of a public as of a private nature, of each of said constituent corporations, and all and singular, the rights, privileges, powers and franchises of each of said corporations, and all property, real, personal and mixed, and all debts due to any of said constituent corporations on whatever account, shall be vested in the corporation resulting from or surviving such consolidation or merger, and all property, rights, privileges, powers, and franchises and all and every other interest shall be thereafter as effectually the property of the resulting or surviving corporation as they were of the several and respective constituent corporations, and the title to any real estate, whether vested by deed or otherwise, under the laws of this State, vested in any such constituent corporations shall not revert or be in any way impaired by reason of such consolidation or merger; provided, however, that all rights of creditors and all liens upon the property of either of or any of said constituent corporations shall be preserved, unimpaired, limited in lien to the property affected by such lien at the time of the merger or consolidation, and all debts, liabilities, and duties of the respective constituent corporations shall thenceforth attach to said resulting or surviving corporation, and may be enforced against it to the same extent as if said debts, liabilities, and duties had been incurred or contracted by it; and further provided that notice of any said liens, debts, liabilities, and duties is given in writing to the resulting or surviving corporation within six months after the date of the filing of the agreement of merger in the office of the Secretary of State. All such liens, debts, liabilities, and duties of which notice is not given as provided herein are forever barred. The certificate of incorporation of the surviving corporation shall be deemed to be amended to the extent, if any, that the changes in its certificates of incorporation are stated in the agreement of merger. All certificates theretofore issued and outstanding by each constituent corporation in good standing upon the date of the filing of such agreement with the Secretary of State without reissuance thereof by the resulting or surviving corporation shall be the contract and agreement of the resulting or surviving corporation with each of the certificate holders thereof and subject to all terms and conditions thereof and of the agreement of merger filed in the office of the Secretary of State.

Any action or proceeding pending by or against any of the corporations consolidated or merged may be prosecuted to judgment as if such consolidation or merger had not taken place, or the corporations resulting from or surviving such consolidation or merger may be substituted in its place.

The liability of such constituent corporations to the certificate holders thereof, and the rights or remedies of the creditors thereof, or persons doing or transacting business with such corporations, shall not, in any way, be lessened or impaired by the consolidation or merger of two or more of such corporations under the provisions of this section, except as provided in this section.

When two or more corporations are consolidated or merged, the corporation resulting from or surviving such consolidation or merger shall have the power and authority to continue any contracts which any of the constituent corporations might have elected to continue. All contracts entered into between any constituent corporations and any other persons shall be and become the contract of the resulting corporations according to the terms and conditions of said contract and the agreement of consolidation or merger.

For the filing of the agreement as hereinabove provided, the Secretary of State is entitled to receive such fees only as he would have received had a new corporation been formed.

Any agreement for merger and/or consolidation as shall conform to the provisions of this section, shall be binding and valid upon all the subscribers, certificate holders and/or members of such constituent corporations, provided only that any subscriber, certificate holder and/or member who shall so indicate his disapproval thereof to the resulting, consolidated or surviving corporation within 90 days after the filing of said agreement with the Secretary of State shall be entitled to receive all unearned portions of premiums paid on his certificate from and after the date of the receipt of the application therefor by the resulting, surviving, or consolidated corporation; each subscriber, certificate holder and/or member who shall not so indicate his or her disapproval of said agreement and said merger within said period of 90 days is deemed and presumed to have approved said agreement and said merger and/or consolidation and shall have waived his or her right to question the legality of said merger and/or consolidation.

No director, officer, subscriber, certificate holder and/or member as such of any such corporation, except as is expressly provided by the plan of merger or consolidation, shall receive any fee, commission, other compensation or valuable consideration whatever, for in any manner aiding, promoting or assisting in the merger or consolidation. (1947, c. 820, s. 8; 1961, c. 1149; 1967, c. 823, s. 25.)

§ 58-65-160: Repealed by Session Laws 1998-3, s. 3.

§ 58-65-165. Commissioner of Insurance determines corporations exempt from this Article and Article 66 of this Chapter.

The Commissioner of Insurance may require from any corporation writing any hospital service contracts and any corporation writing medical and/or dental service contracts or any or all of them, such information as will enable him to determine whether such corporation is subject to the provisions of this Article and Article 66 of this Chapter. (1947, c. 820, s. 9; 1961, c. 1149.)

Part 2. Indemnification.

§ 58-65-166. Policy statement and definitions.

(a) It is the public policy of this State to enable corporations organized under this Chapter to attract and maintain responsible, qualified directors, officers, employees, and agents, and, to that end, to permit corporations organized under this Chapter to allocate the risk of personal liability of directors, officers, employees, and agents through indemnification and insurance as authorized in this Part.

(b) Definitions in this Part:

(1) "Corporation" includes any not for profit domestic hospital, medical, or dental service corporation, or successor of a corporation in a merger or other transaction in which the predecessor's existence ceased upon consummation of the transaction.

(2) "Director" or "Trustee" means an individual who is or was a director of a corporation or an individual who, while a director of a corporation, is or was serving at the corporation's request as a director, officer, partner, trustee, employee, or agent of another foreign or domestic corporation, partnership, joint venture, trust, employee benefit plan, or other enterprise. A director is considered to be serving an employee benefit plan at the corporation's request if his duties to the corporation also impose duties on, or otherwise involve services by, him to the plan or to participants in or beneficiaries of the plan. "Director" or "Trustee" includes, unless the context requires otherwise, the estate or personal representative of a director or trustee.

(3) "Expenses" means expenses of every kind incurred in defending a proceeding, including counsel fees.

(4) "Liability" means the obligation to pay a judgment, settlement, penalty, fine (including an excise tax assessed with respect to an employee benefit plan), or reasonable expenses incurred with respect to a proceeding.

(5) "Official capacity" means: (i) when used with respect to a director or trustee, the office of director or trustee in a corporation; and (ii) when used with respect to an individual other than a director or trustee, as contemplated in G.S. 58-65-172, the office in a corporation held by the officer or the employment or agency relationship undertaken by the employee or agent on behalf of the corporation. "Official capacity" does not include service for any other foreign or domestic corporation or any partnership, joint venture, trust, employee benefit plan, or other enterprise.

(6) "Party" includes an individual who was, is, or is threatened to be made a named defendant or respondent in a proceeding.

(7) "Proceeding" means any threatened, pending, or completed action, suit, or proceeding, whether civil, criminal, administrative, or investigative and whether formal or informal.

(8) "Trustee". Whenever the term "director" or "directors" is used herein it shall include the term "trustee", or a person who is designated as a "trustee" under a corporation governed by this Article. (1989 (Reg. Sess., 1990), c. 1071, s. 1.)

§ 58-65-167. Authority to indemnify.

(a) Except as provided in subsection (d), a corporation may indemnify an individual made a party to a proceeding because he is or was a director against liability incurred in the proceeding if:

(1) He conducted himself in good faith; and

(2) He reasonably believed (i) in the case of conduct in his official capacity with the corporation, that his conduct was in its best interests; and (ii) in all other cases, that his conduct was at least not opposed to its best interests; and

(3) In the case of any criminal proceeding, he had no reasonable cause to believe his conduct was unlawful.

(b) A director's conduct with respect to an employee benefit plan for a purpose he reasonably believed to be in the interests of the participants in and beneficiaries of the plan is conduct that satisfies the requirement of subsection (a)(2)(ii).

(c) The termination of a proceeding by judgment, order, settlement, conviction, or upon a plea of no contest or its equivalent is not, of itself, determinative that the director did not meet the standard of conduct described in this section.

(d) A corporation may not indemnify a director under this section:

(1) In connection with a proceeding by or in the right of the corporation in which the director was adjudged liable to the corporation; or

(2) In connection with any other proceeding charging improper personal benefit to him, whether or not involving action in his official capacity, in which he was adjudged liable on the basis that personal benefit was improperly received by him.

(e) Indemnification permitted under this section in connection with a proceeding by or in the right of the corporation that is concluded without a final adjudication on the issue of liability is limited to reasonable expenses incurred in connection with the proceeding.

(f) The authorization, approval or favorable recommendation by the board of directors of a corporation of indemnification, as permitted by this section, shall not be deemed an act or corporate transaction in which a director has a conflict of interest, and no such indemnification shall be void or voidable on such ground. (1989 (Reg. Sess., 1990), c. 1071, s. 1.)

§ 58-65-168. Mandatory indemnification.

Unless limited by its articles of incorporation, a corporation shall indemnify a director who was wholly successful, on the merits or otherwise, in the defense of any proceeding to which he was a party because he is or was a director of the corporation against reasonable expenses incurred by him in connection with the proceeding. (1989 (Reg. Sess., 1990), c. 1071, s. 1.)

§ 58-65-169. Advance for expenses.

Expenses incurred by a director in defending a proceeding may be paid by the corporation in advance of the final disposition of such proceeding as authorized by the board of directors in the specific case or as authorized or required under any provision in the articles of incorporation or bylaws or by any applicable resolution or contract upon receipt of an undertaking by or on behalf of the director to repay such amount unless it shall ultimately be determined that he is entitled to be indemnified by the corporation against such expenses. (1989 (Reg. Sess., 1990), c. 1071, s. 1.)

§ 58-65-170. Court-ordered indemnification.

Unless a corporation's articles of incorporation provide otherwise, a director of the corporation who is a party to a proceeding may apply for indemnification to the court conducting the proceeding or to another court of competent jurisdiction. On receipt of an application, the court after giving any notice the court considers necessary may order indemnification if it determines:

(1) The director is entitled to mandatory indemnification under G.S. 58-65-168, in which case the court shall also order the corporation to pay the director's reasonable expenses incurred to obtain court-ordered indemnification; or

(2) The director is fairly and reasonably entitled to indemnification in view of all the relevant circumstances, whether or not he met the standard of conduct set forth in G.S. 58-65-167 or was adjudged liable as described in G.S. 58-65-167(d), but if he was adjudged so liable his indemnification is limited to reasonable expenses incurred. (1989 (Reg. Sess., 1990), c. 1071, s. 1.)

§ 58-65-171. Determination and authorization of indemnification.

(a) A corporation may not indemnify a director under G.S. 58-65-167 unless authorized in the specific case after a determination has been made that indemnification of the director is permissible in the circumstances because he has met the standard of conduct set forth in G.S. 58-65-167.

(b) The determination shall be made:

(1) By the board of directors by majority vote of a quorum consisting of directors not at the time parties to the proceeding;

(2) If a quorum cannot be obtained under subdivision (1), by majority vote of a committee duly designated by the board of directors (in which designation directors who are parties may participate), consisting solely of two or more directors not at the time parties to the proceeding;

(3) By special legal counsel (i) selected by the board of directors or its committee in the manner prescribed in subdivision (1) or (2); or (ii) if a quorum of the board of directors cannot be obtained under subdivision (1) and a committee cannot be designated under subdivision (2), selected by majority vote of the full board of directors (in which selection directors who are parties may participate); or

(4) By the shareholders, but shares owned by or voted under the control of directors who are at the time parties to the proceeding may not be voted on the determination.

(c) Authorization of indemnification and evaluation as to reasonableness of expenses shall be made in the same manner as the determination that indemnification is permissible, except that if the determination is made by special legal counsel, authorization of indemnification and evaluation as to reasonableness of expenses shall be made by those entitled under subsection (b)(3) to select counsel. (1989 (Reg. Sess., 1990), c. 1071, s. 1.)

§ 58-65-172. Indemnification of officers, employees, and agents.

Unless a corporation's articles of incorporation provide otherwise:

(1) An officer of the corporation is entitled to mandatory indemnification under G.S. 58-65-168 and is entitled to apply for court-ordered indemnification under G.S. 58-65-170, in each case to the same extent as a director;

(2) The corporation may indemnify and advance expenses under this Part to an officer, employee, or agent of the corporation to the same extent as to a director; and

(3) A corporation may also indemnify and advance expenses to an officer, employee, or agent who is not a director to the extent, consistent with public policy, that may be provided by its articles of incorporation, bylaws, general or specific action of its board of directors, or contract. (1989 (Reg. Sess., 1990), c. 107´, s. 1; 1995, c. 193, s. 56.)

§ 58-65-173. Additional indemnification and insurance.

(a) In addition to and separate and apart from the indemnification provided for in G.S. 58-65-167, 58-65-168, 58-65-170, 58-65-171, and 58-65-172, a corporation may in its articles of incorporation or bylaws or by contract or resolution indemnify or agree to indemnify any one or more of its directors, officers, employees, or agents against liability and expenses in any proceeding (including without limitation a proceeding brought by or on behalf of the corporation itself) arising out of their status as such or their activities in any of the foregoing capacities; provided, however, that a corporation may not indemnify or agree to indemnify a person against liability or expenses he may incur on account of his activities which were at the time taken known or believed by him to be clearly in conflict with the best interests of the corporation. A corporation may likewise and to the same extent indemnify or agree to indemnify any person who, at the request of the corporation, is or was serving as a director, officer, partner, trustee, employee, or agent of another foreign or domestic corporation, partnership, joint venture, trust or other enterprise or as a trustee or administrator under an employee benefit plan. Any provision in any articles of incorporation, bylaw, contract, or resolution permitted under this section may include provisions for recovery from the corporation of reasonable costs, expenses, and attorneys' fees in connection with the enforcement of rights to indemnification granted therein and may further include provisions establishing reasonable procedures for determining and enforcing the rights granted therein.

(b) The authorization, adoption, approval, or favorable recommendation by the board of directors of a corporation of any provision in any articles of incorporation, bylaw, contract or resolution, as permitted in this section, shall not be deemed an act or corporate transaction in which a director has a conflict of interest, and no such articles of incorporation or bylaw provision or contract or resolution shall be void or voidable on such grounds. The authorization, adoption, approval, or favorable recommendation by the board of directors of a corporation of any provision in any articles of incorporation, bylaw, contract or resolution, as permitted in this section, which occurred on or prior to the effective date of this act, shall not be deemed an act or corporate transaction in which a director has a conflict of interest, and no such articles of incorporation, bylaw provision, contract or resolution shall be void or voidable on such grounds.

(c) A corporation may purchase and maintain insurance on behalf of an individual who is or was a director, officer, employee, or agent of the corporation, or who, while a director, officer, employee, or agent of the corporation, is or was serving at the request of the corporation as a director, officer, partner, trustee, employee, or agent of another foreign or domestic corporation, partnership, joint venture, trust, employee benefit plan, or other enterprise, against liability asserted against or incurred by him in that capacity or arising from his status as a director, officer, employee, or agent, whether or not the corporation would have power to indemnify him against the same liability under any provision of this Chapter. (1989 (Reg. Sess., 1990), c. 1071, s. 1; 1991, c. 172.)

§ 58-65-174. Application of Part.

(a)   If articles of incorporation limit indemnification or advance for expenses, indemnification and advance for expenses are valid only to the extent consistent with the articles.

(b)   This Part does not limit a corporation's power to pay or reimburse expenses incurred by a director in connection with his appearance as a witness in a proceeding at a time when he has not been made a named defendant or respondent to the proceeding.

(c)   This Part shall not affect rights or liabilities arising out of acts or omissions occurring before October 1, 1990. (1989 (Reg. Sess., 1990), c. 1071, s. 1.)

Article 66.

Hospital, Medical and Dental Service Corporation Readable Insurance Certificates Act.

§ 58-66-1. Title.

This Article is known and may be cited as the "Hospital, Medical and Dental Service Corporation Readable Insurance Certificates Act." (1979, 2nd Sess., c. 1161, s. 1.)

§ 58-66-5. Purpose.

The purpose of this Article is to provide that insurance certificates and subscriber contracts under this Article and Article 65 of this Chapter be readable by a person of average intelligence, experience, and education. All insurers are required by this Article to use certificate and contract forms and, where applicable, benefit booklets that are written in simple and commonly used language, that are logically and clearly arranged, and that are printed in a legible format. (1979, 2nd Sess., c. 1161, s. 1.)

§ 58-66-10. Scope of application.

(a) Except as provided in subsection (b) of this section, the provisions of this Article apply to the certificates and contracts of direct insurance and health care coverage that are described in G.S. 58-65-60(a) and (b).

(b) Nothing in this Article applies to:

(1) Any group contract or certificate, nor any group certificate delivered or issued for delivery outside of this State;

(2) Insurers who issue benefit booklets on group and nongroup bases explaining the certificates or contracts issued under G.S. 58-65-60. In such cases, the provisions of this Article apply only to the benefit booklets furnished to the persons insured, and not to the certificates.

(c) No other provision of the General Statutes setting language simplification standards shall apply to any certificate forms covered by this Article.

(d) Any non-English language certificate delivered or issued for delivery in this State shall be deemed to be in compliance with this Article if the insurer certifies that such certificate is translated from an English language certificate which does comply with this Article. (1979, 2nd Sess., c. 1161, s. 1.)

§ 58-66-15. Definitions.

As used in this Article, unless the context clearly indicates otherwise:

(1) "Benefit booklet" means any written explanation of insurance coverages or benefits issued by an insurer and which is supplemental to and not a part of an insurance certificate or subscriber contract.

(2) "Commissioner" means the Commissioner of Insurance.

(3) "Flesch scale analysis readability score" means a measurement of the case of readability of an insurance certificate or contract made pursuant to the procedures described in G.S. 58-66-25.

(4) "Insurance certificate or contract" or "policy" or "certificate" means an agreement as defined by G.S. 58-65-60.

(5) "Insurer" means every corporation providing contracts or certificates of coverage of insurance as described in G.S. 58-65-1. (1979, 2nd Sess., c. 1161, s. 1.)

§ 58-66-20. Format requirements.

(a) All certificates and contracts covered by G.S. 58-66-35 must be printed in a type face at least as large as 10 point modern type, one point leaded, be written in a logical and clear order and form, and contain the following items:

(1) On the cover, first, or insert page of the certificate a statement that the certificate is a legal contract between the certificate owner and the insurer, and the statement, printed in larger or other contrasting type or color, "Read your certificate carefully";

(2) An index of the major provisions of the certificate, which may include the following items:

a. The person or persons insured by the certificate;

b. The applicable events, occurrences, conditions, losses, or damages covered by the certificate;

c. The limitations or conditions on the coverage of the certificate;

d. Definitional sections of the certificate;

e. Provisions governing the procedure for filing a claim under the certificate;

f. Provisions governing cancellation, renewal, or amendment of the certificate by either the insurer or the subscriber;

g. Any options under the certificate; and

h. Provisions governing the insurer's duties and powers in the event that suit is filed against the subscriber.

(b) In determining whether or not a certificate is written in a logical and clear order and form the Commissioner must consider the following factors:

(1) The extent to which sections or provisions are set off and clearly identified by titles, headings, or margin notations;

(2) The use of a more readable format, such as narrative or outline forms;

(3) Margin size and the amount and use of space to separate sections of the policy; and

(4) Contrast and legibility of the colors of the ink and paper, and the use of contrasting titles or headings for sections. (1979, 2nd Sess., c. 1161, s. 1.)

§ 58-66-25. Flesch scale analysis readability score; procedures.

(a) A Flesch scale analysis readability score will be measured as provided in this section.

(b) For certificates containing 10,000 words or less of text, the entire certificate must be analyzed. For certificates containing more than 10,000 words, the readability of two 200-word samples per page may be analyzed in lieu of the entire certificate. The samples must be separated by at least 20 printed lines. For the purposes of this subsection a word will be counted as five printed characters or spaces between characters.

(c) The number of words and sentences in the text must be counted and the total number of words divided by the total number of sentences. The figure obtained must be multiplied by a factor of 1.015. The total number of syllables must be counted and divided by the total number of words. The figure obtained must be multiplied by a factor of 84.6. The sum of the figures computed under this subsection subtracted from 206.835 equals the Flesch scale analysis readability score for the certificate.

(d) For the purposes of subsection (c) of this section the following procedures must be used:

(1) A contraction, hyphenated word, or numbers and letters, when separated by spaces, will be counted as one word;

(2) A unit of words ending with a period, semicolon, or colon, but excluding headings, and captions will be counted as a sentence; and

(3) A syllable means a unit of spoken language consisting of one or more letters of a word as divided by an accepted dictionary. Where the dictionary shows two or more equally acceptable pronunciations of a word, the pronunciation containing fewer syllables may be used.

(e) The term "text" as used in this section includes all printed matter except the following:

(1) The name and address of the insurer; the name, number or title of the certificate; the table of contents or index; captions and subcaptions; specification pages, schedules or tables; and

(2) Any certificate language that is drafted to conform to the requirements of any law, regulation, or agency interpretation of any state or the federal government; any certificate language required by any collectively bargained agreement; any medical terminology; and any words that are defined in the certificate: Provided, however, that the insurer submits with his filing under G.S. 58-66-30 a certified document identifying the language or terminology that is entitled to be excepted by this subdivision. (1979, 2nd Sess., c. 1161, s. 1.)

§ 58-66-30. Filing requirements; duties of the Commissioner.

(a) No insurer may make, issue, amend or renew any certificate or contract after the dates specified in G.S. 58-66-35 for the applicable type of insurance unless the certificate is in compliance with the provisions of G.S. 58-66-20 and 58-66-25, and unless the certificate is filed with the Commissioner for this approval. The policy will be deemed approved 90 days after filing unless disapproved within the 90-day period. The Commissioner may not unreasonably withhold this approval. Any disapproval must be delivered to the insurer in writing and must state the grounds for disapproval. Any certificate filed with the Commissioner must be accompanied by a certified Flesch scale readability analysis and test score and by the insurer's certification that the policy is, in the insurer's judgment, readable based on the factors specified in G.S. 58-66-20 and 58-66-25.

(b) The Commissioner must disapprove any certificate covered by subsection (a) of this section if he finds that:

(1) It is not accompanied by a certified Flesch scale analysis readability score of 50 or more;

(2) It is not accompanied by the insurer's certification that the certificate is, in the judgment of the insurer, readable under the standards of this Article; or

(3) It does not comply with the format requirements of G.S. 58-66-20. (1979, 2nd Sess., c. 1161, s. 1; 1995, c. 193, s. 57.)

§ 58-66-35. Application to policies; dates.

(a) The filing requirements of G.S. 58-66-30 apply to all subscribers' contracts of hospital, medical, and dental service corporations as described in G.S. 58-65-60(a) and (b) that are made, issued, amended or renewed after July 1, 1983.

(b) Repealed by Session Laws 1995, c. 193, s. 58, effective June 7, 1995. (1979, 2nd Sess., c. 1161, s. 1; 1995, c. 193, s. 58; 1995 (Reg. Sess., 1996), c. 742, s. 28.)

§ 58-66-40. Construction.

(a) The provisions of this Article will not operate to relieve any insurer from any provision of law regulating the contents or provisions of insurance certificates or contracts nor operate to reduce an insured's, beneficiary's or subscriber's rights or protection granted under any statute or provision of the law.

(b) The provisions of this Article shall not be construed to mandate, require, or allow alteration of the legal effect of any provision of any insurance certificate or contract.

(c) In any action brought by a subscriber or claimant arising out of a certificate approved pursuant to this Article, the subscriber or claimant may base such an action on either or both (i) the substantive language prescribed by such other statute or provision of law, or (ii) the wording of the approved certificate. (1979, 2nd Sess., c. 1161, s. 1.)

Article 67.

Health Maintenance Organization Act.

§ 58-67-1. Short title.

This Article may be cited as the Health Maintenance Organization Act of 1979. (1977, c. 580, s. 1; 1979, c. 876, s. 1.)

§ 58-67-5. Definitions.

(a) "Commissioner" means the Commissioner of Insurance.

(b) "Enrollee" means an individual who is covered by an HMO.

(c) "Evidence of coverage" means any certificate, agreement, or contract issued to an enrollee setting out the coverage to which he is entitled.

(d) "Health care plan" means any arrangement whereby any person undertakes on a prepaid basis to provide, arrange for, pay for, or reimburse any part of the cost of any health care services and at least part of such arrangement consists of arranging for or the provision of health care services, as distinguished from mere indemnification against the cost of such services on a prepaid basis through insurance or otherwise.

(e) "Health care services" means any services included in the furnishing to any individual of medical or dental care, or hospitalization or incident to the furnishing of such care or hospitalization, as well as the furnishing to any person of any and all other services for the purpose of preventing, alleviating, curing, or healing human illness or injury.

(f) "Health maintenance organization" or "HMO" means any person who undertakes to provide or arrange for the delivery of health care services to enrollees on a prepaid basis except for enrollee responsibility for copayments and deductibles. For the purposes of 11 U.S.C. § 109(b) (2) and (d), an HMO is a domestic insurance company.

(g) "Person" includes associations, trusts, or corporations, but does not include professional associations, or individuals.

(h) "Provider" means any physician, hospital, or other person that is licensed or otherwise authorized in this State to furnish health care services.

(i) "Net worth" means the excess of total assets over the total liabilities and may include borrowed funds that are repayable only from the net earned income of the health maintenance organization and repayable only with the advance permission of the Commissioner. For the purposes of this subsection, "assets" means (i) tangible assets and (ii) other investments permitted under G.S. 58-67-60.

(j) "Working capital" means the excess of current assets over current liabilities; provided that the only borrowed funds that may be included in working capital must be those borrowed funds that are repayable only from net earned income and must be repayable only with the advance permission of the Commissioner.

(k) "Subscriber" means an individual whose employment or other status, except family dependency, is the basis for eligibility for enrollment in the HMO;

or in the case of an individual contract, the person in whose name the contract is issued.

(l) "Participating provider" means a provider who, under an express or implied contract with the HMO or with its contractor or subcontractor, has agreed to provide health care services to enrollees with an expectation of receiving payment, directly or indirectly, from the HMO, other than copayment or deductible.

(m) "Insolvent" or "insolvency" means that the HMO has been declared insolvent and is placed under an order of liquidation by a court of competent jurisdiction.

(n) "Carrier" means an HMO, an insurer, a nonprofit hospital or medical service corporation, or other entity responsible for the payment of benefits or provision of services under a group contract.

(o) "Discontinuance" means the termination of the contract between the group contract holder and an HMO due to the insolvency of the HMO and does not mean the termination of any agreement between any individual enrollee and the HMO.

(p) "Uncovered expenditures" means the amounts owed or paid to any provider who provides health care services to an enrollee and where such amount owed or paid is (i) not made pursuant to a written contract that contains the "hold harmless" provisions defined in G.S. 58-67-115; or (ii) not guaranteed or insured by a guaranteeing organization or insurer under the terms of a written guarantee or insurance policy that has been determined to be acceptable to the Commissioner. "Uncovered expenditures" includes amounts owed or paid to providers directly from the HMO as well as payments made by a medical group, independent practice association, or any other similar organization to reimburse providers for services rendered to an enrollee. (1977, c. 580, s. 1; 1979, c. 876, s. 1; 1987, c. 631, s. 1; 1989, c. 776, ss. 2, 3, 15; 1991, c. 195, s. 4; c. 720, s. 40; 2001-417, s. 13; 2003-212, s. 19.)

§ 58-67-10. Establishment of health maintenance organizations.

(a) Notwithstanding any law of this State to the contrary, any person may apply to the Commissioner for a license to establish and operate a health maintenance organization in compliance with this Article. No person shall establish or operate a health maintenance organization in this State, nor sell or offer to sell, or solicit offers to purchase or receive advance or periodic consideration in conjunction with a health maintenance organization without obtaining a license under this Article. A foreign corporation may qualify under this Article, subject to its full compliance with Article 16 of this Chapter.

(b) (1) It is specifically the intention of this section to permit such persons as were providing health services on a prepaid basis on July 1, 1977, or receiving federal funds under Section 254(c) of Title 42, U.S. Code, as a community health center, to continue to operate in the manner which they have heretofore operated.

(2) Notwithstanding anything contained in this Article to the contrary, any person can provide health services on a fee for service basis to individuals who are not enrollees of the organization, and to enrollees for services not covered by the contract, provided that the volume of services in this manner shall not be such as to affect the ability of the health maintenance organization to provide on an adequate and timely basis those services to its enrolled members which it has contracted to furnish under the enrollment contract.

(3) This Article shall not apply to any employee benefit plan to the extent that the Federal Employee Retirement Income Security Act of 1974 preempts State regulation thereof.

(3a) This Article does not apply to any prepaid health service or capitation arrangement implemented or administered by the Department of Health and Human Services or its representatives, pursuant to 42 U.S.C. § 1396n or Chapter 108A of the General Statutes, a provider sponsored organization or other organization certified, qualified, or otherwise approved by the Division of Medical Assistance of the Department of Health and Human Services pursuant to Article 17 of Chapter 131E of the General Statutes, or to any provider of health care services participating in such a prepaid health service or capitation arrangement. Article; provided, however, that to the extent this Article applies to any such person acting as a subcontractor to a Health Maintenance Organization licensed in this State, that person shall be considered a single service Health Maintenance Organization for the purpose of G.S. 58-67-20(4), G.S. 58-67-25, and G.S. 58-67-110.

(4) Except as provided in paragraphs (1), (2), (3), and (3a) of this subsection, the persons to whom these paragraphs are applicable shall be required to comply with all provisions contained in this Article.

(c) Each application for a license shall be verified by an officer or authorized representative of the applicant, shall be in a form prescribed by the Commissioner, and shall be set forth or be accompanied by the following:

(1) A copy of the basic organizational document, if any, of the applicant such as the articles of incorporation, articles of association, partnership agreement, trust agreement, or other applicable documents, and all amendments thereto. Any proposed articles of incorporation for the formation of a domestic health maintenance organization shall be filed with the Commissioner. The Commissioner shall examine the proposed articles. If the Commissioner finds that the proposed articles meet the requirements of the insurance laws of this State and otherwise determines that the articles should be approved, the Commissioner shall place a certificate of approval on the articles and submit the approved articles to the Secretary of State;

(2) A copy of the bylaws, rules and regulations, or similar document, if any, regulating the conduct of the internal affairs of the applicant;

(3) A list of the names, addresses, and official positions of persons who are to be responsible for the conduct of the affairs of the applicant, including all members of the board of directors, board of trustees, executive committee, or other governing board or committee, the principal officers in the case of a corporation, and the partners or members in the case of a partnership or association;

(4) A copy of any contract form made or to be made between any class of providers and the HMO and a copy of any contract form made or to be made between third party administrators, marketing consultants, or persons listed in subdivision (3) of this subsection and the HMO;

(5) A statement generally describing the health maintenance organization, its health care plan or plans, facilities, and personnel;

(6) A copy of the form of evidence of coverage to be issued to the enrollees;

(7) A copy of the form of the group contract, if any, which is to be issued to employers, unions, trustees, or other organizations;

(8) Financial statements showing the applicant's assets, liabilities, and sources of financial support. If the applicant's financial affairs are audited by independent certified public accountants, a copy of the applicant's most recent

regular certified financial statement shall be deemed to satisfy this requirement unless the Commissioner directs that additional or more recent financial information is required for the proper administration of this Article;

(9) A financial feasibility plan, which includes detailed enrollment projections, the methodology for determining premium rates to be charged during the first 12 months of operations certified by an actuary or a recognized actuarial consultant, a projection of balance sheets, cash flow statements, showing any capital expenditures, purchase and sale of investments and deposits with the State, and income and expense statements anticipated from the start of operations until the organization has had net income for at least one year; and a statement as to the sources of working capital as well as any other sources of funding;

(10) A power of attorney duly executed by such applicant, if not domiciled in this State, appointing the Commissioner and his successors in office, and duly authorized deputies, as the true and lawful attorney of such applicant in and for this State upon whom all lawful process in any legal action or proceeding against the health maintenance organization on a cause of action arising in this State may be served;

(11) A statement reasonably describing the geographic area or areas to be served;

(12) A description of the procedures to be implemented to meet the protection against insolvency requirements of G.S. 58-67-110;

(13) A description of the internal grievance procedures to be utilized for the investigation and resolution of enrollee complaints and grievances; and

(14) Such other information as the Commissioner may require to make the determinations required in G.S. 58-67-20.

(d) (1) A health maintenance organization shall file a notice describing any significant modification of the operation set out in the information required by subsection (c) of this section. Such notice shall be filed with the Commissioner prior to the modification. If the Commissioner does not disapprove within 90 days after the filing, such modification shall be deemed to be approved. Changes subject to the terms of this section include expansion of service area, changes in provider contract forms and group contract forms where the distribution of risk is significantly changed, and any other changes that the Commissioner describes in properly promulgated rules. Every HMO shall report to the Commissioner for his information material changes in the provider network, the addition or deletion of Medicare risk or Medicaid risk arrangements and the addition or deletion of employer groups that exceed ten percent (10%) of the health maintenance organization's book of business or such other information as the Commissioner may require. Such information shall be filed with the Commissioner within 15 days after implementation of the reported changes. Every HMO shall file with the Commissioner all subsequent changes in the information or forms that are required by this Article to be filed with the Commissioner.

(1a) Any proposed change to the articles of incorporation shall be filed with the Commissioner. The Commissioner shall examine the proposed change to the articles. If the Commissioner determines that the proposed change should be approved, the Commissioner shall place a certificate of approval on the change and submit the approved change to the Secretary of State.

(2) The Commissioner may promulgate rules and regulations exempting from the filing requirements of subdivision (1) those items he deems unnecessary. (1977, c. 580, s. 1; 1979, c. 876, s. 1; 1983, c. 386, s. 1; 1985 (Reg. Sess., 1986), c. 1027, s. 49; 1987, c. 631, ss. 6, 7; 1989, c. 776, ss. 4-8; 1991, c. 720, ss. 41, 69; 1993, c. 529, s. 7.2; 1993 (Reg. Sess., 1994), c. 769, s. 25.48; 1997-443, s. 11A.118(a); 1998-227, s. 2; 2005-215, s. 23.)

§ 58-67-11. Additional HMO application information.

(a) In addition to the information filed under G.S. 58-67-10(c), each application shall include a description of the following:

(1) The program to be used to evaluate whether the applicant's provider network is sufficient, in numbers and types of providers, to assure that all health care services will be accessible without unreasonable delay.

(2) The program to be used for verifying provider credentials.

(3) The quality management program to assure quality of care and health care services managed and provided through the health care plan.

(4)   The utilization review program for the review and control of health care services provided or paid for.

(5)   The applicant's provider network and evidence of the ability of that network to provide all health care services to the applicant's prospective enrollees.

(b)   G.S. 58-67-10(d) applies to the information specified in this section. (1997-519, s. 1.2.)

§§ 58-67-12 through 58-67-14. Reserved for future codification purposes.

§ 58-67-15. Health maintenance organization of bordering states may be admitted to do business; reciprocity.

A federally qualified health maintenance organization approved and regulated under the laws of a state bordering this State may be admitted to do business in this State by satisfying the Commissioner that it is fully and legally organized under the laws of that state, and that it complies with all requirements for health maintenance organizations organized within this State; provided that the bordering state has a law or regulation substantially similar to this section. (1985, c. 666, s. 69.)

§ 58-67-20. Issuance and continuation of license.

(a)   Before issuing or continuing any such license, the Commissioner of Insurance may make such an examination or investigation as he deems expedient. The Commissioner of Insurance shall issue a license upon the payment of the application fee prescribed in G.S. 58-67-160 and upon being satisfied on the following points:

(1)   The applicant is established as a bona fide health maintenance organization as defined by this Article;

(2)   The rates charged and benefits to be provided are fair and reasonable;

(3) The amounts provided as working capital are repayable only out of earned income in excess of amounts paid and payable for operating expenses and expenses of providing services and such reserve as the Department of Insurance deems adequate, as provided hereinafter;

(4) That the amount of money actually available for working capital be sufficient to carry all acquisition costs and operating expenses for a reasonable period of time from the date of the issuance of the license and that the health maintenance organization is financially responsible and may reasonably be expected to meet its obligations to enrollees and prospective enrollees. Such working capital shall initially be a minimum of one million five hundred thousand dollars ($1,500,000) for any full service medical health maintenance organization. Initial working capital for a single service health maintenance organization shall be a minimum of one hundred thousand dollars ($100,000) or such higher amount as the Commissioner shall determine to be adequate.

(b) In making the determinations required under this section, the Commissioner shall consider:

(1) The financial soundness of the health care plan's arrangements for health care services and the schedule of premiums used in connection therewith;

(2) The adequacy of working capital;

(3) Any agreement with an insurer, a hospital or medical service corporation, a government, or any other organization for insuring the payment of the cost of health care services or the provision for automatic applicability of alternative coverage in the event of discontinuance of the plan;

(4) Any agreement with providers for the provision of health care services; and

(5) Any firm commitment of federal funds to the health maintenance organization in the form of a grant, even though such funds have not been paid to the health maintenance organization, provided that the health maintenance organization certifies to the Commissioner that such funds have been committed, that such funds are to be paid to the health maintenance organization with a current fiscal year and that such funds may be used directly

for operating purposes and for the benefit of enrollees of the health maintenance organization.

(c) A license shall be denied only after compliance with the requirements of G.S. 58-67-155. (1977, c. 580, s. 1; 1979, c. 876, s. 1; 1983, c. 386, s. 2; 1987, c. 631, ss. 2, 4, 8; 1987 (Reg. Sess., 1988), c. 975, s. 1; 2003-212, s. 26(n).)

§ 58-67-25. Deposits.

(a) The Commissioner shall require a minimum deposit of five hundred thousand dollars ($500,000) for all full service medical health maintenance organizations or such higher amount as he deems necessary for the protection of enrollees.

(b) The Commissioner shall require a minimum deposit of twenty-five thousand dollars ($25,000) for all single service health maintenance organizations or such higher amount as he deems necessary for the protection of enrollees.

(c) All deposits required by this section shall be administered in accordance with the provisions of Article 5 of this Chapter. (1987, c. 631, s. 3; 2005-215, s. 18.)

§ 58-67-30. Management and exclusive agreements; custodial agreements.

(a) No health maintenance organization shall enter into an exclusive agency, management, or custodial agreement unless the agreement is first filed with the Commissioner and approved under this section within 45 days after filing or such reasonable extended period as the Commissioner shall specify by notice that is given within the 45 day period.

(b) The Commissioner shall disapprove an agreement submitted under subsection (a) of this section if the Commissioner determines that the agreement:

(1) Subjects the health maintenance organization to excessive charges;

(2) Extends for an unreasonable period of time;

(3) Does not contain fair and adequate standards of performance;

(4) Enables persons under the contract to manage the health maintenance organization who are not sufficiently trustworthy, competent, experienced, and free from conflict of interest to manage the health maintenance organization with due regard for the interests of its enrollees, creditors, or the public; or

(5) Contains provisions that impair the interests of the organization's enrollees, creditors, or the public. (1987, c. 631, s. 10; 2001-223, s. 20.5.)

§ 58-67-35. Powers of health maintenance organizations.

(a) The powers of a health maintenance organization include, but are not limited to the following:

(1) The purchase, lease, construction, renovation, operation, or maintenance of hospitals, medical facilities, or both, and their ancillary equipment, and such property as may reasonably be required for its principal office or for such other purposes as may be necessary in the transaction of the business of the organization;

(2) The making of loans to a medical group under contract with it in furtherance of its program or the making of loans to a corporation or corporations under its control for the purpose of acquiring or constructing medical facilities and hospitals or in furtherance of a program providing health care services to enrollees;

(3) The furnishing of health care services through providers which are under contract with or employed by the health maintenance organization;

(4) The contracting with any person for the performance on its behalf of certain functions such as marketing, enrollment and administration;

(5) The contracting with an insurance company licensed in this State, or with a hospital or medical service corporation authorized to do business in this State, for the provision of insurance, indemnity, or reimbursement against the cost of health care services provided by the health maintenance organization;

(6) The offering and contracting for the provision or arranging of, in addition to health care services, of:

a. Additional health care services;

b. Indemnity benefits, covering out-of-area or emergency services;

c. Indemnity benefits, in addition to those relating to out-of-area and emergency services, provided through insurers or hospital or medical service corporations; and

d. Point-of-service products, for which an HMO may precertify out-of-plan covered services on the same basis as it precertifies in-plan covered services, and for which the Commissioner shall adopt rules governing:

1. The percentage of an HMO's total health care expenditures for out-of-plan covered services for all of its members that may be spent on those services, which may not exceed twenty percent (20%);

2. Product limitations, which may provide for payment differentials for services rendered by providers who are not in an HMO network, subject to G.S. 58-3-200(d).

3. Deposit and other financial requirements; and

4. Other requirements for marketing and administering those products.

(b) (1) A health maintenance organization shall file notice, with adequate supporting information, with the Commissioner prior to the exercise of any power granted in subsections (a)(1) or (2). The Commissioner shall disapprove such exercise of power if in his opinion it would substantially and adversely affect the financial soundness of the health maintenance organization and endanger its ability to meet its obligations. If the Commissioner does not disapprove within 30 days of the filing, it shall be deemed approved.

(2) The Commissioner may promulgate rules and regulations exempting from the filing requirement of subdivision (1) those activities having a de minimis effect. (1977, c. 580, s. 1; 1979, c. 876, s. 1; 1991 (Reg. Sess., 1992), c. 837, s. 8; 1997-519, s. 3.18; 2001-334, s. 8.2.)

§ 58-67-40: Repealed by Session Laws 2003-212, s. 20, effective October 1, 2003.

§ 58-67-45. Fiduciary responsibilities.

Any director, officer or partner of a health maintenance organization who receives, collects, disburses, or invests funds in connection with the activities of such organization shall be responsible for such funds in a fiduciary relationship to the enrollees. (1977, c. 580, s. 1; 1979, c. 876, s. 1.)

§ 58-67-50. Evidence of coverage and premiums for health care services.

(a) (1) Every enrollee residing in this State is entitled to evidence of coverage under a health care plan. If the enrollee obtains coverage under a health care plan through an insurance policy or a contract issued by a hospital or medical service corporation, whether by option or otherwise, the insurer or the hospital or medical service corporation shall issue the evidence of coverage. Otherwise, the health maintenance organization shall issue the evidence of coverage.

(2) No evidence of coverage, or amendment thereto, shall be issued or delivered to any person in this State until a copy of the form of the evidence of coverage, or amendment thereto, has been filed with and approved by the Commissioner.

(3) An evidence of coverage shall contain:

a. No provisions or statements which are unjust, unfair, inequitable, misleading, deceptive, which encourage misrepresentation, or which are untrue, misleading or deceptive as defined in G.S. 58-67-65(a); and

b. A clear and complete statement, if a contract, or a reasonably complete summary, if a certificate of:

1. The health care services and insurance or other benefits, if any, to which the enrollee is entitled under the health care plan;

2. Any limitations on the services, benefits, or kind of benefits, to be provided, including any deductible or copayment feature;

3. Where and in what manner information is available as to how services may be obtained;

4. The total amount of payment for health care services and the indemnity or service benefits, if any, which the enrollee is obligated to pay with respect to individual contracts, or an indication whether the plan is contributory or noncontributory with respect to group certificates;

5. A clear and understandable description of the health maintenance organization's method of resolving enrollee complaints;

6. A description of the reasons, if any, for which an enrollee's enrollment may be terminated for cause, which reasons may include behavior that seriously impairs the health maintenance organization's ability to provide services or an inability to establish and maintain a satisfactory physician-patient relationship after reasonable efforts to do so have been made.

Any subsequent change may be evidenced in a separate document issued to the enrollee.

(4) A copy of the form of the evidence of coverage to be used in this State, and any amendment thereto, shall be subject to the filing and approval requirements of subsection (b) unless it is subject to the jurisdiction of the Commissioner under the laws governing health insurance or hospital or medical service corporations in which event the filing and approval provisions of such laws shall apply. To the extent, however, that such provisions do not apply the requirements in subsection (c) shall be applicable.

(b) (1) Premium approval. - No schedule of premiums for coverage for health care services, or any amendment to the schedule, shall be used in conjunction with any health care plan until a copy of the schedule or amendment has been filed with and approved by the Commissioner.

(2) Individual coverage. - Premiums shall be established in accordance with actuarial principles for various categories of enrollees. Premiums applicable to

an enrollee shall not be individually determined based on the status of the enrollee's health. Premiums shall not be excessive, inadequate or unfairly discriminatory; and shall exhibit a reasonable relationship to the benefits provided by the evidence of coverage. The premiums or any premium revisions for nongroup enrollee coverage shall be guaranteed, as to every enrollee covered under the same category of enrollee coverage, for a period of not less than 12 months. As an alternative to giving this guarantee for nongroup enrollee coverage, the premium or premium revisions may be made applicable to all similar categories of enrollee coverage at one time if the health maintenance organization chooses to apply for the premium revision with respect to the categories of coverages no more frequently than once in any 12-month period. The premium revision shall be applicable to all categories of nongroup enrollee coverage of the same type; provided that no premium revision may become effective for any category of enrollee coverage unless the HMO has given written notice of the premium revision to the enrollee 45 days before the effective date of the revision. The enrollee must then pay the revised premium in order to continue the contract in force. The Commissioner may adopt reasonable rules, after notice and hearing, to require the submittal of supporting data and such information as the Commissioner considers necessary to determine whether the rate revisions meet the standards in this subdivision. In adopting the rules under this subsection, the Commissioner may require identification of the types of rating methodologies used by filers and may also address standards for data in HMO rate filings for initial filings, filings by recently licensed HMOs, and rate revision filings; data requirements for service area expansion requests; policy reserves used in rating; incurred loss ratio standards; and other recognized actuarial principles of the NAIC, the American Academy of Actuaries, and the Society of Actuaries.

(3)   Group coverage. - Employer group premiums shall be established in accordance with actuarial principles for various categories of enrollees, provided that premiums applicable to an enrollee shall not be individually determined based on the status of the enrollee's health. Premiums shall not be excessive, inadequate, or unfairly discriminatory, and shall exhibit a reasonable relationship to the benefits provided by the evidence of coverage. The premiums or any revisions to the premiums for employer group coverage shall be guaranteed for a period of not less than 12 months. No premium revision shall become effective for any category of group coverage unless the HMO has given written notice of the premium revision to the master group contract holder upon receipt of the group's finalized benefits or 45 days before the effective date of the revision, whichever is earlier. The master group contract holder thereafter must pay the revised premium in order to continue the contract in force. The Commissioner

may adopt reasonable rules, after notice and hearing, to require the submittal of supporting data and such information as the Commissioner considers necessary to determine whether the rate revisions meet the standards in this subdivision.

(c) The Commissioner shall, within a reasonable period, approve any form if the requirements of subsection (a) of this section are met and any schedule of premiums if the requirements of subsection (b) of this section are met. It shall be unlawful to issue the form or to use the schedule of premiums until approved. If the Commissioner disapproves the filing, the Commissioner shall notify the filer. In the notice, the Commissioner shall specify the reasons for disapproval. A hearing will be granted within 30 days after a request in writing by the person filing. If the Commissioner does not approve or disapprove any form or schedule of premiums within 90 days after the filing for forms and within 45 days after the filing for premiums, they shall be deemed to be approved.

(d) The Commissioner may require the submission of whatever relevant information he deems necessary in determining whether to approve or disapprove a filing made pursuant to this section.

(e) Every health maintenance organization shall provide at least minimum cost and utilization information for group contracts of 100 or more subscribers on an annual basis when requested by the group. Such information shall be compiled in accordance with the Data Collection Form developed by the Standardized HMO Date Form Task Force as endorsed by the Washington Business Group on Health and the Group Health Association of America on November 19, 1986, and any subsequent amendments. (1977, c. 580, s. 1; 1979, c. 876, s. 1; 1987, c. 631, s. 9; 1989, c. 485, s. 59; 1991, c. 195, s. 1; c. 644, s. 13; c. 720, s. 36; 1995, c. 193, s. 59; 1997-474, s. 3; 1997-519, s. 1.3; 2001-334, ss. 8.1, 17.4; 2001-487, ss. 106(a), 106(b); 2008-124, s. 5.3; 2009-173, s. 1.)

§ 58-67-55. Statements filed with Commissioner.

Every HMO subject to this Article is subject to G.S. 58-2-165. (1977, c. 580, s. 1; 1979, c. 876, s. 1; 1999-244, s. 12.)

§ 58-67-60. Investments.

With the exception of investments made in accordance with G.S. 58-67-35(a)(1) and (2) and G.S. 58-67-35(b), the funds of a health maintenance organization shall be invested or maintained only in securities, other investments, or other assets permitted by the laws of this State for the investment of assets constituting the legal reserves of life insurance companies or such other securities or investments as the Commissioner may permit. (1977, c. 580, s. 1; 1979, c. 876, s. 1; 2001-223, s. 8.18.)

§ 58-67-65. Prohibited practices.

(a) No health maintenance organization, or representative thereof, may cause or knowingly permit the use of advertising which is untrue or misleading, solicitation which is untrue or misleading, or any form of evidence of coverage which is deceptive. For purposes of this Article:

(1) A statement or item of information shall be deemed to be untrue if it does not conform to fact in any respect which is or may be significant to an enrollee of, or person considering enrollment in, a health care plan.

(2) A statement or item of information shall be deemed to be misleading, whether or not it may be literally untrue, if, in the total context in which such statement is made or such item of information is communicated, such statement or item of information may be reasonably understood by a reasonable person, not possessing special knowledge regarding health care coverage, as indicating any benefit or advantage or the absence of any exclusion, limitation, or disadvantage of possible significance to an enrollee of, or person considering enrollment in a health care plan, if such benefit or advantage or absence of limitation, exclusion or disadvantage does not in fact exist.

(3) An evidence of coverage shall be deemed to be deceptive if the evidence of coverage taken as a whole, and with consideration given to typography and format, as well as language, shall be such as to cause a reasonable person, not possessing special knowledge regarding health care plans and evidences of coverage therefor, to expect benefits, services, premiums, or other advantages which the evidence of coverage does not provide or which the health care plan issuing such evidence of coverage does not regularly make available for enrollees covered under such evidence of coverage.

(b) Article 63 of this Chapter applies to health maintenance organizations and their agents and representatives.

(c) An enrollee may not be cancelled or not renewed because of any deterioration in the health of the enrollee.

(d) No health maintenance organization, unless licensed as an insurer, may use in its name, contracts, or literature any of the words "insurance", "casualty", "surety", "mutual", or any other words descriptive of the insurance, casualty, or surety business or deceptively similar to the name or description of any insurance or surety corporation doing business in this State.

(e) The HMO shall not refuse to enroll employees except when they can demonstrate they are unable to arrange adequate services.

(f) No health maintenance organization shall refuse to enroll an individual or refuse to continue enrollment of an individual in a health care plan; limit the amount, extent, or kinds of health care plans available to an individual; or charge an individual a different rate for the same health plan, because of the race, color, or national or ethnic origin of that individual. (1977, c. 580, s. 1; 1979, c. 876, s. 1; 1989, c. 485, s. 24; 1999-244, s. 14.)

§ 58-67-66. Collaboration with local health departments.

A health maintenance organization and a local health department shall collaborate and cooperate within available resources regarding health promotion and disease prevention efforts that are necessary to protect the public health. (1997-474, s. 4.)

§ 58-67-70. Coverage for chemical dependency treatment.

(a) As used in this section, the term "chemical dependency" means the pathological use or abuse of alcohol or other drugs in a manner or to a degree that produces an impairment in personal, social or occupational functioning and which may, but need not, include a pattern of tolerance and withdrawal.

(b) On and after January 1, 1985, every health maintenance organization that writes a health care plan on a group basis and that is subject to this Article shall offer benefits for the necessary care and treatment of chemical dependency that are not less favorable than benefits under the health care plan generally. Except as provided in subsection (c) of this section, benefits for chemical dependency shall be subject to the same durational limits, dollar limits, deductibles, and coinsurance factors as are benefits under the health care plan generally.

(c) Every group health care plan that provides benefits for chemical dependency treatment and that provides total annual benefits for all illnesses in excess of eight thousand dollars ($8,000) is subject to the following conditions:

(1) The plan shall provide, for each 12-month period, a minimum benefit of eight thousand dollars ($8,000) for the necessary care and treatment of chemical dependency.

(2) The plan shall provide a lifetime minimum benefit of sixteen thousand dollars ($16,000) for the necessary care and treatment of chemical dependency for each enrollee.

(d) Provisions for benefits for necessary care and treatment of chemical dependency in group health care plans shall provide for benefit payments for the following providers of necessary care and treatment of chemical dependency:

(1) The following units of a general hospital licensed under Article 5 of General Statutes Chapter 131E:

a. Chemical dependency units in facilities licensed after October 1, 1984;

b. Medical units;

c. Psychiatric units; and

(2) The following facilities or programs licensed after July 1, 1984, under Article 2 of General Statutes Chapter 122C:

a. Chemical dependency units in psychiatric hospitals;

b. Chemical dependency hospitals;

c. Residential chemical dependency treatment facilities;

d. Social setting detoxification facilities or programs;

e. Medical detoxification facilities or programs; and

(3) Duly licensed physicians and duly licensed practicing psychologists and certified professionals working under the direct supervision of such physicians or psychologists in facilities described in (1) and (2) above and in day/night programs or outpatient treatment facilities licensed after July 1, 1984, under Article 2 of General Statutes Chapter 122C.

Provided, however, that nothing in this subsection shall prohibit any plan from requiring the most cost effective treatment setting to be utilized by the person undergoing necessary care and treatment for chemical dependency.

(e) Coverage for chemical dependency treatment as described in this section shall not be applicable to any group that rejects the coverage in writing.

(f) Notwithstanding any other provision of this section or Article, any health maintenance organization subject to this Article that becomes a qualified health maintenance organization under Title XIII of the United States Public Health Service Act shall provide the benefits required under that federal Act, which shall be deemed to constitute compliance with the provisions of this section; and any health maintenance organization may provide that the benefits provided under this section must be obtained through providers affiliated with the health maintenance organization.

(g) Notwithstanding any other provisions of this section, a group health benefit plan that covers both medical and surgical benefits and chemical dependency treatment benefits shall, with respect to the chemical dependency treatment benefits, comply with all applicable standards of Subtitle B of Title V of Public Law 110-343, known as the Paul Wellstone and Pete Domenici Mental Health Parity and Addiction Equity Act of 2008.

(h) Subsection (g) of this section applies only to a group health benefit plan covering a large employer as defined in G.S. 58-68-25(a)(10). (1983 (Reg. Sess., 1984), c. 1110, s. 9; 1985, c. 589, s. 43(a), (b); 1989, c. 175, s. 3; 1991, c. 720, s. 64; 2009-382, s. 22.)

§ 58-67-74. Coverage for certain treatment of diabetes.

(a) Every health care plan written by a health maintenance organization and in force, issued, renewed, or amended on or after October 1, 1997, that is subject to this Article, shall provide coverage for medically appropriate and necessary services, including diabetes outpatient self-management training and educational services, and equipment, supplies, medications, and laboratory procedures used to treat diabetes. Diabetes outpatient self-management training and educational services shall be provided by a physician or a health care professional designated by the physician. The health maintenance organization shall determine who shall provide and be reimbursed for the diabetes outpatient self-management training and educational services. The same deductibles, coinsurance, and other limitations as apply to similar services covered under the policy, contract, or plan shall apply to the diabetes coverage required under this section.

(b) For the purposes of this section, "physician" is a person licensed to practice in this State under Article 1 or Article 7 of Chapter 90 of the General Statutes. (1997-225, s. 3.)

§ 58-67-75. No discrimination against mentally ill or chemically dependent individuals.

(a) Definitions. - As used in this section, the term:

(1) "Mental illness" has the same meaning as defined in G.S. 122C-3(21), with a mental disorder defined in the Diagnostic and Statistical Manual of Mental Disorders, DSM-IV, or subsequent editions published by the American Psychiatric Association, except those mental disorders coded in the DSM-IV or subsequent editions as substance-related disorders (291.0 through 292.9 and 303.0 through 305.9), those coded as sexual dysfunctions not due to organic disease (302.70 through 302.79), and those coded as "V" codes.

(2) "Chemical dependency" has the same meaning as defined in G.S. 58-67-70, with a mental disorder defined in the Diagnostic and Statistical Manual of Mental Disorders, DSM-IV, or subsequent editions published by the American Psychiatric Association.

(b) Coverage of Physical Illness. - No health maintenance organization governed by this Chapter shall, solely because an individual has or had a mental illness or chemical dependency:

(1) Refuse to enroll that individual in any health care plan covering physical illness or injury;

(2) Have a higher premium rate or charge for physical illness or injury coverages or benefits for that individual; or

(3) Reduce physical illness or injury coverages or benefits for that individual.

(b1) [Expired October 1, 2001.]

(c) Chemical Dependency Coverage Not Required. - Nothing in this section requires an HMO to offer coverage for chemical dependency, except as provided in G.S. 58-67-70.

(d) Applicability. - This section applies only to group contracts, other than excepted benefits as defined in G.S. 58-68-25. For purposes of this section, "group health insurance contracts" include MEWAs, as defined in G.S. 58-49-30(a).

(e) Nothing in this section requires an insurer to cover treatment or studies leading to or in connection with sex changes or modifications and related care. (1989, c. 369, s. 2; 1991, c. 720, s. 83; 1997-259, s. 23; 1999-132, s. 4.4; 2007-268, s. 4.)

§ 58-67-76. Coverage for mammograms and cervical cancer screening.

(a) Every health care plan written by a health maintenance organization and in force, issued, renewed, or amended on or after January 1, 1992, that is subject to this Article, shall provide coverage for examinations and laboratory tests for the screening for the early detection of cervical cancer and for low-dose screening mammography. The same deductibles, coinsurance, and other limitations as apply to similar services covered under the plan shall apply to coverage for examinations and laboratory tests for the screening for the early detection of cervical cancer and low-dose screening mammography.

(a1) As used in this section, "examinations and laboratory tests for the screening for the early detection of cervical cancer" means conventional PAP smear screening, liquid-based cytology, and human papilloma virus (HPV) detection methods for women with equivocal findings on cervical cytologic analysis that are subject to the approval of and have been approved by the United States Food and Drug Administration.

(b) As used in this section, "low-dose screening mammography" means a radiologic procedure for the early detection of breast cancer provided to an asymptomatic woman using equipment dedicated specifically for mammography, including a physician's interpretation of the results of the procedure.

(c) Coverage for low-dose screening mammography shall be provided as follows:

(1) One or more mammograms a year, as recommended by a physician, for any woman who is determined to be at risk for breast cancer. For purposes of this subdivision, a woman is at risk for breast cancer if any one or more of the following is true:

a. The woman has a personal history of breast cancer;

b. The woman has a personal history of biopsy-proven benign breast disease;

c. The woman's mother, sister, or daughter has or has had breast cancer; or

d. The woman has not given birth prior to the age of 30;

(2) One baseline mammogram for any woman 35 through 39 years of age, inclusive;

(3) A mammogram every other year for any woman 40 through 49 years of age, inclusive, or more frequently upon recommendation of a physician; and

(4) A mammogram every year for any woman 50 years of age or older.

(d) Reimbursement for a mammogram authorized under this section shall be made only if the facility in which the mammogram was performed meets mammography accreditation standards established by the North Carolina Medical Care Commission.

(e) Coverage for the screening for the early detection of cervical cancer shall be in accordance with the most recently published American Cancer Society guidelines or guidelines adopted by the North Carolina Advisory Committee on Cancer Coordination and Control. Coverage shall include the examination, the laboratory fee, and the physician's interpretation of the laboratory results. Reimbursements for laboratory fees shall be made only if the laboratory meets accreditation standards adopted by the North Carolina Medical Care Commission. (1991, c. 490, s. 3; 2003-186, s. 4.)

§ 58-67-77. Coverage for prostate-specific antigen (PSA) tests.

(a) Every health care plan written by a health maintenance organization and in force, issued, renewed, or amended on or after January 1, 1994, that is subject to this Article, shall provide coverage for prostate-specific antigen (PSA) tests or equivalent tests for the presence of prostate cancer. The same deductibles, coinsurance, and other limitations as apply to similar services covered under the plan shall apply to coverage for prostate-specific antigen (PSA) tests or equivalent tests for the presence of prostate cancer.

(b) As used in this section, "prostate-specific antigen (PSA) tests or equivalent tests for the presence of prostate cancer" means serological tests for determining the presence of prostate cytoplasmic protein (PSA) and the generation of antibodies to it, as a novel marker for prostatic disease.

(c) Coverage for prostate-specific antigen (PSA) tests or equivalent tests for the presence of prostate cancer shall be provided when recommended by a physician. (1993, c. 269, s. 3.)

§ 58-67-78. Coverage of certain prescribed drugs for cancer treatment.

(a) No health care plan written by a health maintenance organization and in force, issued, renewed, or amended on or after January 1, 1994, and that provides coverage for prescribed drugs approved by the federal Food and Drug Administration for the treatment of certain types of cancer shall exclude coverage of any drug on the basis that the drug has been prescribed for the treatment of a type of cancer for which the drug has not been approved by the federal Food and Drug Administration. The drug, however, must be approved by the federal Food and Drug Administration and must have been proven effective and accepted for the treatment of the specific type of cancer for which the drug has been prescribed in any one of the following established reference compendia:

(1) The National Comprehensive Cancer Network Drugs & Biologics Compendium;

(2) The ThomsonMicromedex DrugDex;

(3) The Elsevier Gold Standard's Clinical Pharmacology; or

(4) Any other authoritative compendia as recognized periodically by the United States Secretary of Health and Human Services.

(b) Notwithstanding subsection (a) of this section, coverage shall not be required for any experimental or investigational drugs or any drug that the federal Food and Drug Administration has determined to be contraindicated for treatment of the specific type of cancer for which the drug has been prescribed.

(c) This section shall apply only to cancer drugs and nothing in this section shall be construed, expressly or by implication, to create, impair, alter, limit, notify, enlarge, abrogate, or prohibit reimbursement for drugs used in the treatment of any other disease or condition. (1993, c. 506, s. 4.3; 2009-170, s. 3.)

§ 58-67-79. Coverage for reconstructive breast surgery following mastectomy.

(a) Every health care plan written by a health maintenance organization that is subject to this Article and that provides coverage for mastectomy shall provide coverage for reconstructive breast surgery following a mastectomy. The coverage shall include coverage for all stages and revisions of reconstructive breast surgery performed on a nondiseased breast to establish symmetry if reconstructive surgery on a diseased breast is performed, as well as coverage for prostheses and physical complications in all stages of mastectomy, including lymphademas. The same deductibles, coinsurance, and other limitations as apply to similar services covered under the policy, contract, or plan shall apply to coverage for reconstructive breast surgery. Reconstruction of the nipple/areolar complex following a mastectomy is covered without regard to the lapse of time between the mastectomy and the reconstruction, subject to the approval of the treating physician.

(b) As used in this section, the following terms have the meanings indicated:

(1) "Mastectomy" means the surgical removal of all or part of a breast as a result of breast cancer or breast disease.

(2) "Reconstructive breast surgery" means surgery performed as a result of a mastectomy to reestablish symmetry between the two breasts, and includes reconstruction of the mastectomy site, creation of a new breast mound, and creation of a new nipple/areolar complex. "Reconstructive breast surgery" also includes augmentation mammoplasty, reduction mammoplasty, and mastopexy of the nondiseased breast.

(c) A policy, contract, or plan subject to this section shall not:

(1) Deny coverage described in subsection (a) of this section on the basis that the coverage is for cosmetic surgery;

(2) Deny to a woman eligibility or continued eligibility to enroll or to renew coverage under the terms of the contract, policy, or plan, solely for the purpose of avoiding the requirements of this section;

(3) Provide monetary payments or rebates to a woman to encourage her to accept less than the minimum protections available under this section;

(4) Penalize or otherwise reduce or limit the reimbursement of an attending provider because the provider provided care to an individual participant or beneficiary in accordance with this section; or

(5) Provide incentives, monetary or otherwise, to an attending provider to induce the provider to provide care to an individual participant or beneficiary in a manner inconsistent with this section.

(d) Written notice of the availability of the coverage provided by this section shall be delivered to every subscriber under the plan upon enrollment and annually thereafter. The notice required by this subsection may be included as a part of any yearly informational packet sent to the subscriber. (1997-312, s. 3; 1999-351, s. 3.3; 2001-334, s. 13.3.)

§ 58-67-80. Meaning of terms "accident", "accidental injury", and "accidental means".

(a) Effective October 1, 1989, this section applies to all health maintenance organization plans under this Article.

(b) "Accident", "accidental injury", and "accidental means" shall be defined to imply "result" language and shall not include words that establish an accidental means test. (1989, c. 485, s. 12.)

§ 58-67-85. Master group contracts, filing requirement; required and prohibited provisions.

(a) A health maintenance organization may issue a master group contract with the approval of the Commissioner of Insurance provided the contract and the individual certificates issued to members of the group, shall comply in substance to the other provisions of this Article. Any such contract may provide for the adjustment of the rate of the premium or benefits conferred as provided in the contract, and in accordance with an adjustment schedule filed with and approved by the Commissioner of Insurance. If the master group contract is issued, altered or modified, the enrollees' contracts issued in pursuance thereof are altered or modified accordingly, all laws and clauses in the enrollees' contracts to the contrary notwithstanding. Nothing in this Article shall be construed to prohibit or prevent the same. Forms of such contract shall at all times be furnished upon request of enrollees thereto.

(b), (c) Repealed by Session Laws 1997-259, s. 18.

(d) Employees shall be added to the master group coverage no later than 90 days after their first day of employment. Employment shall be considered continuous and not be considered broken except for unexcused absences from work for reasons other than illness or injury. The term "employee" is defined as a nonseasonal person who works on a full-time basis, with a normal work week of 30 or more hours and who is otherwise eligible for coverage, but does not include a person who works on a part-time, temporary, or substitute basis.

(d1) When determining employee eligibility for a large employer, as defined in G.S. 58-68-25(10), an individual proprietor, owner, or operator shall be defined as an "employee" for the purpose of obtaining coverage under the employee group health plan and shall not be held to a minimum workweek requirement as imposed on other eligible employees.

(e) Whenever an employer master group contract replaces another group contract, whether the contract was issued by a corporation under Articles 1 through 67 of this Chapter, the liability of the succeeding corporation for insuring persons covered under the previous group contract is:

(1) Each person who is eligible for coverage in accordance with the succeeding corporation's plan of benefits with respect to classes eligible and activity at work and nonconfinement rules must be covered by the succeeding corporation's plan of benefits; and

(2) Each person not covered under the succeeding corporation's plan of benefits in accordance with (e)(1) must nevertheless be covered by the succeeding corporation if that person was validly covered, including benefit extension, under the prior plan on the date of discontinuance and if the person is a member of the class of persons eligible for coverage under the succeeding corporation's plan. (1989, c. 775, s. 5; 1991, c. 720, ss. 38, 88; 1991 (Reg. Sess., 1992), c. 837, s. 4; 1993, c. 408, ss. 5, 5.1; 1995, c. 507, s. 23A.1(f); 1997-259, s. 18; 2005-223, s. 2(b).)

§ 58-67-88. Continuity of care.

(a) Definitions. - As used in this section:

(1) "Ongoing special condition" means:

a. In the case of an acute illness, a condition that is serious enough to require medical care or treatment to avoid a reasonable possibility of death or permanent harm.

b. In the case of a chronic illness or condition, a disease or condition that is life-threatening, degenerative, or disabling, and requires medical care or treatment over a prolonged period of time.

c. In the case of pregnancy, pregnancy from the start of the second trimester.

d. In the case of a terminal illness, an individual has a medical prognosis that the individual's life expectancy is six months or less.

(2) "Terminated or termination". - Includes, with respect to a contract, the expiration or nonrenewal of the contract, but does not include a termination of the contract by an HMO for failure to meet applicable quality standards or for fraud.

(b) Termination of Provider. - If a contract between an HMO benefit plan that is not a point-of-service plan and a health care provider is terminated by the provider or by the HMO, or benefits or coverage provided by the HMO are terminated because of a change in the terms of provider participation in a health benefit plan of an HMO that is not a point-of-service plan, and an individual is covered by the plan and is undergoing treatment from the provider for an ongoing special condition on the date of the termination, then, the HMO shall:

(1) Upon termination of the contract by the HMO or upon receipt by the HMO of written notification of termination by the provider, notify the individual on a timely basis of the termination and of the right to elect continuation of coverage of treatment by the provider under this section if the individual has filed a claim with the HMO for services provided by the terminated provider or the individual is otherwise known by the HMO to be a patient of the provider.

(2) Subject to subsection (h) of this section, permit the individual to elect to continue to be covered with respect to the treatment by the provider of the ongoing special condition during a transitional period provided under this section.

(c) Newly Covered Insured. - Each health benefit plan offered by an HMO that is not a point-of-service plan shall provide transition coverage to individuals who are undergoing treatment from a provider for an ongoing special condition and are newly covered under the health benefit plan because the individual's employer has changed health benefit plans, and the HMO shall:

(1) Notify the individual on the date of enrollment of the right to elect continuation of coverage of treatment by the provider under this section.

(2) Subject to subsection (h) of this section, permit the individual to elect to continue to be covered with respect to the treatment by the provider of the ongoing special condition during a transitional period provided under this section.

(d) Transitional Period: In General. - Except as otherwise provided in subsections (e), (f), and (g) of this section, the transitional period under this subsection shall extend up to 90 days, as determined by the treating health care provider, after the date of the notice to the individual described in subdivision (b)(1) of this section or the date of enrollment in a new plan described in subdivision (c)(1) of this section.

(e) Transitional Period: Scheduled Surgery, Organ Transplantation, or Inpatient Care. - If surgery, organ transplantation, or other inpatient care was scheduled for an individual before the date of the notice required under subdivision (b)(1) of this section, or the date of enrollment in a new plan described in subdivision (c)(1) of this section, or if the individual on that date was on an established waiting list or otherwise scheduled to have the surgery, transplantation, or other inpatient care, the transitional period under this subsection with respect to the surgery, transplantation, or other inpatient care shall extend beyond the period under subsection (d) of this section through the date of discharge of the individual after completion of the surgery, transplantation, or other inpatient care, and through postdischarge follow-up care related to the surgery, transplantation, or other inpatient care occurring within 90 days after the date of discharge.

(f) Transitional Period: Pregnancy. - If an insured has entered the second trimester of pregnancy on the date of the notice required under subdivision (b)(1) of this section, or the date of enrollment in a new plan described in subdivision (c)(1) of this section, and the provider was treating the pregnancy before the date of the notice, or the date of enrollment in the new plan, the transitional period with respect to the provider's treatment of the pregnancy shall extend through the provision of 60 days of postpartum care.

(g)   Transitional Period: Terminal Illness. - If an insured was determined to be terminally ill at the time of a provider's termination of participation under subsection (b) of this section, or at the time of enrollment in the new plan under subdivision (c)(1) of this section, and the provider was treating the terminal illness before the date of the termination or enrollment in the new plan, the transitional period shall extend for the remainder of the individual's life with respect to care directly related to the treatment of the terminal illness or its medical manifestations.

(h)   Permissible Terms and Conditions. - An HMO may condition coverage of continued treatment by a provider under subdivision (b)(2) or (c)(2) of this section upon the following terms and conditions:

(1)   When care is provided pursuant to subdivision (b)(2) of this section, the provider agrees to accept reimbursement from the HMO and individual involved, with respect to cost-sharing, at the rates applicable before the start of the transitional period as payment in full. When care is provided pursuant to subdivision (c)(2) of this section, the provider agrees to accept the prevailing rate based on contracts the insurer has with the same or similar providers in the same or similar geographic area, plus the applicable copayment, as reimbursement in full from the HMO and the insured for all covered services.

(2)   The provider agrees to comply with the quality assurance programs of the HMO responsible for payment under subdivision (1) of this subsection and to provide to the HMO necessary medical information related to the care provided. The quality assurance programs shall not override the professional or ethical responsibility of the provider or interfere with the provider's ability to provide information or assistance to the patient.

(3)   The provider agrees otherwise to adhere to the HMO's established policies and procedures for participating providers, including procedures regarding referrals and obtaining prior authorization, providing services pursuant to a treatment plan, if any, approved by the HMO, and member hold harmless provisions.

(4)   The insured or the insured's representative notifies the HMO within 45 days of the date of the notice described in subdivision (b)(1) of this section or

the new enrollment described in subdivision (c)(1) of this section, that the insured elects to continue receiving treatment by the provider.

(5) The provider agrees to discontinue providing services at the end of the transition period pursuant to this section and to assist the insured in an orderly transition to a network provider. Nothing in this section shall prohibit the insured from continuing to receive services from the provider at the insured's expense.

(i) Construction. - Nothing in this section:

(1) Requires the coverage of benefits that would not have been covered if the provider involved remained a participating provider or, in the case of a newly covered insured, requires the coverage of benefits not provided under the new policy under which the person is covered.

(2) Requires an HMO to offer a transitional period when the HMO terminates a provider's contract for reasons relating to quality of care or fraud; and refusal to offer a transitional period under these circumstances is not subject to the grievance review provisions of G.S. 58-50-62.

(3) Prohibits an HMO from extending any transitional period beyond that specified in this section.

(4) Prohibits an HMO from terminating the continuing services of a provider as described in this section when the HMO has determined that the provider's continued provision of services may result in, or is resulting in, a serious danger to the health or safety of the insured. Such terminations shall be in accordance with the contract provisions that the provider would otherwise be subject to if the provider's contract were still in effect.

(j) Disclosure of Right to Transitional Period. - Each HMO shall include a clear description of an insured's rights under this section in its evidence of coverage and summary plan description. (2001-446, s. 1.)

§ 58-67-90. Licensing and regulation of agents.

Every agent of any HMO authorized to do business in this State under this Article is subject to the licensing provisions of Article 33 of this Chapter and all other provisions in this Chapter applicable to life and health insurance agents.

(1977, c. 580, s. 1; 1979, c. 876, s. 1; 1985 (Reg. Sess., 1986), c. 928, s. 5; 1987, c. 629, s. 3; 1999-244, s. 8.)

§ 58-67-95. Powers of insurers and hospital and medical service corporations.

(a) An insurance company licensed in this State, or a hospital or medical service corporation authorized to do business in this State, may either directly or through a subsidiary or affiliate organize and operate a health maintenance organization under the provisions of this Article. Notwithstanding any other law which may be inconsistent herewith, any two or more such insurance companies, hospital or medical service corporations, or subsidiaries or affiliates thereof, may jointly organize and operate a health maintenance organization. The business of insurance is deemed to include the arranging of health care by a health maintenance organization owned or operated by an insurer or a subsidiary thereof.

(b) Notwithstanding any provision of the insurance and hospital or medical service corporation laws contained in Articles 1 through 66 of this Chapter, an insurer or a hospital or medical service corporation may contract with a health maintenance organization to provide insurance or similar protection against the cost of care provided through health maintenance organizations and to provide coverage in the event of the failure of the health maintenance organization to meet its obligations. The enrollees of a health maintenance organization constitute a permissible group under such laws. Among other things, under such contracts, the insurer or hospital or medical service corporation may make benefit payments to health maintenance organizations for health care services rendered by providers pursuant to the health care plan. (1977, c. 580, s. 1; 1979, c. 876, s. 1.)

§ 58-67-100. Examinations.

(a) The Commissioner may make an examination of the affairs of any health maintenance organization and the contracts, agreements or other arrangements pursuant to its health care plan as often as the Commissioner deems it necessary for the protection of the interests of the people of this State but not less frequently than once every five years. Examinations shall otherwise be conducted under G.S. 58-2-131 through G.S. 58-2-134.

(b) Repealed by Session Laws 1997-519, s. 1, effective January 1, 1998.

(c) Repealed by Session Laws 1995, c. 360, s. 2(m).

(d) Instead of conducting an examination, the Commissioner may accept the report of an examination made by the HMO regulator of another state. (1977, c. 580, s. 1; 1979, c. 876, s. 1; 1995, c. 360, s. 2(m); 1997-519, s. 1.4; 1999-132, s. 11.10; 2007-127, s. 16.)

§ 58-67-105. Hazardous financial condition.

(a) Whenever the financial condition of any health maintenance organization indicates a condition such that the continued operation of the health maintenance organization might be hazardous to its enrollees, creditors, or the general public, then the Commissioner may order the health maintenance organization to take such action as may be reasonably necessary to rectify the existing condition, including but not limited to one or more of the following steps:

(1) To reduce the total amount of present and potential liability for benefits by reinsurance;

(2) To reduce the volume of new business being accepted;

(3) To reduce the expenses by specified methods;

(4) To suspend or limit the writing of new business for a period of time; or

(5) To require an increase to the health maintenance organization's net worth by contribution.

(b) The Commissioner may adopt rules to set uniform standards and criteria for the early warning that the continued operation of any health maintenance organization might be hazardous to its enrollees, creditors, or the general public, and to set standards for evaluating the financial condition of any health maintenance organization, which standards shall be consistent with the purposes expressed in subsection (a) of this section. (1987, c. 631, s. 5.)

§ 58-67-110. Protection against insolvency.

(a) The Commissioner shall require deposits in accordance with the provisions of G.S. 58-67-25.

(b) Each full service health maintenance organization shall maintain a minimum net worth equal to the greater of one million dollars ($1,000,000) or the amount required pursuant to the risk-based capital provisions of Article 12 of this Chapter. Each single service health maintenance organization shall maintain a minimum net worth equal to the greater of fifty thousand dollars ($50,000) or that amount required pursuant to the risk-based capital provisions of Article 12 of this Chapter.

(c), (d) Repealed by Session Laws 2003-212, s. 21, effective October 1, 2003.

(e) Every full service medical health maintenance organization shall have and maintain at all times an adequate plan for protection against insolvency acceptable to the Commissioner. In determining the adequacy of such a plan, the Commissioner may consider:

(1) A reinsurance agreement preapproved by the Commissioner covering excess loss, stop loss, or catastrophes. The agreement must provide that the Commissioner will be notified no less than 60 days prior to cancellation or reduction of coverage.

(2) A conversion policy or policies that will be offered by an insurer to the enrollees in the event of the health maintenance organization's insolvency.

(3) Any other arrangements offering protection against insolvency that the Commissioner may require. (1987, c. 631, s. 5; 1989, c. 776, ss. 11, 12; 2003-212, s. 21.)

§ 58-67-115. Hold harmless agreements or special deposit.

(a) Unless the HMO maintains a special deposit in accordance with subsection (b) of this section, each contract between every HMO and a participating provider of health care services shall be in writing and shall set forth that in the event the HMO fails to pay for health care services as set forth in the contract, the subscriber or enrollee shall not be liable to the provider for any sums owed by the HMO. No other provisions of such contracts shall, under any circumstances, change the effect of such a provision. No participating provider, or agent, trustee, or assignee thereof, may maintain any action at law against a subscriber or enrollee to collect sums owed by the HMO.

(b) In the event that the participating provider contract has not been reduced to writing or that the contract fails to contain the required prohibition, the HMO shall maintain a special deposit in cash or cash equivalent as follows:

(1) Every HMO that has incurred uncovered health care expenditures in an amount that exceeds ten percent (10%) of its total expenditures for health care services for the immediately preceding six months, shall do either of the following:

a. Calculate as of the first day of every month and maintain for the remainder of the month, cash or cash equivalents acceptable to the Commissioner, as an account to cover claims for uncovered health care expenditures at least equal to one hundred twenty percent (120%) of the sum of the following:

1. All claims for uncovered health care expenditures received for reimbursement, but not yet processed; and

2. All claims for uncovered health care expenditures denied for reimbursement during the previous 60 days; and

3. All claims for uncovered health care expenditures approved for reimbursement, but not yet paid; and

4. An estimate for uncovered health care expenditures incurred, but not reported; and

5. All claims for uncovered emergency services and uncovered services rendered outside the service area.

b. Maintain adequate insurance, or a guaranty arrangement approved in writing by the Commissioner, to pay for any loss to enrollees claiming reimbursement due to the insolvency of the HMO. The Commissioner shall approve a guaranty arrangement if the guaranteeing organization has been in operation for at least 10 years and has a net worth, including organization-related land, buildings, and equipment, of at least fifty million dollars ($50,000,000); unless the Commissioner finds that the approval of such guaranty may be financially hazardous to enrollees. In order to qualify under the terms of this subsection, the guaranteeing organization shall (i) submit to the jurisdiction of this State for actions arising under the guarantee; (ii) submit certified, audited annual financial statements to the Commissioner; and (iii) appoint the Commissioner to receive service of process in this State.

(2) Whenever the reimbursements described in this subsection exceed ten percent (10%) of the HMO's total costs for health care services over the immediately preceding six months, the HMO shall file a written report with the Commissioner containing the information necessary to determine compliance with sub-subdivision (b)(1)a. of this section with its financial statements filed pursuant to G.S. 58-2-165. Upon an adequate showing by the HMO that the requirements of this section should be waived or reduced, the Commissioner may waive or reduce these requirements to such an amount as he deems sufficient to protect enrollees of the HMO consistent with the intent and purpose of this Article.

(3) Any cash or cash equivalents maintained pursuant to the terms of this section shall be maintained as a special deposit controlled by and administered by the Commissioner in accordance with the provisions of G.S. 58-5-1. (1989, c. 776, s. 13; 2005-215, s. 19.)

§ 58-67-120. Continuation of benefits.

(a) The Commissioner shall require that each HMO have a plan for handling insolvency, which plan allows for continuation of benefits for the duration of the contract period for which premiums have been paid and continuation of benefits to enrollees who are confined in an inpatient facility until their discharge or expiration of benefits. In considering such a plan, the Commissioner may require:

(1) Insurance to cover the expenses to be paid for benefits after an insolvency;

(2) Provisions in provider contracts that obligate the provider to provide services for the duration of the period after the HMO's insolvency for which

premium payment has been made and until the enrollees' discharge from inpatient facilities;

(3)   Insolvency reserves such as the Commissioner may require;

(4)   Letters of credit acceptable to the Commissioner;

(5)   Any other arrangements to assure that benefits are continued as specified above. (1989, c. 776, s. 13.)

§ 58-67-125. Enrollment period.

(a)   In the event of an insolvency of an HMO upon order of the Commissioner, all other carriers that participated in the enrollment process with the insolvent HMO at a group's last regular enrollment period shall offer such group's enrollees of the insolvent HMO a 30-day enrollment period commencing upon the date of insolvency. Each carrier shall offer such enrollees of the insolvent HMO the same coverages and rates that it had offered to the enrollees of the group at its last regular enrollment period.

(b)   If no other carrier had been offered to some groups enrolled in the insolvent HMO, or if the Commissioner determines that the other health benefit plan or plans lack sufficient health care delivery resources to assure that health care services will be available and accessible to all of the group enrollees of the insolvent HMO, then the Commissioner shall allocate the insolvent HMO's group contracts for such groups among all other HMOs that operate within a portion of the insolvent HMO's service area, taking into consideration the health care delivery resources of each HMO. Each HMO to which a group or groups are so allocated shall offer such group or groups that HMO's existing coverage that is most similar to each group's coverage with the insolvent HMO at rates determined in accordance with the successor HMO's existing rating methodology.

(c)   The Commissioner shall also allocate the insolvent HMO's nongroup enrollees who are unable to obtain other coverage among all HMOs that operate within a portion of the insolvent HMO's service area, taking into consideration the health care delivery resources of each such HMO. Each HMO to which nongroup enrollees are allocated shall offer such nongroup enrollees that HMO's existing coverage for individual or conversion coverage as determined by his type of coverage in the insolvent HMO at rates determined in accordance with the successor HMO's existing rating methodology. Successor HMOs that do not offer direct nongroup enrollment may aggregate all of the allocated nongroup enrollees into one group for rating and coverage purposes. (1989, c. 776, s. 13.)

§ 58-67-130. Replacement coverage.

(a) Any carrier providing replacement coverage with respect to group hospital, medical, or surgical expense or service benefits, within a period of 60 days from the date of discontinuance of a prior HMO contract or policy providing such hospital, medical or surgical expense or service benefits, shall immediately cover all enrollees who were validly covered under the previous HMO contract or policy at the date of discontinuance and who would otherwise be eligible for coverage under the succeeding carrier's contract, regardless of any provisions of the contract relating to active employment or hospital confinement or pregnancy.

(b) Except to the extent benefits for the condition would have been reduced or excluded under the prior carrier's contract or policy, no provision in a succeeding carrier's contract of replacement coverage that would operate to reduce or exclude benefits on the basis that the condition giving rise to benefits preceded the effective date of the succeeding carrier's contract shall be applied with respect to those enrollees validly covered under the prior carrier's contract or policy on the date of discontinuance. (1989, c. 776. s. 13.)

§ 58-67-135. Incurred but not reported claims.

(a) Every HMO shall, when determining liability, include an amount estimated in the aggregate to provide for any unearned premium and for the payment of all claims for health care expenditures that have been incurred, whether reported or unreported, that are unpaid and for which such HMO is or may be liable; and to provide for the expense of adjustment or settlement of such claims.

(b)   Such liabilities shall be computed in accordance with rules adopted by the Commissioner upon reasonable consideration of the ascertained experience and character of the HMO. (1989, c. 776, s. 13.)

§ 58-67-140. Suspension or revocation of license.

(a)   The Commissioner may suspend or revoke an HMO license if the Commissioner finds that the HMO:

(1)   Is operating significantly in contravention of its basic organizational document, or in a manner contrary to that described in and reasonably inferred from any other information submitted under G.S. 58-67-10, unless amendments to such submissions have been filed with and approved by the Commissioner.

(2)   Issues evidences of coverage or uses a schedule of premiums for health care services that do not comply with G.S. 58-67-50.

(3)   Is no longer financially responsible and may reasonably be expected to be unable to meet its obligations to enrollees or prospective enrollees.

(4)   Has itself or through any person on its behalf advertised or merchandised its services in an untrue, misrepresentative, misleading, deceptive or unfair manner.

(5)   Is operating in a manner that would be hazardous to its enrollees.

(6)   Knowingly or repeatedly fails or refuses to comply with any law or rule applicable to the HMO or with any order issued by the Commissioner after notice and opportunity for a hearing.

(7)   Has knowingly published or made to the Department or to the public any false statement or report, including any report or any data that serves as the basis for any report, required to be submitted under G.S. 58-3-191.

(b)   A license shall be suspended or revoked only after compliance with G.S. 58-67-155.

(c)   When an HMO license is suspended, the HMO shall not, during the suspension, enroll any additional enrollees except newborn children or other newly acquired dependents of existing enrollees, and shall not engage in any advertising or solicitation.

(d) When an HMO license is revoked, the HMO shall proceed, immediately following the effective date of the order of revocation, to wind up its affairs, and shall conduct no further business except as may be essential to the orderly conclusion of the affairs of the HMO. The HMO shall engage in no advertising or solicitation. The Commissioner may, by written order, permit such further operation of the HMO as the Commissioner may find to be in the best interest of enrollees, to the end that enrollees will be afforded the greatest practical opportunity to obtain continuing health care coverage. (1977, c. 580, s. 1; 1979, c. 876, s. 1; 1997-519, s. 1.5; 2003-212, ss. 22, 23, 26(l).)

§ 58-67-145. Rehabilitation, liquidation, or conservation of health maintenance organization.

Any rehabilitation, liquidation or conservation of a health maintenance organization shall be deemed to be the rehabilitation, liquidation, or conservation of an insurance company and shall be conducted under the supervision of the Commissioner pursuant to the law governing the rehabilitation, liquidation, or conservation of insurance companies, except that the provisions of Articles 48 and 62 of this Chapter shall not apply to health maintenance organizations. The Commissioner may apply for an order directing him to rehabilitate, liquidate, or conserve a health maintenance organization upon one or more grounds set out in Article 30 of this Chapter or when in his opinion the continued operation of the health maintenance organization would be hazardous either to the enrollees or to the people of this State. (1977, c. 580, s. 1; 1979, c. 876, s. 1; 1989, c. 452, s. 2; c. 776, s. 14; 1998-211, s. 5.)

§ 58-67-150. Regulations.

The Commissioner may, after notice and hearing, promulgate reasonable rules and regulations as are necessary or proper to carry out the provisions of this Article. Such rules and regulations shall be subject to review in accordance with G.S. 58-67-155. (1977, c. 580, s. 1; 1979, c. 876, s. 1.)

§ 58-67-155. Administrative procedures.

(a) When the Commissioner has cause to believe that grounds for the denial of an application for a certificate of authority exist, or that grounds for the suspension or revocation of a certificate of authority exist, he shall notify the health maintenance organization in writing specifically stating the grounds for denial, suspension, or revocation and fixing a time of at least 30 days thereafter for a hearing on the matter.

(b) After such hearing, or upon the failure of the health maintenance organization to appear at such hearing, the Commissioner shall take action as is deemed advisable or written findings which shall be mailed to the health maintenance organization. The action of the Commissioner shall be subject to review by the Superior Court of Wake County. The court may, in disposing of the issue before it, modify, affirm, or reverse the order of the Commissioner in whole or in part.

(c) The provisions of Chapter 150B of the General Statutes of this State shall apply to proceedings under this section to the extent that they are not in conflict with subsections (a) and (b). (1977, c. 580, s. 1; 1979, c. 876, s. 1; 1987, c. 827, s. 1.)

§ 58-67-160. Fees.

Every health maintenance organization subject to this Article shall pay to the Commissioner a fee of five hundred dollars ($500.00) for filing an application for a license and an annual license continuation fee of two thousand dollars ($2,000) for each license. The license shall continue in full force and effect, subject to timely payment of the annual license continuation fee in accordance with G.S. 58-6-7 and subject to any other applicable provisions of the insurance laws of this State. (1977, c. 580, s. 1; 1979, c. 876, s. 1; 1989 (Reg. Sess., 1990), c. 1069, s. 6; 1995, c. 507, s. 11A(c); 1999-435, s. 6; 2003-212, s. 26(m); 2005-424, s. 1.6; 2009-451, s. 21.10(a).)

§ 58-67-165. Penalties and enforcement.

(a) The Commissioner may, in addition to or in lieu of suspending or revoking a license under G.S. 58-67-140, proceed under G.S. 58-2-70, provided that the health maintenance organization has a reasonable time within which to remedy the defect in its operations that gave rise to the procedure under G.S. 58-2-70.

(b) Any person who violates this Article or any other provision of this Chapter that expressly applies to health maintenance organizations shall be guilty of a Class 1 misdemeanor.

(c) (1) If the Commissioner shall for any reason have cause to believe that any violation of this Article or any other provision of this Chapter that expressly applies to health maintenance organizations has occurred or is threatened, the Commissioner may give notice to the health maintenance organization and to the representatives or other persons who appear to be involved in such suspected violation to arrange a conference with the alleged violators or their authorized representatives for the purpose of attempting to ascertain the facts relating to such suspected violation, and, in the event it appears that any violation has occurred or is threatened, to arrive at an adequate and effective means of correcting or preventing such violation.

(2) Proceedings under this subsection shall not be governed by any formal procedural requirements, and may be conducted in such manner as the Commissioner may deem appropriate under the circumstances.

(d) (1) The Commissioner may issue an order directing a health maintenance organization or a representative of a health maintenance organization to cease and desist from engaging in any act or practice in violation of the provisions of this Article or any other provision of this Chapter that expressly applies to health maintenance organizations.

(2) Within 30 days after service of the cease and desist order, the respondent may request a hearing on the question of whether acts or practices have occurred that are in violation of this Article or any other provision of this Chapter that expressly applies to health maintenance organizations. The hearing shall be conducted under Article 3A of Chapter 150B of the General Statutes, and judicial review shall be available as provided by Article 4 of Chapter 150B of the General Statutes.

(e) In the case of any violation of the provisions of this Article or any other provision of this Chapter that expressly applies to health maintenance organizations, if the Commissioner elects not to issue a cease and desist order, or in the event of noncompliance with a cease and desist order issued under subsection (d) of this section, the Commissioner may institute a proceeding to obtain injunctive relief, or seeking other appropriate relief, in the Superior Court of Wake County. (1977, c. 580, s. 1; 1979, c. 876, s. 1; 1985, c. 666, s. 52; 1987, c. 827, s. 1; 1993, c. 539, s. 470; 1994, Ex. Sess., c. 24, s. 14(c); 2001-5, s. 1.)

§ 58-67-170. Statutory construction and relationship to other laws.

(a) Except as otherwise provided in this Chapter, provisions of the insurance laws and service corporation laws do not apply to any health maintenance organization licensed under this Article. This subsection does not apply to an insurer or service corporation licensed and regulated under the insurance laws or the service corporation laws of this State except with respect to its health maintenance organization activities authorized and regulated under this Article or any other provision of this Chapter that expressly applies to health maintenance organizations.

(b) Solicitation of enrollees by a health maintenance organization granted a license, or its representatives, shall not be construed to violate any provision of law relating to solicitation or advertising by health professionals.

(c) Any health maintenance organization authorized under this Article shall not be deemed to be practicing medicine or dentistry and shall be exempt from the provisions of Chapter 90 of the General Statutes relating to the practice of medicine and dentistry; provided, however, that this exemption does not apply to individual providers under contract with or employed by the health maintenance organization. (1977, c. 580, s. 1; 1979, c. 876, s. 1; 1985, c. 30; 2001-5, s. 2.)

§ 58-67-171. Other laws applicable to HMOs.

The following provisions of this Chapter are applicable to HMOs that are subject to this Article:

G.S. 58-2-125.	Authority over all insurance companies; no exemptions from license.
G.S. 58-2-150.	Oath required for compliance with law.
G.S. 58-2-155.	Investigation of charges.
G.S. 58-2-160.	Reporting and investigation of insurance and reinsurance fraud and the financial condition of licensees; immunity from liability.
G.S. 58-2-162.	Embezzlement by insurance agents, brokers, or administrators.
G.S. 58-2-185.	Record of business kept by companies and agents; Commissioner may inspect.
G.S. 58-2-190.	Commissioner may require special reports.
G.S. 58-2-195.	Commissioner may require records, reports, etc., for agencies, agents, and others.
G.S. 58-2-200.	Books and papers required to be exhibited.
G.S. 58-3-50.	Companies must do business in own name; emblems, insignias, etc.
G.S. 58-3-100(c),(e).	Insurance company licensing provisions.
G.S. 58-3-115.	Twisting with respect to insurance policies; penalties.
G.S. 58-7-46.	Notification to Commissioner for president or chief executive officer changes.
G.S. 58-7-73.	Dissolution of insurers.
Part 7 of Article 10.	Annual Financial Reporting.
G.S. 58-50-35	Notice of nonpayment of premium required before forfeiture.

G.S. 58-51-15(a)(2)b.	Accident and health policy provisions.
G.S. 58-51-17	Portability for accident and health insurance.
G.S. 58-51-25.	Policy coverage to continue as to mentally retarded or physically handicapped children.
G.S. 58-51-35.	Insurers and others to afford coverage to mentally retarded and physically handicapped children.
G.S. 58-51-45.	Policies to be issued to any person possessing the sickle-cell trait or hemoglobin C trait. (1999-244, s. 2; 2005-215, s. 20; 2009-382, s. 7; 2009-384, s. 4.)

§ 58-67-175. Filings and reports as public documents.

All applications, filings and reports required under this Article shall be treated as public documents. (1977, c. 580, s. 1; 1979, c. 876, s. 1.)

§ 58-67-180. Confidentiality of medical information.

Any data or information pertaining to the diagnosis, treatment, or health of any enrollee or applicant obtained from such person or from any provider by any health maintenance organization shall be held in confidence and shall not be disclosed to any person except to the extent that it may be necessary to carry out the purposes of this Article; or upon the express consent of the enrollee or applicant; or pursuant to statute; or pursuant to court order for the production of evidence or the discovery thereof; or in the event of claim or litigation between such person and the health maintenance organization wherein such data or information is pertinent. A health maintenance organization shall be entitled to claim any statutory privileges against such disclosure which the provider who furnished such information to the health maintenance organization is entitled to claim. (1977, c. 580, s. 1; 1979, c. 876, s. 1; 1999-272, s. 1.)

§ 58-67-185. Severability.

f any section, term, or provision of this Article shall be adjudged invalid for any reason, such judgments shall not affect, impair, or invalidate any other section, term, or provision of this Article, but the remaining sections, terms, and provisions shall be and remain in full force and effect. (1977, c. 580, s. 1; 1979, c. 876, s. 1.)

Article 68.

Health Insurance Portability and Accountability.

§§ 58-68-1 through 58-68-20: Repealed by Session Laws 1997-259, s. 1(a).

Part A. Group Market Reforms.

Subpart 1. Portability, Access, and Renewability Requirements.

§ 58-68-25. Definitions; excepted benefits; employer size rule.

(a) Definitions. - In addition to other definitions throughout this Article, the following definitions and their cognates apply in this Article:

(1) "Bona fide association". - With respect to health insurance coverage offered in this State, an association that:

a. Has been actively in existence for at least five years.

b. Has been formed and maintained in good faith for purposes other than obtaining insurance.

c. Does not condition membership in the association on any health status-related factor relating to an individual (including an employee of an employer or a dependent of an employee).

d. Makes health insurance coverage offered through the association available to all members regardless of any health status-related factor relating to the members (or individuals eligible for coverage through a member).

e. Does not make health insurance coverage offered through the association available other than in connection with a member of the association.

f. Meets the additional requirements as may be imposed under State law.

(2) "COBRA continuation provision". - Any of the following:

a. Section 4980B of the Internal Revenue Code of 1986, other than subdivision (f)(1) of the section insofar as it relates to pediatric vaccines.

b. Part 6 of subtitle B of title I of the Employee Retirement Income Security Act of 1974, other than section 609 of the Act.

c. Title XXII of the Public Health Service Act (42 U.S.C.S. § 300bb, et seq.,) as requirements for certain group health plans for certain State and local employees.

d. Article 53 of this Chapter or the health insurance continuation law of another state.

(3) "Employee". - The meaning given the term under section 3(6) of the Employee Retirement Income Security Act of 1974.

(4) "Employer". - The meaning given the term under section 3(5) of the Employee Retirement Income Security Act of 1974, except that the term shall include only employers of two or more employees.

(4a) "Group health insurance coverage". - Health insurance coverage offered in connection with a group health plan.

(4b) "Group health plan". - The meaning given the term under 45 C.F.R. § 146.145(a).

(4c) "Group market." - The market for health insurance coverage offered in connection with a group health plan.

(5) "Health insurance coverage" or "coverage" or "health insurance plan" or "plan". - Benefits consisting of medical care, provided directly through insurance or otherwise and including items and services paid for as medical care, under any accident and health insurance policy or certificate, hospital or medical service plan contract, or health maintenance organization contract, written by a health insurer. Health insurance coverage includes group health insurance coverage and individual health insurance coverage.

(6) "Health insurer". - An insurance company subject to this Chapter, a hospital or medical service corporation subject to Article 65 of this Chapter, a health maintenance organization subject to Article 67 of this Chapter, or a multiple employer welfare arrangement subject to Article 49 of this Chapter, that offers and issues health insurance coverage.

(7) "Health status-related factor". - Any of the factors described in G.S. 58-68-35(a)(1).

(8) "Individual health insurance coverage". - Health insurance coverage offered to individuals in the individual market, but not short-term limited duration insurance.

(9) "Individual market". - The market for health insurance coverage offered to individuals.

(10) "Large employer". - An employer who employed an average of at least 51 employees on business days during the preceding calendar year and who employs at least two employees on the first day of the health insurance plan year.

(11) "Large group market". - The health insurance market under which individuals obtain health insurance coverage, directly or through any arrangement, on behalf of themselves and their dependents through a group health insurance plan maintained by a large employer.

(12) "Medical care". - Amounts paid for:

a. The diagnosis, cure, mitigation, treatment, or prevention of disease, or amounts paid for the purpose of affecting any structure or function of the body.

b. Amounts paid for transportation primarily for and essential to medical care referred to in sub-subdivision a. of this subdivision.

282

c.   Amounts paid for insurance covering medical care referred to in sub-subdivisions a. and b. of this subdivision.

(13)   "Network plan". - Health insurance coverage of a health insurer under which the financing and delivery of medical care (including items and services paid for as medical care) are provided, in whole or in part, through a defined set of health care providers under contract with the health insurer.

(14)   "Participant". - The meaning given the term under section 3(7) of the Employee Retirement Income Security Act of 1974.

(15)   "Placed for adoption". - The assumption and retention by a person of a legal obligation for total or partial support of a child in anticipation of adoption of the child. The child's placement with the person terminates upon the termination of the legal obligation.

(16)   "Small employer". - The meaning given to the term in G.S. 58-50-110(22).

(17)   "Small group market". - The health insurance market under which individuals obtain health insurance coverage, directly or through any arrangement, on behalf of themselves and their dependents through a group health insurance plan maintained by a small employer.

(b)   Excepted Benefits. - For the purposes of this Article, "excepted benefits" means benefits under one or more or any combination of the following:

(1)   Benefits not subject to requirements. -

a.   Coverage only for accident or disability income insurance or any combination of these.

b.   Coverage issued as a supplement to liability insurance.

c.   Liability insurance, including general liability insurance and automobile liability insurance.

d.   Workers' compensation or similar insurance.

e.   Automobile medical payment insurance.

f. Credit-only insurance.

g. Coverage for on-site medical clinics.

h. Other similar insurance coverage, specified in federal regulations, under which benefits for medical care are secondary or incidental to other insurance benefits.

i. Short-term limited-duration health insurance policies as defined in Part 144 of Title 45 of the Code of Federal Regulations.

(2) Benefits not subject to requirements if offered separately. -

a. Limited scope dental or vision benefits.

b. Benefits for long-term care, nursing care, home health care, community-based care, or any combination of these.

c. The other similar, limited benefits as are specified in federal regulations.

(3) Benefits not subject to requirements if offered as independent, noncoordinated benefits. -

a. Coverage only for a specified disease or illness.

b. Hospital indemnity or other fixed indemnity insurance.

(4) Benefits not subject to requirements if offered as separate insurance policy. - Medicare supplemental health insurance (as defined under section 1882(g)(1) of the Social Security Act), coverage supplemental to the coverage provided under chapter 55 of title 10, United States Code, and similar supplemental coverage provided to coverage under a group health insurance plan.

(c) Application of certain rules in determination of employer size. - For the purposes of this Article:

(1) Application of aggregation rule for employers. - All persons treated as a single employer under subsection (b), (c), (m), or (o) of section 414 of the Internal Revenue Code of 1986 shall be treated as one employer.

(2) Employers not in existence in preceding year. - In the case of an employer that was not in existence throughout the preceding calendar year, the determination of whether the employer is a small or large employer shall be based on the average number of employees that it is reasonably expected the employer will employ on business days in the current calendar year.

(3) Predecessors. - Any reference in this subsection to an employer shall include a reference to any predecessor of the employer. (1997-259, s. 1(c); 2002-187, s. 5.1; 2009-382, ss. 2, 3.)

§ 58-68-30. Increased portability through limitation on preexisting condition exclusions.

(a) Limitation on Preexisting Condition Exclusion Period; Crediting for Periods of Previous Coverage. - Subject to subsection (d) of this section, a group health insurer may, with respect to a participant or beneficiary, impose a preexisting condition exclusion only if:

(1) The exclusion relates to a condition, whether physical or mental, regardless of the cause of the condition, for which medical advice, diagnosis, care, or treatment was recommended or received within the six-month period ending on the enrollment date.

(2) The exclusion extends for a period of not more than 12 months, or 18 months in the case of a late enrollee, after the enrollment date.

(3) The period of any preexisting condition exclusion is reduced by the aggregate of the periods of creditable coverage, if any, applicable to the participant or beneficiary as of the enrollment date.

(b) Definitions. - For the purposes of this Part:

(1) Enrollment date. - With respect to an individual covered under a group health insurance plan, the date of enrollment of the individual in the coverage or, if earlier, the first day of the waiting period for the enrollment. An individual's enrollment date does not change if the individual receiving benefits under a group health insurance plan changes benefit packages or if the plan changes health insurers.

(2) Late enrollee. - With respect to coverage under a group health insurance plan, a participant or beneficiary who enrolls under the plan other than during:

a. The first period in which the individual is eligible to enroll under the plan, or

b. A special enrollment period under subsection (f) of this section.

(3) Preexisting condition exclusion. -

a. In general. - "Preexisting condition exclusion" means, with respect to coverage, a limitation or exclusion of benefits relating to a condition based on the fact that the condition was present before the effective date of coverage under a group health plan or group health insurance coverage, whether or not any medical advice, diagnosis, care, or treatment was recommended or received before that day. A preexisting condition exclusion includes any exclusion applicable to an individual as a result of information relating to an individual's health status before the individual's effective date of coverage under a group health plan or group health insurance coverage, such as a condition identified as a result of a preenrollment questionnaire or physical examination given to the individual, or review of medical records relating to the preenrollment period.

b. Treatment of genetic information. - Genetic information shall not be treated as a condition described in subdivision (a)(1) of this subsection in the absence of a diagnosis of the condition related to the information.

(4) Waiting period. -

a. With respect to a group health insurance plan and an individual who is a potential participant or beneficiary in the plan, the period that must pass with respect to the individual before the individual is eligible to be covered for benefits under the terms of the plan.

b. If an employee or dependent enrolls as a late enrollee or special enrollee, any period before the late or special enrollment is not a waiting period.

c. If an individual seeks individual health insurance coverage, a waiting period begins on the date the individual submits a substantially complete application and ends on: (i) the date coverage begins if the application results in coverage; or (ii) the date on which the application is denied by the health insurer or the date on which the offer for coverage lapses if the application does not result in coverage.

(c) Rules Relating to Crediting Previous Coverage. -

(1) Creditable coverage defined. - For the purposes of this Article, "creditable coverage" means, with respect to an individual, coverage of the individual under any of the following:

a. A group health plan.

b. Health insurance coverage without regard to whether the coverage is offered in the group market, the individual market, or otherwise.

c. Part A or part B of title XVIII of the Social Security Act.

d. Title XIX of the Social Security Act, other than coverage consisting solely of benefits under section 1928.

e. Chapter 55 of title 10, United States Code.

f. A medical care program of the Indian Health Service or of a tribal organization.

g. A State health benefits risk pool.

h. A health plan offered under chapter 89 of title 5, United States Code.

i. A public health plan (as defined in federal regulations).

j. A health benefit plan under section 5(e) of the Peace Corps Act (22 U.S.C. § 2504(e)).

k. Title XXI of the Social Security Act (State Children's Health Insurance Program).

"Creditable coverage" does not include coverage consisting solely of coverage of excepted benefits. However, short-term limited-duration health insurance coverage shall be considered creditable coverage for purposes of this section.

(2) Not counting periods before significant breaks in coverage. -

a. In general. - A period of creditable coverage shall not be counted, with respect to enrollment of an individual under a group health insurance plan, if, after the period and before the enrollment date, there was a 63-day period during all of which the individual was not covered under any creditable coverage.

b. Waiting period not treated as a break in coverage. - For the purposes of sub-subdivision a. of this subdivision and subdivision (d)(4) of this subsection, any period that an individual is in a waiting period for any coverage under a group health insurance plan or is in an affiliation period shall not be taken into account in determining the continuous period under sub-subdivision a. of this subdivision.

c. Time spent on short term limited duration health insurance not treated as a break in coverage. - For the purposes of sub-subdivision a. of this subdivision, any period that an individual is enrolled on a short term limited duration health insurance policy shall not be taken into account in determining the continuous period under sub-subdivision a. of this subdivision so long as the period of time spent on the short term limited duration health insurance policy or policies does not exceed 12 months.

d. For an individual who elects COBRA continuation coverage during the second election period provided under the Trade Act of 2002, the days between the date the individual lost group health plan coverage and the first day of the second COBRA election period shall not be considered when determining whether a significant break in coverage has occurred.

(3) Method of crediting coverage. -

a. Standard method. - Except as otherwise provided under sub-subdivision b. of this subdivision for the purposes of applying subdivision (a)(3) of this subsection, a group health insurer shall count a period of creditable coverage without regard to the specific benefits covered during the period.

b. Election of alternative method. - A group health insurer may elect to apply subdivision (a)(3) of this subsection based on coverage of benefits within each of several classes or categories of benefits specified in federal regulations rather than as provided under sub-subdivision a. of this subdivision. This election shall be made on a uniform basis for all participants and beneficiaries. Under this election a group health insurer shall count a period of creditable coverage with respect to any class or category of benefits if any level of benefits is covered within the class or category.

c. Health insurer notice. - In the case of an election under sub-subdivision b. of this subdivision with respect to health insurance coverage in the small or large group market, the health insurer: (i) shall prominently state in any disclosure statements concerning the coverage, and to each employer at the time of the offer or sale of the coverage, that the health insurer has made the election, and (ii) shall include in the statements a description of the effect of the election.

(4) Establishment of period. - Periods of creditable coverage for an individual shall be established through presentation of certifications described in subsection (e) of this section or in another manner that is specified in federal regulations.

(5) Determination of creditable coverage. -

a. Determination within reasonable time. - If a group health insurer receives creditable coverage information under subsection (e) of this section, the group health insurer shall, within a reasonable time following receipt of the information, make a determination regarding the amount of the individual's creditable coverage and the length of any exclusion that remains. Whether this determination is made within a reasonable time depends on the relevant facts and circumstances. Relevant facts and circumstances include whether a plan's application of a preexisting condition exclusion would prevent an individual from having access to urgent medical care.

b. No time limit on presenting evidence of creditable coverage. - A group health insurer shall not impose any limit on the amount of time that an individual has to present a certificate or other evidence of creditable coverage.

(d) Exceptions. -

(1) Exclusion not applicable to certain newborns. - Subject to subdivision (4) of this subsection, a group health insurer shall not impose any preexisting condition exclusion in the case of an individual who, as of the last day of the 30-day period beginning with the individual's date of birth, is covered under creditable coverage.

(2) Exclusion not applicable to certain adopted children. - Subject to subdivision (4) of this subsection, a group health insurer shall not impose any preexisting condition exclusion in the case of a child who is adopted or placed for adoption before attaining 18 years of age and who, as of the last day of the 30-day period beginning on the date of the adoption or placement for adoption, is covered under creditable coverage. The previous sentence does not apply to coverage before the date of the adoption or placement for adoption.

(3) Exclusion not applicable to pregnancy. - A group health insurer shall not impose any preexisting condition exclusion relating to pregnancy as a preexisting condition.

(4) Loss if break in coverage. - Subdivisions (1) and (2) of this subsection shall no longer apply to an individual after the end of the first 63-day period during all of which the individual was not covered under any creditable coverage.

(5) Condition first diagnosed under previous coverage. - A group health insurer shall not impose any preexisting condition exclusion for a condition for which medical advice, diagnosis, care, or treatment was recommended or received for the first time while the covered person held qualifying previous coverage or prior creditable coverage and the condition was covered under the qualifying previous coverage or prior creditable coverage; provided that the qualifying previous coverage or prior creditable coverage was continuous to a date not more than 63 days before the enrollment date for the new coverage.

(e) Certifications and Disclosure of Coverage. -

(1) Requirement for certification of period of creditable coverage. -

a. In general. - A group health insurer shall provide the certification described in sub-subdivision b. of this subdivision: (i) at the time an individual ceases to be covered under the plan or otherwise becomes covered under a COBRA continuation provision, (ii) in the case of an individual becoming covered under a COBRA continuation provision, at the time the individual ceases to be covered under the COBRA continuation provision, and (iii) on the request on behalf of an individual made not later than 24 months after the date of cessation of the coverage described in clause (i) or (ii) of this sub-subdivision, whichever is later.

The certification under clause (i) of this sub-subdivision may be provided, to the extent practicable, at a time consistent with notices required under any applicable COBRA continuation provision.

b. Certification. - The certification described in this sub-subdivision is a written certification of: (i) the period of creditable coverage of the individual under the plan and any coverage under the COBRA continuation provision, and (ii) any waiting period and affiliation period, if applicable, imposed with respect to the individual for any coverage under the plan.

(2) Disclosure of information on previous benefits. - In the case of an election described in sub-subdivision (c)(3)b. of this subsection by a group health insurer, if the health insurer enrolls an individual for coverage under the plan and the individual provides a certification of coverage of the individual under subdivision (1) of this subsection:

a. Upon request of the health insurer, the entity that issued the certification provided by the individual shall promptly disclose to the requesting plan or health insurer information on coverage of classes and categories of health benefits available under the entity's coverage.

b. The entity may charge the requesting plan or health insurer for the reasonable cost of disclosing the information.

(f) Special Enrollment Periods. -

(1) Individuals losing other coverage. - A group health insurer shall permit an employee who is eligible, but not enrolled, for coverage under the terms of the plan (or a dependent of the employee if the dependent is eligible, but not enrolled, for coverage under the terms) to enroll for coverage under the terms of the plan if each of the following conditions is met:

a. The employee or dependent was covered under an ERISA group health plan or had health insurance coverage at the time coverage was previously offered to the employee or dependent.

b. The employee stated in writing at the time that coverage under the group health plan or health insurance coverage was the reason for declining enrollment, but only if the health insurer required the statement at the time and provided the employee with notice of the requirement and the consequences of the requirement at the time.

c. With respect to the employee's or dependent's coverage described in sub-subdivision a. of this subsection: (i) the coverage was under a COBRA continuation provision and the coverage under the provision was exhausted; (ii) the coverage was not under that provision and either the coverage was terminated because of loss of eligibility for the coverage, including legal separation, divorce, cessation of dependent status (such as attaining the maximum age to be eligible as a dependent child under the plan), death of an employee, termination of employment, reduction in the number of hours of employment, and any loss of eligibility for coverage after a period that is measured by reference to any of the foregoing; (iii) employer contributions toward the coverage were terminated; (iv) in the case of coverage offered through an arrangement that does not provide benefits to individuals who no longer reside, live, or work in a service area, there has been loss of coverage because an individual no longer resides, lives, or works in the service area (whether or not within the choice of the individual), and no other benefit package is available to the individual; (v) an individual incurs a claim that would meet or exceed a lifetime limit on all benefits; or (vi) a plan no longer offers any benefits to the class of similarly situated individuals that includes the individual; or (vii) the health insurer terminated coverage under G.S. 58-68-45(c)(2).

d. Under the terms of the plan, the employee requests the enrollment not later than 30 days after the date of the applicable event described in sub-subdivision c. of this subdivision.

(2) For dependent beneficiaries. -

a. In general. - If: (i) a group health insurance plan makes coverage available with respect to a dependent of an individual, (ii) the individual is a participant under the plan (or has met any waiting period applicable to becoming a participant under the plan and is eligible to be enrolled under the plan but for a failure to enroll during a previous enrollment period), and (iii) a person becomes the dependent of the individual through marriage, birth, or adoption or placement for adoption.

The plan shall provide for a dependent special enrollment period described in sub-subdivision b. of this subdivision during which the person (or, if not otherwise enrolled, the individual) may be enrolled under the plan as a dependent of the individual, and in the case of the birth or adoption of a child, the spouse of the individual may be enrolled as a dependent of the individual if the spouse is otherwise eligible for coverage.

b. Dependent special enrollment period. - A dependent special enrollment period under this sub-subdivision shall be a period of not less than 30 days and shall begin on the later of: (i) the date dependent coverage is made available, or (ii) the date of the marriage, birth, or adoption or placement for adoption described in sub-subdivision a.(iii) of this subdivision.

c. No waiting period. - If an individual seeks to enroll a dependent during the first 30 days of the dependent's special enrollment period, the coverage of the dependent shall become effective: (i) in the case of marriage, not later than the first day of the first month beginning after the date the completed request for enrollment is received; (ii) in the case of a dependent's birth, as of the date of the birth; or (iii) in the case of a dependent's adoption or placement for adoption, the date of the adoption or placement for adoption.

(3) Treatment of special enrollees.

a. If an individual requests enrollment while the individual is entitled to special enrollment under this subsection, the individual is a special enrollee, even if the request for enrollment coincides with a late enrollment opportunity under the plan. Therefore, the individual cannot be considered a late enrollee.

b. Special enrollees shall be offered all of the benefit packages available to similarly situated individuals who enroll when first eligible. For this purpose, any difference in benefits or cost-sharing requirements for different individuals constitutes a different benefit package. In addition, a special enrollee cannot be required to pay more for coverage than a similarly situated individual who enrolls in the same coverage when first eligible. The length of any preexisting condition exclusion that may be applied to a special enrollee cannot exceed the length of any preexisting condition exclusion that is applied to similarly situated individuals who enroll when first eligible.

(4) Special rules for application in case of Medicaid or State Children's Health Insurance Program (Title XXI of the Social Security Act). - A group health insurer shall permit an employee who is eligible, but not enrolled, for coverage under the terms of the plan (or a dependent of the employee if the dependent is eligible, but not enrolled, for coverage under the terms) to enroll for coverage under the terms of the plan if either of the following conditions is met:

a. Termination of Medicaid or State Children's Health Insurance Program. - The employee or dependent is covered under a Medicaid plan under Title XIX of the Social Security Act or under a State children's health plan under Title XXI of the Social Security Act and coverage of the employee or dependent under such a plan is terminated as a result of the loss of eligibility for such coverage and the employee requests coverage under the group health insurance coverage not later than 60 days after the termination of such coverage.

b. Eligibility for employment assistance under Medicaid or State Children's Health Insurance Program. - The employee or dependent becomes eligible for assistance, with respect to coverage under the group health insurance coverage, under such Medicaid plan or State child health plan (including any waiver or demonstration project conducted under or in relation to such a plan), if the employee requests coverage under the group health insurance coverage not later than 60 days after the date the employee or dependent is determined to be eligible for such assistance.

(g) Use of Affiliation Period by HMO as Alternative to Preexisting Condition Exclusion. -

(1) In general. - A health maintenance organization that does not impose any preexisting condition exclusion allowed under subsection (a) of this section with respect to any particular coverage option may impose an affiliation period for the coverage option, but only if:

a. The period is applied uniformly without regard to any health status-related factors.

b. The period does not exceed two months (or three months in the case of a late enrollee).

(2) Affiliation period. -

a. Defined. - For the purposes of this Subpart, "affiliation period" means a period that, under the terms of the health insurance coverage offered by the health maintenance organization, must expire before the health insurance coverage becomes effective. The health maintenance organization is not required to provide health care services or benefits during the period and no premium shall be charged to the participant or beneficiary for any coverage during the period.

b. Beginning. - The period shall begin on the enrollment date.

c.   Runs concurrently with waiting periods. - An affiliation period under a plan shall run concurrently with any waiting period under the plan.

(3)   Alternative methods. - A health maintenance organization described in subdivision (1) of this subsection may use alternative methods, as approved by the Commissioner, from those described in that subdivision, to address adverse selection.

(h)   General Notice of Preexisting Condition Exclusion. - A group health insurer offering group health insurance coverage subject to a preexisting condition exclusion shall provide a written general notice of preexisting condition exclusion to participants under the plan; and shall not impose a preexisting condition exclusion with respect to a participant or a dependent of the participant until the notice is provided.

A group health insurer shall provide the general notice of preexisting condition exclusion as part of any written application materials distributed by the insurer for enrollment. If the insurer does not distribute these materials, the notice shall be provided by the earliest date following a request for enrollment that the insurer, acting in a reasonable and prompt fashion, can provide the notice.

The general notice of preexisting condition exclusion shall notify participants of the following:

(1)   The existence and terms of any preexisting condition exclusion under the plan. This description includes the length of the plan's look-back period, which shall not exceed six months under subdivision (a)(1) of this section; the maximum preexisting condition exclusion period under the plan, which shall not exceed 12 months (18 months for late enrollees) under subdivision (a)(2) of this section; and how the plan will reduce the maximum preexisting condition exclusion period by creditable coverage, as described in subsection (c) of this section.

(2)   A description of the rights of individuals to demonstrate creditable coverage, and any applicable waiting periods, through a certificate of creditable coverage, as required by subsection (e) of this section, or through other means as described in federal regulations. This shall include a description of the right of the individual to request a certificate from a prior insurer, if necessary, and a statement that the current insurer will assist in obtaining a certificate from any prior plan or insurer, if necessary.

(3) A person to contact, including an address or telephone number for obtaining additional information or assistance about the preexisting condition exclusion.

Nothing in this subsection affects a group health insurer's responsibility under this section to fully disclose in the master group policy, the certificate or evidence of coverage, and the member handbook the plan's preexisting condition limitation, the rules relating to creditable coverage, including how an individual may provide proof of creditable coverage, and the methods of counting and crediting coverage.

(i) Individual Notice of Period of Preexisting Condition Exclusion. - After an individual has presented evidence of creditable coverage and the group health insurer has made a determination of creditable coverage under subdivision (c)(5) of this section, the group health insurer shall provide the individual a written notice of the length of preexisting condition exclusion that remains after offsetting for prior creditable coverage. In the notice, the insurer is not required to identify any medical conditions specific to the individual that could be subject to the exclusion. A group health insurer is not required to provide this notice if the plan does not impose any preexisting condition exclusion on the individual or if the plan's preexisting condition exclusion is completely offset by the individual's prior creditable coverage.

The individual notice must be provided by the earliest date following a determination that the group health insurer, acting in a reasonable and prompt fashion, can provide the notice.

A group health insurer shall disclose:

(1) Its determination of any preexisting condition exclusion period that applies to the individual, including the last day on which the preexisting condition exclusion applies.

(2) The basis for that determination, including the source and substance of any information on which the plan or insurer relied.

(3) An explanation of the individual's right to submit additional evidence of creditable coverage.

(4) A description of any applicable appeal procedures established by the group health insurer.

(j) Determination Modification. - Nothing in this section prevents a plan or insurer from modifying an initial determination of creditable coverage if it determines that the individual did not have the claimed creditable coverage, provided that:

(1) A notice of the new determination, consistent with the requirements of subsection (i) of this section, is provided to the individual; and

(2) Until the notice of the new determination is provided, the group health insurer, for purposes of approving access to medical services (such as a presurgery authorization), acts in a manner consistent with the initial determination.

(k) Notice Form and Content. - Any notices required under this section shall be in the form and content and be delivered as prescribed by, in accordance with, or as specified in federal regulations, unless otherwise provided in this Chapter. (1997-259, s. 1(c); 1998-211, s. 7; 2001-334, s. 9; 2005-224, ss. 1, 4, 2.1, 2.2; 2007-298, ss. 2.3-2.5; 2009-382, ss. 4, 23.)

§ 58-68-35. Prohibiting discrimination against individual participants and beneficiaries based on health status.

(a) In Eligibility To Enroll. -

(1) In general. - Subject to subdivision (2) of this subsection, a group health insurer shall not establish rules for eligibility, including continued eligibility, of any individual to enroll under the terms of the health insurer's plan based on any of the following health status-related factors in relation to the individual or a dependent of the individual:

a. Health status.

b. Medical condition (including both physical and mental illnesses).

c. Claims experience.

d. Receipt of health care.

e. Medical history.

f. Genetic information.

g. Evidence of insurability (including conditions arising out of acts of domestic violence).

h. Disability.

(2) No application to benefits or exclusions. - To the extent consistent with G.S. 58-68-30, subdivision (1) of this subsection shall not be construed:

a. To require a group health insurance plan to provide particular benefits other than those provided under the terms of the plan, or

b. To prevent the plan from establishing limitations or restrictions on the amount, level, extent, or nature of the benefits or coverage for similarly situated individuals enrolled in the plan.

(3) Construction. - For the purposes of subdivision (1) of this subsection, rules for eligibility to enroll under a plan include rules defining any applicable waiting periods for the enrollment.

(b) In Premium Contributions. -

(1) In general. - A group health insurance plan shall not require any individual (as a condition of enrollment or continued enrollment under the plan) to pay a premium or contribution that is greater than the premium or contribution for a similarly situated individual enrolled in the plan on the basis of any health status-related factor in relation to the individual or to an individual enrolled under the plan as a dependent of individual.

(2) Construction. - Nothing in subdivision (1) of this subsection shall be construed:

a. To restrict the amount that an employer may be charged for coverage under a group health insurance plan; or

b. To prevent a group health insurer from establishing premium discounts or modifying otherwise applicable copayments or deductibles in return for adherence to programs of health promotion and disease prevention. (1997-259, s. 1(c).)

Subpart 2. Health Insurance Availability and Renewability.

§ 58-68-40. Guaranteed availability of coverage for employers in the small group market.

(a)   Issuance of Coverage in the Small Group Market. -

(1)   In general. - Subject to subsections (c) through (f) of this section, each health insurer that offers health insurance coverage in the small group market in this State:

a.   Must accept every small employer that applies for the coverage; and

b.   Must accept for enrollment under the coverage every eligible individual who applies for enrollment during the period in which the individual first becomes eligible to enroll under the terms of the group health insurance plan and shall not place any restriction that is inconsistent with G.S. 58-68-35 on an eligible individual being a participant or beneficiary.

(2)   Eligible individual defined. - For the purposes of this section, "eligible individual" means, with respect to a health insurer that offers health insurance coverage to a small employer in the small group market, such an individual in relation to the employer as shall be determined:

a.   In accordance with the terms of the plan,

b.   As provided by the health insurer under rules of the health insurer that are uniformly applicable in this State to small employers in the small group market, and

c.   In accordance with all applicable State laws governing the health insurer and the market.

(b)   Special Rules for Network Plans. -

(1) In general. - In the case of a health insurer that offers health insurance coverage in the small group market through a network plan, the health insurer may:

a. Limit the employers that may apply for coverage to those with eligible individuals who live, work, or reside in the service area for the network plan; and

b. Within the service area of the network plan, deny coverage to the employers if the health insurer has demonstrated to the Commissioner that: (i) it will not have the capacity to deliver services adequately to enrollees of any additional groups because of its obligations to existing group contract holders and enrollees, and (ii) it is applying this subdivision uniformly to all employers without regard to the claims experience of those employers and their employees (and their dependents) or any health status-related factor relating to the employees and dependents.

(2) 180-day suspension upon denial of coverage. - A health insurer, upon denying health insurance coverage in any service area in accordance with sub-subdivision (1)b. of this subsection, shall not offer coverage in the small group market within the service area for a period of 180 days after the date the coverage is denied.

(c) Application of Financial Capacity Limits. -

(1) In general. - A health insurer may deny health insurance coverage in the small group market if the health insurer has demonstrated to the Commissioner that:

a. It does not have the financial reserves necessary to underwrite additional coverage; and

b. It is applying this subdivision uniformly to all employers in the small group market in the State consistent with this Chapter and without regard to the claims experience of those employers and their employees (and their dependents) or any health status-related factor relating to the employees and dependents.

(2) 180-day suspension upon denial of coverage. - A health insurer upon denying health insurance coverage in accordance with subdivision (1) of this subsection shall not offer coverage in the small group market in the State for a period of 180 days after the date the coverage is denied or until the health

insurer has demonstrated to the Commissioner that the health insurer has sufficient financial reserves to underwrite additional coverage, whichever is later. The Commissioner may apply this subsection on a service-area-specific basis.

(d) Exception to Requirement for Failure to Meet Certain Minimum Participation or Contribution Rules. -

(1) In general. - Subsection (a) of this section does not preclude a health insurer from establishing employer contribution rules or group participation rules for the offering of health insurance coverage in connection with a group health insurance plan in the small group market, as allowed under this Chapter.

(2) Rules defined. - For the purposes of subdivision (1) of this subsection:

a. "Employer contribution rule" means a requirement relating to the minimum level or amount of employer contribution toward the premium for enrollment of participants and beneficiaries; and

b. "Group participation rule" means a requirement relating to the minimum number of participants or beneficiaries that must be enrolled in relation to a specified percentage or number of eligible individuals or employees of an employer.

(e) Exception for Coverage. - Subsection (a) of this section does not apply to:

(1) Health insurance coverage offered by a health insurer if the coverage is made available in the small group market only through one or more bona fide associations.

(2) A self-employed individual as defined in G.S. 58-50-110(21a), except as otherwise provided for the basic and standard health care plans or other plans under G.S. 58-50-126 under the North Carolina Small Employer Group Health Coverage Reform Act. (1997-259, s. 1(c); 1999-132, s. 4.6; 2006-154, s. 4.)

§ 58-68-45. Guaranteed renewability of coverage for employers in the group market.

(a) In General. - Except as provided in this section, if a health insurer offers health insurance coverage in the small or large group market, the health insurer must renew or continue in force the coverage at the option of the employer.

(b) General Exceptions. - A health insurer may nonrenew or discontinue health insurance coverage in the small or large group market based only on one or more of the following:

(1) Nonpayment of premiums. - The policyholder has failed to pay premiums or contributions in accordance with the terms of the health insurance coverage or the health insurer has not received timely premium payments.

(2) Fraud. - The policyholder has performed an act or practice that constitutes fraud or made an intentional misrepresentation of material fact under the terms of the coverage.

(3) Violation of participation or contribution rules. - The policyholder has failed to comply with a material plan provision relating to employer contribution or group participation rules, as permitted under G.S. 58-68-40(d) in the case of the small group market or pursuant to this Chapter in the case of the large group market.

(4) Termination of coverage. - The health insurer is ceasing to offer coverage in the market in accordance with subsection (c) of this section and this Chapter.

(5) Movement outside service area. - In the case of a health insurer that offers health insurance coverage in the market through a network plan, there is no longer any enrollee in connection with the network plan who lives, resides, or works in the service area of the health insurer or in the area for which the health insurer is authorized to do business and, in the case of the small group market, the health insurer would deny enrollment with respect to the network plan under G.S. 58-68-40(c)(1)a.

(6) Association membership ceases. - In the case of health insurance coverage that is made available in the small or large group market only through one or more bona fide associations, the membership of an employer in the association, on the basis of which the coverage is provided, ceases but only if the coverage is terminated under this subdivision uniformly without regard to any health status-related factor relating to any covered individual.

(c) Requirements for Uniform Termination of Coverage. -

(1) Particular type of coverage not offered. - In any case in which a health insurer decides to discontinue offering a particular type of group health insurance coverage offered in the small or large group market, coverage of the type may be discontinued by the health insurer in accordance with this Chapter in the market only if:

a. The health insurer provides notice to each policyholder provided coverage of this type in the market and to the participants and beneficiaries covered under the coverage of the discontinuation at least 90 days before the date of the discontinuation of the coverage;

b. The health insurer offers to each policyholder provided coverage of this type in the market the option to purchase all, or in the case of the large group market, any other health insurance coverage currently being offered by the health insurer to a group health insurance plan in the market; and

c. In exercising the option to discontinue coverage of this type and in offering the option of coverage under sub-subdivision b. of this subdivision, the health insurer acts uniformly without regard to the claims experience of those sponsors or any health status-related factor relating to any participants or beneficiaries covered or new participants or beneficiaries who may become eligible for the coverage.

(2) Discontinuance of all coverage. -

a. In general. - In any case in which a health insurer elects to discontinue offering all health insurance coverage in the small group market or the large group market, or both markets, in this State, health insurance coverage may be discontinued by the health insurer only in accordance with this Chapter and if: (i) the health insurer provides notice to the Commissioner and to each policyholder and to the participants and beneficiaries covered under the coverage of the discontinuation at least 180 days before the date of the discontinuation of the coverage; and (ii) all health insurance issued or delivered for issuance in this State in the market or markets are discontinued and coverage under the health insurance coverage in the market or markets is not renewed.

b. Prohibition on market reentry. - In the case of a discontinuation under sub-subdivision a. of this subdivision in a market, the health insurer shall not provide for the issuance of any health insurance coverage in that market in this

State during the five-year period beginning on the date of the discontinuation of the last health insurance coverage not so renewed.

(d) Exception for Uniform Modification of Coverage. - At the time of coverage renewal, a health insurer may modify the health insurance coverage for a product offered to a group health insurance plan:

(1) In the large group market; or

(2) In the small group market if, for coverage that is available in the market other than only through one or more bona fide associations, the modification is consistent with this Chapter and effective on a uniform basis among group health insurance plans with that product.

(e) Application to Coverage Offered Only Through Associations. - In applying this section in the case of health insurance coverage that is made available by a health insurer in the small or large group market to employers only through one or more associations, a reference to "policyholder" is deemed, with respect to coverage provided to an employer member of the association, to include a reference to the employer. (1997-259, s. 1(c); 1997-456, s. 42.)

Vision Books Order Form

Fax Orders:	1-980-299-5965
Phone Orders:	1-704-898-0770
E-mail Orders:	www.visionbooks.org
Mail Orders:	Vision Books, LLC P.O. Box 42406 Charlotte, NC 28215

Shipp To:
Name_____
Address_____
City_____State_____Zip_____
Phone_____Fax_____
Email_____@_____

Bill To: We can bill a third party on your behalf.
Name_____
Address_____
City_____State_____Zip_____
Phone____(_____)_____Fax_____
Email_____@_____

Pamphlet Number ($15.00 Each)	Qty	Total Cost
_____	_____	_____
_____	_____	_____
_____	_____	_____
_____	_____	_____
_____	_____	_____
_____	_____	_____
_____	_____	_____
_____	_____	_____
<u>Full Volume Set 1-92</u>	<u>92 Pamphlets</u>	<u>1,380.00</u>

Free Shipping Shipping & Handling on Full Volume Orders
Add $1.00 Shipping & Handling per pamphlet $_____

Total Cost $_____

Thank you for your support. Management!

DID YOU ENJOY THIS BOOK?

Vision Books, LLC would like to hear from you! If you or someone you know has been fasely imprisoned, we would like to hear your story. If the 'North Carolina Criminal Law and Procedure' has had an effect in your life or if you have suggestions, we would like to hear from you. Send your letters to:

Vision Books, LLC
Attn: Staff Writers
P.O. Box 42406
Charlotte, NC 28215
Email: staff@visionbooks.org

Order Additional Copies:

Fax Orders:	1-980-299-5965
Phone Orders:	1-704-898-0770
E-mail Orders:	www.visionbooks.org
Mail Orders:	Vision Books, LLC P.O. Box 42406 Charlotte, NC 28215

www.ingramcontent.com/pod-product-compliance
Lightning Source LLC
Chambersburg PA
CBHW051627170526
45167CB00001B/94